Early Modern Cultural Studies 1500–1700

Series Editors
Jean Howard
Department of English
Columbia University
New York, NY, USA

Ivo Kamps
General
University of Mississippi
University, MS, USA

In the twenty first century, literary criticism, literary theory, historiography and cultural studies have become intimately interwoven, and the formerly distinct fields of literature, society, history, and culture no longer seem so discrete. The Early Modern Cultural Studies series encourages scholarship that crosses boundaries between disciplines, time periods, nations, and theoretical orientations. The series assumes that the early modern period was marked by incipient processes of transculturation brought about through exploration, trade, colonization, and the migration of texts and people. These phenomena set in motion the processes of globalization that remain in force today. The purpose of this series is to publish innovative scholarship that is attentive to the complexity of this early modern world and bold in the methods it employs for studying it.

More information about this series at
http://www.palgrave.com/gp/series/14956

Lynn M. Maxwell

Wax Impressions, Figures, and Forms in Early Modern Literature

Wax Works

Lynn M. Maxwell
Spelman College
Atlanta, GA, USA

Early Modern Cultural Studies 1500–1700
ISBN 978-3-030-16931-2   ISBN 978-3-030-16932-9   (eBook)
https://doi.org/10.1007/978-3-030-16932-9

This Palgrave Macmillan imprint is published by the registered company Springer Nature
Switzerland AG
The registered company address is: Gewerbestrasse 11, 6330 Cham, Switzerland

ACKNOWLEDGEMENTS

Research for this book was made possible by the generous support of Spelman College and Emory University. A grant from Emory University allowed me to travel to Spain and Italy and see many of the paintings and waxworks discussed in this project firsthand. A research leave from Spelman and the support of my colleagues helped me bring the final manuscript to fruition.

A section of Chapter 2 was originally published as "Writing Women, Writing Wax: Metaphors of Impression—Possibilities of Agency in Shakespeare's *Rape of Lucrece* and *Twelfth Night*" in *Criticism: A Quarterly for Literature and the Arts* 58, no. 3 (2016): 433–458. I am grateful to Wayne State University for permission to republish it in this book. A section of Chapter 5 originally appeared as "Wax Magic and *The Duchess of Malfi*" in *The Journal for Early Modern Cultural Studies* 14, no. 3 (2014): 31–54. I would like to thank University of Pennsylvania Press for permission to reprint that material here. I am also thankful for the editorial team at Palgrave, which has been very helpful through the process, and indebted to the two anonymous reviewers provided by Palgrave, who provided valuable insight into how this project might be strengthened.

I am forever grateful for my colleagues and mentors who provided me feedback on various stages of this manuscript. Jonathan Goldberg always pushed me to think harder and to embrace suggestive readings over determinative ones. He also filled my inbox with wax moments and brought the *Like Life* exhibit at The Met Breuer to my attention. Patricia Cahill has been a generous and insightful reader of my work and has helped move this project forward in many ways. I am grateful to Richard Rambuss, who provided feedback on early drafts of the project and to Karen Newman who invited me to teach a session of her graduate course on early modern things. Together with her students at Brown, she pushed me to think about wax in relation to posthumanism.

I am grateful to my academic friends and my fellow Emory early modernists: Kate Doubler, Rebecca Kumar, Maureen McCarthy, Dominick Rolle, Brent Dawson, Perry Guevara, and Bellee Jones-Pierce provided me with support and camaraderie on a regular basis. My colleagues at Spelman and most especially Michelle Hite, Stephen Knadler, and Sarah Rudewalker have also been invaluable supports. I am thankful also for Margaret Boyle and Erin McCarthy, who mentored me through the publishing process and generally cheered me on.

I would not be where I am without my family and friends: Stephen Maxwell, Kim Maxwell, Lachy Maxwell, Jenna Maxwell, Kristen Maxwell, Maggie Schirm, Supraja Narasimhan, and most especially Shannen Naegel, who has read more versions of this book than anyone else, and who has always believed in its value.

I dedicate this book to Kevin, Roric, and Freya, whose prints indelibly shape my heart.

CONTENTS

CHAPTER 1

Introduction: Wax Concepts

In Tintoretto's *The Temptation of St. Anthony* (c. 1577), the Savior swoops in to rescue the beleaguered saint from the devils who tempt him.[1] While the painting captures all of the figures in suspended motion—Anthony reaches up toward heaven, as the devils clutch at him and simultaneously twist away from the light—it is the Christ figure that arrests the viewer's eye. The foreshortened form seems on the verge of soaring through the canvas; arms outstretched with mercy and radiating light, he is a figure of hope and power for saint and viewer alike (Fig. 1.1).

At first glance, this masterpiece of oil and canvas seems to have nothing to do with wax; yet wax played an integral part in Tintoretto's process. As Carlo Ridolfi explains in *Le Maraviglie dell'arte* (1648), Tintoretto learned about perspective and light through wax. He discovered that:

> by making little models out of wax or clay and dressing them in scraps of cloth and carefully draping them so that the folds emphasized the shape of the limbs. These small models he placed in little houses and perspective boxes. He would place little lights in the windows so that light and shade would be produced. Still other models he suspended from the beams of his ceiling. This enabled him to observe the effect they made when seen from below, from which he learned how to make foreshortenings for ceiling frescoes.[2]

© The Author(s) 2019
L. M. Maxwell, *Wax Impressions, Figures, and Forms in Early Modern Literature*, Early Modern Cultural Studies 1500–1700, https://doi.org/10.1007/978-3-030-16932-9_1

Fig. 1.1 Tintoretto,
*The Temptation of Saint
Anthony*, 1577–1588,
San Trovaso, Venice
(photographed by Didier
Descouens / https://
creativecommons.org/
licenses/by-sa/4.0/
legalcode)

Tintoretto's models provided him with perfectly manipulable subjects, figures that he could push beyond the limits of human models and view from unlikely and extreme angles. Lightweight enough to seem unaffected by gravity, such figures might have allowed Tintoretto to study the possibilities of a human body in flight and ultimately convey the Savior's power and dynamism. Tintoretto's dramatic forms in flight were technical achievements, as Marco Boschini remarks in *Ricche Minere della Pittura Venezia* (1674): "difficult as foreshortening is on a flat surface, it is still more difficult to do in the air. Nor can one make statues fly. But our learned Venetian painters make human figures fly."[3] By freeing his figures from the constraints of gravity, Tintoretto pushed the limits of perspective and canvas, conveying truths about the human form in motion that revolutionized the visual arts.

Almost a hundred years later, at a crucial moment in the *Meditations* (1641), René Descartes takes up wax to discover what it is possible to know about it as a material object. What starts as a seemingly insignificant inquiry into the nature of wax becomes an investigation into the nature and limits of the human mind and by extension the human. He begins by describing a specific piece of wax in detail; the wax "has just been taken from the honeycomb; it has not yet quite lost the taste of the honey; it retains some of the scent of the flowers from which it was gathered; its colour, shape, and size are plain to see; it is hard, cold and can be handled without difficulty."[4] He then applies fire to the wax and registers how completely the wax has changed in every material attribute: "the residual taste is eliminated, the smell goes away, the colour changes, the shape is lost, the size increases; it becomes liquid and hot; you can hardly touch it, and if you strike it, it no longer makes a sound."[5] The experiment has transformed the wax and his knowledge of it, leading Descartes to conclude that the true nature of wax must inhere in those qualities that remain once you "take away everything which does not belong to the wax, and see what is left: merely something extended, flexible, and changeable."[6] Since these qualities of extension, flexibility, and changeability can only be comprehended in the mind and reveal more about the nature and existence of the mind than of the wax, his consideration of wax leads to his cogito, a foundational moment for philosophy that severs subject from object and establishes the priority of the individual mind.

These two uses of wax are fundamentally different from each other—one involves actual wax models, the other uses wax metaphorically; one seeks to understand the human body, the other the human mind—and yet both artist and philosopher seem to be using wax to discover on some level the nature and limits of humanity. Together they begin to suggest the power of wax as a conceptual material in the early modern period. This book is about that power. With Tintoretto we will consider how wax figures can teach us about human ones, with Descartes we will contemplate the nature of wax and what it might teach us about the human mind and the relationship of man and God, man and woman, mind and the world, and man and machine. We will read wax in a variety of early modern cultural spaces such as the stage and the artist's studio and in literary and philosophical texts, including those by William Shakespeare, John Donne, Margaret Cavendish, and Edmund Spenser, ultimately discovering that just as wax was vital to the projects of both Tintoretto and Descartes; it was also integral to early modern attempts to understand human relationality and what it might mean to be human.

1.1   Conceiving Wax

First though, we must pause over wax itself and consider, like Descartes, what kind of a material it is. Descartes begins to answer that question when he defines wax as an "extended, flexible, and changeable" substance.[7] This definition highlights wax's malleability, perhaps its most salient quality, and without a doubt the quality that matters most for Descartes' own project. Indeed, wax has a long history in philosophy as a material to model the mind, in part because of wax's capacity for change. Similarly, as we saw with Tintoretto, wax proves useful in the artist's studio because it can be easily molded into different shapes. Throughout this book, we will think about the importance of wax's malleability. For now, it is enough to register the importance of the simple fact that wax waxes.

Descartes' narrative also reveals wax's status as a natural material. Again, as we saw earlier, the wax that he holds in his hand has "just been taken from the honeycomb; it has not yet lost the taste of honey; it retains some scent of the flowers from which it was gathered."[8] As Descartes' brief description begins to reveal, early modern ideas about wax production do not align perfectly with modern science. While we now know that wax is produced by bees whose glands convert sugar into little white flakes which are secreted, masticated, and then used to construct honeycomb, early moderns followed Aristotle in believing that wax was gathered by bees.[9] In his *History of Animals*, Aristotle writes, "the honeycomb is made from flowers, and the materials for the wax they gather from the resinous gum of trees, while honey is what falls from the air, and is deposited chiefly at the risings of the constellations or when a rainbow is in the sky."[10] Later in the same volume, Aristotle revisits the question of wax, explaining "Bees scramble up the stalks of flowers and rapidly gather the bees-wax with their front legs; the front legs wipe it off on to the middle legs, and these pass it on to the hollow curves of the hind-legs; when thus laden, they fly away home, and one may see plainly that their load is a heavy one."[11] We can hear echoes of Aristotle in early bee-keeping treatises. In Thomas Hill's *A pleasaunt instruction of the parfit ordering of Bees* (1568), he glosses over the details, writing that on "a cleare and fayre morning … [The bees] flye forth and returne againe to their hyues, laden with the substance of the flowers on their legges."[12] Rev. Charles Butler's *The Feminine Monarchie* (1609) is more detailed in its treatment. According to Butler, "the wax they gather with their fágs" or flaps.[13] Once they have gathered it, the same "being kept soft with the heat of their little bodies, of the aire, and of their hiues is easily wrought into combs."[14] While the difference in believing wax to be a product gathered from flowers, or produced by bees might seem subtle, it impacts literary representations of wax in the early modern period. For example, In *The Second Part of Henry the Fourth*, King Henry likens fathers to bees:

> Our thighs packed with wax, our mouths with honey,
> We bring it to the hive; and, like the bees
> Are murdered for our pains.[15]

Shakespeare depicts worker bees as overburdened, laden down with both honey and wax for which they will ultimately be killed. The bearing of the wax heightens the sense of bodily sacrifice in the work the bees do and the reward that they receive from that work.

If we continue thinking about Descartes' wax, we also notice that it has an almost prelapsarian status. As he describes the virgin wax, he borders on the poetic, emphasizing that neither the "taste of honey," nor the "scent of flowers" has yet been "lost." While his wax may be destined for use, at this moment in *The Meditations*, it retains its connection to the natural world, the pastoral landscape, and the innocence presumed in such spaces. Again, these associations of wax manifest in literary, philosophical, and other cultural locations. In Michael Drayton's "The Quest of Cynthia," for example, Cynthia invites her would-be lover to join her in the Edenic forest, promising:

> But here our sports shall be:
> Such as the golden world first sawe,
> Most Innocent and free.[16]

Once in the forest, one of their first "sports" will be to examine a hive:

> The waxen Pallace of the Bee,
> We seeking will surprise
> The curious workmanship to see,
> Of her full-laden thighes.[17]

Here, Cynthia registers fascination with the "curious workmanship" of the hive and the way that construction connects to the bee's body, and specifically to "her full-laden thighs." Yet what starts as a desire "to see" is transformed by the next stanza to a desire to "suck the sweets out of the Combe" and enjoy food fit for the gods. The "chaste desires" that the lovers imagine are sensual. The wax palace of the bee satisfies both curiosity and hunger, substituting for other bodily desires, while simultaneously evoking them.

The purity of virgin wax also aligns it metaphorically with the chaste female body, as we will explore further in Chapters 1 and 5. Thus, in Philip Sidney's *Old Arcadia*, Pyrocles describes Philoclea's navel as "a dainty seal of virgin wax, / Where nothing but impression lacks."[18] Philoclea's purity, like that of Descartes' wax, is offered only a liminal status, both are not yet lost, and for both, transformation seems inevitable. At the same time, Pyrocles insists that his print on Philoclea's navel will give it completeness, suggesting that as admirable as a virginal state may be, it is also one of lack. Untouched wax might be purer and more valuable than other forms of wax, but its value lies primarily in the promise of use and transformation. Indeed, virgin wax is the most apt to take impression, as detailed in John Trevisa's translation of *Bartholomeus De Proprietatibus Rerum*, "the more new waxe is the better it smelleth, & to the more pure & the better to work, & the more able to take impression & printing."[19] It should come as small surprise then, that natural philosophers from Aristotle on used wax to figure procreation, imagining that the womb is like wax, waiting to take on a man's print.

Descartes, of course, does not stop with a consideration of virgin wax. Instead, he writes about what happens to the wax after it has been subjected to heat. It loses the smell of flowers and the taste of honey and becomes "liquid and hot."[20] This change is what convinces Descartes that the only thing which can be known about wax is its changeability. When wax is put to use—to seal letters, to make candles, or as modeling wax—it is transformed, and that possibility or promise of transformation is an integral part of wax's literary and cultural value.

1.2   PRODUCING WAX

While beeswax occurs naturally, as a commercial product it must be gathered, processed, and refined. By the seventeenth century, West Africa was one of the largest producers of beeswax, with wax from West Africa traveling to both the Americas and Europe.[21] An early account by Alvise Cadamosto suggests that prior to contact with the Europeans, Africans discarded wax as a useless byproduct of honey.[22] In his 1455 treatise, he writes that the West Africans:

> marveled much on seeing a candle burning in a candlestick, for here they do not know how to make any other light than that of a fire. To them the sight of the candle never seen before, was beautiful and miraculous. As, in this country, honey is found, they suck the honey from the comb, and throw away the wax. Having bought a little honeycomb, I showed them how to extract the honey from the wax, and then asked whether they knew what it was that remained. They replied it was good for nothing. In their presence, therefore, I had some candles made, and lighted.[23]

Cadamosto is clearly invested in providing an account that celebrates Europeans as the bearers of the light of civilization, a bias which calls the veracity of this account into question. Yet it is undeniable that a brisk trade in wax soon developed between the two regions. André Alvarres d'Almada wrote of the Gambia River, in 1594, "it is a river which possesses a large trade in slaves, in black and white cotton cloths, in raw cotton, and in wax — although no hives are built, the bees are so numerous, and the forest so great, that honey and wax are plentiful."[24] In return for wax, Africans received wine, paper, gems, and weapons.[25] The wax trade impacted the balance of power in West Africa and reveals the complexity of the European and African relations. Despite this robust trade, wax does not seem to be strongly associated with Africa in the cultural imagination of the period—except perhaps in anecdotes of maternal impression in where the surprising birth of a Black child to a European woman is explained by her exposure to a painting of a Black man.[26] Still, by and large there seems to have been an erasure of any African or dark associations with wax together with a simultaneous whitening of the material.

Once in Europe, raw beeswax had to be processed in order to be made into candles. This refinement process doubles the symbolic whitening mentioned above by literally lightening and purifying the wax.

As early as Pliny (the elder), we can find a detailed description of this process:

> Wax is made after the honey has been extracted from the combs, but these must be first cleaned with water and dried for three days in the dark; then on the fourth day they are melted in a new earthen vessel on the fire, with just enough water to cover them, and then strained in a wicker basket. The wax is boiled again with the same water in the same pot, and poured into other water, this is to be cold, contained in vessels smeared all round inside with honey.[27]

The process that Pliny describes, by which honeycombs are melted and strained, is almost identical to the processes described in the early modern bee-keeping treatises of Hill and Butler. All stress the need for pure wax and offer methods by which wax can be refined. Pliny, for example, suggests that the best wax is Punic wax, which is yellow wax that is bleached and boiled three additional times to further purify it and give it "the greatest whiteness."[28]

In England, concern over the purity of wax led to the regulation of the wax trade. The wax chandler's guild was intrusted with protecting the purity of wax in order to maintain its economic value. In 1581, "An Acte for the true melting making and working of Waxe" was passed. It stated:

> Where by the goodnes of God this Land doth yeeld great plentie of Honye and Waxe, as not onelye doth suffice the necessarye uses of the Queenes Majestie and her Subjectes to be spent within this Realme, but also a greate quantitie to be spared to be transported unto other Realmes and Contreys beyond the Seas by waye of Merchaundize, to the greate Benefite of her Majestie and the Realme; And yet nevertheless a greate parte of the Waxe made and melted within this Realme hathe byn founde to bee of late verye corrupt, by reason of the deceyptfull mixture thereof... Be yt therefore enacted by the Aucthoritie of this present Parliament, That everye person within this Realme or the Dominions of the same, which shall after the Feaste of Pentecost next ensuing, in the making and melting of Waxe, by any waye or meanes use or practise or cause to bee used and practized any manner deceypte, by mixture and mingling the same, with Rosen Tallowe Turpentyne or any other decyptfull thing, to the intent to sell and utter the same or offer the same to bee solde or uttered for Waxe to any person or persons whatsoever, shall forfeyt and lose the same mingled or

corrupted Waxe... And to the intent that the Offendors in these kind of deceyptes maye bee the better and sooner knowne and found out, Be yt enacted by that acuthoritie aforesaid, That everye Melter and Maker up of unwrought Waxe, shall have for himselfe a Stampe or Marke of the Breadeth of Sixe Pence, wherein Two Letters shalbee playnelye graven signifieng his Name and Surname, and with the same shall stampe everye Piece of Waxe, to bee printed or stamped Triangle in three places, uppon the outsyde of the upper parte of everye piece so melted and cast; upon the payne to forfeyte the valewe of everye piece or cake solde or offered to bee solde, and not so stamped or marked.[29]

The act obsesses over the need to ensure that the wax being sold is free from "deceyptfull mixture" and requires producers of wax to mark their wax, not once, but repeatedly to ensure that corrupters can be traced. It also attaches a penalty for selling contaminated wax of 2s per pound, an amount that would purchase approximately the same quantity of goods as £40 would now.[30] Again, these concerns connect metaphorically to other cultural preoccupations. Just as the value of wax depends on its lack of corruption, so too does a woman's value in marriage. The practice of stamping the wax with the creator's signet to signal purity might connect to the role that fathers were supposed to play as guarantors of their daughters' virtue. We will return to these issues of purity, virtue, and ownership in this chapter when we look at the association of female bodies with wax in Shakespeare's work and especially in *The Rape of Lucrece*.

Once purified, wax could be sold. Most beeswax went into the production of candles, which were consumed primarily by the elite, and by the Catholic Church.[31] Candles made of tallow, a substance derived from animal fats, substituted for wax in poorer households. The fact that beeswax was an elite material adds to its positive cultural valences, especially since beeswax burns more cleanly than tallow, which gives off a foul odor and significantly more smoke. While the association of candles with Catholicism might have tainted their virtue for some Protestant authors, outside of conversations about religion they seem to have retained their association with virtue. After all, candles were the purest way to bring light to the darkness. In Shakespeare's *True Tragedy of Richard Duke of York and the Good King Henry the Sixth* (*3 Henry VI*), Clifford, dying, compares his life to a candle, "Here burns my candle out — ay, here it dies, / Which, whiles it lasted, gave King Henry light."[32] The candlelight represents both Clifford's life and the hope that he was able to offer the King. In *The Tragedy of Macbeth*, Macbeth also associates candlelight with life, mournfully lamenting, "out, out, brief Candle. / Life's but a walking shadow" after hearing the news of his wife's death.[33] For Shakespeare's villain, it is the shadow cast by candlelight that signifies his own life's path in fraught relation to the path of light, or virtue.[34]

1.3   Using Wax

The demand for candles drove the wax trade, but candles were not the only important use of wax. Wax was also used medicinally, as a material for writing, and as a material of artistic creation. Each of these uses adds additional resonances to the meanings wax takes on in the early modern period. All of the treatises on bee-keeping that I mentioned earlier detail the medicinal uses of wax. According to Butler, "[w]axe hath no certaine elementar quality, but is a meane betweene hot and cold, and betweene dry and moist, it mollifieth the sinews, [and] it ripeneth & resolveth ulcers."[35] This Galenic description of the value of wax as medicine ascribes it a place as the "meane" between the four humoral qualities. It straddles the difference between "hot and cold" and between "dry and moist," which allows it to soothe both "sinewes" and "ulcers." Further, this in-between quality makes wax like skin, leading Pliny to suggest, "all wax … is emollient, warming, and restorative of flesh; the fresher it is the better."[36]

Again in the medicinal uses of wax, we see an association of wax with bodies and particularly with female bodies. Butler suggests that wax is particularly useful for women struggling to breastfeed:

> The quantity of a pease in waxe beeing swallowed down of nurces doth dissolue the milke curded in the paps, and ten round pieces of wax of the bignes of so many graines of millet or hepseede will not suffer the milke to curdle in the stomach.[37]

Hill provides an almost identical list of medicinal uses for wax. These medicinal associations double the humoral and reproductive associations that we will explore in this chapter.

Another form wax takes in the world is as a material of writing. Wax tablets, for example, were used as writing surfaces in ancient Rome and Greece, and the practice continued throughout the Middle Ages and into the sixteenth and seventeenth centuries. As a result of its characteristics as a writing surface, wax accrues additional meaning in literary texts. Wax is well suited for writing because even in its most solid state wax is soft enough that it can easily be scratched with a stylus and firm enough that it can retain inscription. Moreover, because wax can be remodeled, wax tablets, like slates can be wiped clean and reused. Since wax writing has a temporary quality, it has never been a medium for official documents. Instead, wax tablets were used during the classical period for writing poetry and making private notations.[38] The classical practice of writing on wax continued into the Middle Ages where wax tablets were used by schoolboys, and accountants, and provided useful surfaces for note taking, and private correspondence.[39]

Wax is a surface suited to ephemeral inscriptions, not wholly unlike the whitewashed walls that Juliet Fleming describes in *Graffiti and the Writing Arts of Early Modern England*.[40] While wax tablets might be more private than walls, both offered surfaces for externalizing thought and both suggest that the "early modern period had a way of understanding the relation of writing to the mind, and to the world outside it, that was not that of representation or reference" but rather "a mode of knowledge that simultaneously thinks through matter and accords it a sensibility of its own."[41] Which is to say, that the materiality of wax informs the meaning of the text inscribed upon it and also has meaning itself.

We might see this in Shakespeare's Sonnet 122, in which the speaker rejects the young man's gift of a writing tablet:

> Thy gift, thy tables, are within my brain
> Fully charactered with lasting memory,
> Which shall above that idle rank remain
> Beyond all date, even to eternity;
> Or at least so long as brain and heart
> Have faculty by nature to subsist,
> Till each to razed oblivion yield his part
> Of thee, thy record never can be missed.
> That poor retention could not so much hold,
> Nor need I tallies thy dear love to score;
> Therefore to give them from me was I bold,
> To trust those tables that receive thee more.
> To keep an adjunct to remember thee
> Were to import forgetfulness in me.[42]

While the speaker never names the material of the "tables," Amanda Watson suggests that these "'writing tables' or 'table-books'" were "made of paper covered in wax for easier erasure."[43] Thus, they materially contain the possibility of erasure in a way that paper alone would not. Jonathan Goldberg, paying attention to the indeterminacy of the tablets, argues "the gift returned is a pad whose space of inscription is at the same time a space of erasure. Whether a pad full of tallies is rejected, or whether filling a pad with tallies is rejected, both possibilities — of the written pad and the blank pad — are apparently the same scene of inscription and erosion."[44] Rejecting the tablets, the speaker insists on the superiority of his mind and that his beloved is "fully charactered" there "with lasting memory."[45] Moreover, the speaker suggests that to accept the gift would be an admission of fallibility: "To keep an adjunct to remember thee / Were to import forgetfulness in me." Still, the possibility of forgetting is intrinsic to the act of memory when memory is made physically a part of the body. Thus even as the speaker advocates the superiority of his own memory, he worries about what will happen to that record when he dies. The claim that memory will last "Beyond all date, even to eternity" gives way to the admission, "Or at least as long as brain and heart / Have faculty by nature to subsist." Yet since the speaker believes that his memory will last for all the eternity he will experience, he chooses to return the tables and to reject the physical reminder of erasure that they embody.

It is not just the temporary nature of writing on wax that differentiates the practice of writing on wax from other practices of writing and gives it additional poetic resonances. Since words are carved into the body of the wax with a stylus, they become part of the wax, giving it form until they are wiped away.[46] Writing on paper or slate requires a writing instrument that leaves a residue of ink, graphite, or chalk to make meaning, while writing on wax is a more physical experience and depends only on the pressure of the stylus to make a mark. In classical cultures, wax tablets were fashioned together to form diptych and triptych booklets. These booklets could be closed and sealed, protecting the contents inside and often were filled with love poems which the recipient could wipe away and then replace with a reply.[47] The form of these booklets together with the wax tablets provided a surface for both lover and beloved to express themselves, functioning as locations of intimate inscription that were themselves almost bodily, as we can see in Ovid's poetry. In *Amores* 1.11 and 1.12, which I will return to again in Chapter 4, he foregrounds the wax surface on which his poem is inscribed. In 1.11, he instructs a servant:

> Receive and take early to your mistress these tablets I have inscribed, and care that nothing hinder or delay! ... Should she ask how I fare, you will say my hope of her favour lets me live; as for the rest, it is charactered in the wax by my fond hand.[48]

The wax not only holds the words of Ovid's poems, it "show[s] the stroked words, softened by a passionate heat."[49] Thus, wax tablets do not merely become a location where writing can happen. They also affect the process of writing itself, making it a more physical and intimate experience. Moreover, as Quintilian claims in his *Institutes of Oratory*, wax might facilitate writing because the process of writing on wax more closely resembles the flow of thought than writing with ink, he explains, "we can write best on *waxen tablets...* parchment, though it assists the sight, yet from the frequent movement of the hand backwards and forwards, while dipping the pen in ink, causes delay, and interrupts the current of thought."[50] Thus, it is not simply that wax makes the experience of writing more bodily, it also makes it more like thought.

In addition, wax also becomes a material of writing when used for sealing letters; this further expands the range of meanings available to textual and artistic deployments of wax. Wax seals are fundamentally iconographic in nature and are used to signal authorship and ownership of a letter or document as well as to testify to its authenticity and, at times, the secrecy of its contents. Wax is a good material for sealing since it can be melted and imprinted with signet rings as it begins to re-solidify. It both holds an impression and proves a good binding material, adhering to the paper it is melted onto. Again, like the process of inscribing poetry in wax, the process of sealing a letter with wax becomes associated with bodies and sex. As we will explore in this chapter and Chapter 2, the trope of signet–seal is taken up in philosophy and poetry to figure epistemological and biological reproduction. We encounter the trope in Plato, Aristotle, Shakespeare's *Rape of Lucrece* and *Twelfth Night*, Donne's "Sappho to Philaenis," and Margaret Cavendish's *Philosophical Letters*. While both the process of inscribing a wax tablet and sealing a letter depend on some measure of force, the latter becomes more strongly associated with forceful encounters and attached to binaries of passive and active.

Wax is also an important material for art as we began to see in our discussion of Tintoretto. The use of wax in sculpture started in ancient Rome and Greece and continues to this day. During the early modern period, wax was put to several sculptural uses. Wax effigies were made of saints and recently departed nobility.[51] In Italy, it was also common for wealthy individuals to have miniature portraits commissioned in wax. In his *Lives of the Artists*, Giorgio Vasari notes "it would take too long if I were to speak of all those who execute portrait-medals of wax, seeing that every goldsmith at the present day makes them."[52] Generally, wax sculpture was regarded as inferior to the carving of stone, a judgment we can begin to hear in Vasari's dismissive mention that "every goldsmith at the present day makes them." In a letter to Benedetto Varchi, Michelangelo argues for the superiority of sculpture over painting and makes the point to clarify that, "by sculpture I mean the sort that is executed by cutting away from the block: the sort that is executed by adding resembles painting."[53] As a sculptural material of addition, wax belongs to the latter, and for Michelangelo, lesser category. Vasari similarly defines sculpture as, "an art which by removing all that is superfluous from the material under treatment reduces it to that form designed in the artist's mind."[54] There is no room in Vasari's definition for a sculpture of "adding on."[55]

Yet despite this dismissive attitude toward wax sculpture as an end in itself, wax played an important role in the production of the marble sculptures that both men valued. Vasari explains, "[s]culptors, when they wish to work a figure in marble, are accustomed to make what is called a model for it in clay or wax or plaster...because they can exhibit in it the attitude and proportion of the figure that they wish to make."[56] The process of addition allows the artist to work "with judgement and manipulation."[57] He "impresses the wax by means of tools made of bone, iron, or wood, and again putting on more he alters and refines till with the fingers the utmost finish is given to the model."[58] The models that Vasari describes are not quick sketches or rough-hewn approximations of the form that the marble will take; instead, they are given "utmost finish," refined until they "exhibit the attitude and the proportion of the figure" that will be carved in marble. Vasari's text reveals that the process of translating vision to marble all but requires the mediation of wax. While a sculptor could begin directly with marble, Vasari warns, "many errors in statues spring from [the] impatience of the artist to see the round figure out of the block at once, so that often an error is revealed that can only be remedied by joining on pieces... [which] is ugly and despicable and worthy of the greatest blame."[59] The malleability of wax allows the material rendering of artistic vision to be a gradual process during which errors can be corrected. Once a sculptor perfects his wax model, he can translate wax form to marble with relative ease and accuracy since the wax model is a site that can be mapped and measured.

Similarly, wax also served as an important intermediary for painters who, as we saw with Tintoretto, used wax models to work out composition, lighting, figure, and form. In *On the True Precepts of the Art of Painting* (1586), Giovanni Battista Armenini asks, "Is there anyone who does not yet know that simply turning one or two figures in round relief in different ways, one can derive many diverse models for one's paintings?"[60] He then suggests that:

> By looking at Michelangelo's *Last Judgment*, one can see that he followed the procedure I have described. And there have been some who have said that he used some wax models he had made himself and that he would first immerse the joints in hot water to soften them and would then twist the limbs to suit his needs. I leave the proof of the possible success of this method up to you.[61]

Armenini is hesitant to assert too strongly that Michelangelo employed wax models, qualifying his claim with "there have been some who said" and eventually specifying that "Leonardo da Vinci had the courage to say, according to what one of his pupils in Milan told me, that he was displeased by *The Last Judgment* only because too few figures had been used in too many ways and, therefore, it seemed he saw as many muscles in the figure of a youth as in that of an old person."[62] By including this statement and attributing it to da Vinci, Armenini both distances himself from the critique and suggests a limitation of the models: The same figure should not be used to represent a wide variety of bodies as the differences in human forms make it dangerous to repeat the same figure in a painting too often if one wants to create a realistic scene. Yet the advantages of using wax figures seem to outweigh the disadvantages. Wax sculptures provided artists with the ability to work out conceptual problems before committing to more permanent mediums and to explore possibilities, such as a flying human form, that would otherwise be inaccessible. Wax's role as an intermediary material in these artistic processes begins to reveal some of its conceptual power; it models the artistic process itself, the translation of artistic conception into material form.

1.4   THINKING WAX

The uses of wax outlined above have begun to suggest that wax is a material that is useful to think with. We can see the same in wax's history as a philosophical model for the mind, heart, and soul, locations of selfhood that have at times been largely interchangeable. Starting with Plato's reading of Homer and extending through Aristotle and the scholastic tradition, wax placed in relation to a signet or stamp served as the dominant model for understanding the production of knowledge and memory. That is until Descartes' cogito broke from tradition by considering wax alone. Wax's role in philosophy underlies the literary uses that we will be exploring in this book. Thus, I want to pause for a moment and trace the philosophical uses of wax as a model for the self.

The connection between wax and a consideration of what we can loosely term the soul can be traced to Homer's *Iliad*. Homer refers to the heart as "shaggy," which, at least for Plato, implies a wax materiality.[63] While Homer only mentions the shaggy heart in passing, it seems to be valenced positively.[64] More importantly, for Plato, Homer is the source for the idea that impressions are made on the waxen block. He explains, impressions are made in "the heart of the soul, as Homer says in a parable, meaning to indicate the likeness of the soul to wax (κῆρ κηὸς)."[65] The linguistic similarity between κῆρ (soul) and κηὸς (wax) becomes the basis for connecting the two first in poetry and then philosophy.

In the *Theaetetus*, Plato's Socrates builds upon this possibility, when he proposes a wax block as a model for the mind. He imagines that all sensory experience and knowledge could be imprinted on the mind "as from the seal of a ring."[66] The model offers a theory as to how external stimuli could be internalized. Yet it does not stop there. Socrates also uses wax to figure the variation in the capacity of the human mind to learn and retain information. He explains that the block of wax might be "of different sizes in different men; harder, moister, and having more or less of purity in one than another, and in some of an intermediate quality."[67] These differences in size and quality of the wax block begin to

explain variations in how much information minds store and how crisply
or clearly they retain information.

While the model of the wax mind is compelling, Socrates ultimately
abandons it because it fails to explain certain kind of errors. The mind
as wax can explain errors of misrecognition or forgetfulness; however, it
cannot explain why people make simple arithmetic errors, such as believing that five and seven add to eleven rather than twelve. According to
Socrates, the person who makes such a mistake knows both eleven and
twelve and thus "does think one thing which he knows to be another
thing which he knows; but this, as we said, was impossible... because
otherwise the same person would inevitably know and not know the
same thing at the same time."[68] To explain this kind of error, Socrates
abandons the model of the mind as a block of wax and offers a second
model for the mind. Instead of conceiving of the mind as a block of wax,
he figures it as an aviary in which "the birds are kinds of knowledge."[69]
This aviary is empty when we are children and "whenever a man has got-
ten and detained in the enclosure a kind of knowledge, he may be said to
have learned or discovered the thing which is the subject of the knowledge: and this is to know."[70] The analogy of the aviary allows Socrates to
explain the difference between having knowledge and using it:

> when the various numbers and forms of knowledge are flying about in
> the aviary, and wishing to capture a certain sort of knowledge out of the
> general store, he takes the wrong one by mistake, that is to say, when he
> thought eleven to be twelve, he got hold of the ring-dove which had in his
> mind when he wanted the pigeon.[71]

Socrates solves the problem of abstract errors through his alternative model of the mind. Yet even this solution proves unsatisfactory
since it does not explain how a person could recognize his own false
opinion.

Ultimately, Socrates refuses to resolve on any model. Yet as he rejects
the aviary model, he recalls the model of the mind as wax, asking
Theaetetus, "will you tell me that there are other forms of knowledge
which distinguish the right and wrong birds, and which the owner keeps
in some other aviaries or graven on waxen blocks according to your foolish images, and which he may be said to know while he possesses them,
even though he have them not at hand in his mind."[72] While Socrates
implies that such an extension of either model would be absurd, this

pairing of the two together also could suggest that there is as much truth in the model of the mind as wax as there is in the model of the mind as aviary. Neither model is privileged, and no perfect model is offered in their place. Instead, the attempt to define knowledge fails. Socrates and Theaetetus agree that Socrates' "art show[s] that [he has] brought forth wind, and that the offspring of [his] brain are not worth bringing up."[73] The dialogue ends with an admission of failure rather than with any positive claims.[74]

Despite the fact that Plato does not ultimately claim that wax is a satisfactory model of the mind, his formulation was very influential. Aristotle's treatment of the senses in *On the Soul* seems to build on this understanding of the mind, while avoiding the philosophical problems of error and knowledge. Aristotle explains that "generally about all perception, we can say that a sense is what has the power of receiving into itself the sensible form of things without the matter, in the way in which a piece of wax takes on the impress of a signet-ring without the iron or gold."[75] Like Plato, Aristotle is using wax as a model or analogy. He does not explicitly render the mind as wax. Instead, he understands sense perception to work on the mind in just the way that a signet would work upon a block of wax. Yet Aristotle's insistence on the perfect symmetry between the two processes stands in stark contrast to the Platonic dialogue's refusal to adopt any model to explain perception.

The Aristotelian engagement with wax is not limited to sense perception. He also uses wax to explain the relationship between body and soul and to help lay out the distinction between passion and action. In *On the Soul*, while discussing the relationship of the soul to the body, Aristotle invokes wax to settle definitively the question of the unity of body and soul. He claims we "can dismiss as unnecessary the question whether the soul and the body are one" because "it is as though we were to ask whether the wax and its shape are one, or generally the matter of a thing and that of which it is the matter. Unity has many senses (as many as 'is' has), but the proper one is that of actuality."[76] For Aristotle, the body is material and the soul is form, or that "of which" body "is the matter." The two together are inseparable and intrinsically intertwined. They form a unity in which the material is actuality, the form potentiality, and both require each other.

Aristotle's choice of wax as an exemplary object seems to be rooted in the special properties of wax. Yet, if we return to Aristotle's invocation of wax, we must still ask the question of whether wax allows us "to dismiss as unnecessary the question whether the soul and the body are one?" When Aristotle arrives at a consideration of the "whole living body" he tells us the:

> soul plus the body constitutes the animal. From this it is clear that the soul is inseparable from its body, or at least that certain parts of it are (if it has parts) – for the actuality of some of them is the actuality of the parts themselves. Yet some may be separable because they are not the actualities of any body at all. Further, we have no light on the problem whether the soul may not be the actuality of its body in the sense in which the sailor is the actuality of the ship. This must suffice as our sketch or outline of the nature of soul.[77]

Aristotle leaves his discussion of the nature of the soul on a mark of uncertainty that is quite far from the claim that we can quickly dismiss the question of the unity of soul and body. Instead, by the end of this section of *On the Soul*, Aristotle seems only to be comfortable in claiming that some part of the soul must be inseparable from the body, because some part of the soul consists in providing functionality to the various parts of the body—such as enabling the eye to see. However, in some ways, that relationship was problematized from the very beginning when Aristotle chose wax to exemplify it rather than a more stable and less complex object.

Wax's ability to model the mind, sense perception, the distinction between passive and active, and the relationship between body and soul make it useful for the philosophers that followed Plato and Aristotle. For example, Cicero's *Dialogue Concerning Oratorical Partitions* (*De Partitiones Oratoriae*) gives voice to a theory of how memory connects to acts of writing. Cicero explains, "for as [writing] consists of the characters of letters, and of that substance on which those characters are impressed, so a perfect memory uses topics, as writing does wax, and on them arranges its images as if they were letters."[78] Here, Cicero explicitly makes memory an act of writing, and not simply impression, expanding on the Platonic and Aristotelian formulations of the mind. Similarly, in Ovid's *Metamorphoses*, his Pythagoras seems to respond to the Aristotelian association of wax with the question of the relationship between body and soul. For Ovid's Pythagoras, wax's malleability figures the capacity of the soul to take on many forms (bodies) and still remain the same:

> As yielding wax is stamped with new designs
> And changes shape and seems not still the same,
> Yet is indeed the same, even so our souls
> Are still the same for ever, but adopt
> In their migrations ever-varying forms.[79]

This vision of the relationship between soul and body (and form and matter) is radically different from the Aristotelian version: Where Aristotle holds that the soul and body are inextricable and, consequently, that the soul has no life outside the body, Pythagoras's soul is capable of taking on a plenitude of bodily forms. Still, both philosophers use wax to figure the tension between continuity and change. Wax also becomes, in Augustine, a material to model the trinity, and to conceptualize the relationship between the Old Testament and the New.[80] In Augustine, both of these traditions come together to theorize questions of religion.

When Descartes turns to wax in the *Meditations*, he is responding to this long tradition of modeling the mind and soul as wax stamped by external pressures. By considering wax alone, without signet, he breaks from scholasticism and reshapes a classic philosophical model. At the same time, by continuing to use wax as a model for the mind, he also signals his connection to that philosophical history. Descartes arrives at wax as though by digression. He has already laid out his argument for the priority of the mind, but finds himself in doubt of his own conclusions:

> But it still appears — and I cannot stop thinking this — that the corporeal things of which images are formed in my thought, and which the senses investigate, are known with much more distinctness than this puzzling 'I' which cannot be pictured in the imagination. And yet it is surely surprising that I should have a more distinct grasp of things which I realize are doubtful, unknown and foreign to me, than I have of that which is true and known — my own self. But I see what it is: my mind enjoys wandering off and will not yet submit to being restrained within the bounds of truth. Very well then; just this once let us give it completely free rein, so that after a while, when it is time to tighten the reins, it may more readily submit to being curbed.[81]

Descartes' framing of the wax argument suggests, at first, that it is a digression away from the main line of inquiry, and not in fact a pivotal moment within his *Meditations*. He treats the turn to wax as a backtracking of sorts. The meditator has already discarded sensory observations as unreliable, and yet "cannot stop thinking" that he knows "corporeal things... with much more distinctness than this puzzling 'I.'" Since he cannot rid the mind of these thoughts, the meditator chooses to indulge the mind so that "when it is time to tighten the reins, it may more readily submit to being curbed" and wax becomes the object with which the meditator indulges his mind, seemingly in error. Yet this framing of the wax passages as a "wandering" is mere sleight of hand. By the end of the discussion of wax, Descartes has used the material to return to his main assertion, that the mind must be the primary object of all knowledge, and that "every consideration whatsoever which contributes to my perception of the wax, or of any other body, cannot but establish even more effectively the nature of my own mind."[82] His discussion of wax then proves a second path to establish the same conclusion that the mind's nature is the most certain object of philosophy.

Descartes is able to use wax to establish the preeminence of the mind, in part, because wax changes. As we have already seen, Descartes begins by describing wax in detail, moving through every sensory register of the wax, before placing the wax by the fire and observing the way that it changes. The difference between the wax before and after the application of heat leads to the question, "what was it in the wax that I understood with such distinctness?"[83] By abstracting from his observations, the meditator finds the answer. He exhorts his reader, "let us concentrate, take away everything which does not belong the wax and see what is left."[84] The mutability of wax leads the meditator to reject the specific sensory characteristics of wax as the qualities that define it. Instead, he argues that only those qualities that are always true of the wax can be ascribed to it.

It turns out such qualities are only graspable in the mind, and not through sensory perception or even imagination. Again, Descartes turns to wax to illustrate the point. The meditator asks:

> but what is meant here by 'flexible' and 'changeable'? Is it what I picture in my imagination: that this piece of wax is capable of changing from a round shape to a square shape, or from a square shape to a triangular shape? Not at all; for I can grasp that the wax is capable of countless changes of this kind, yet I am unable to run through this immeasurable number of changes in my imagination, from which it follows that it is not the faculty of imagination that gives me my grasp of the wax as flexible and changeable.[85]

While the imagination can picture wax in a great number of shapes, the move to abstraction requires the mind. Moreover, as the meditator insists, "the nature of this piece of wax is in no way revealed by my imagination, but is perceived by the mind alone."[86] Since the truth of wax only can be known through thought, the meditator deduces "the perception I have of it is a case not of vision or touch or imagination — nor has it ever been despite previous appearances — but of purely mental scrutiny."[87] Even this mental scrutiny is ultimately insufficient to ensure our knowledge of wax. While it might seem that we now know wax, having derived an abstract understanding of it as "something extended, flexible and changeable," the meditator insists that in that process of abstracting we have actually more firmly confirmed the nature of our mind than any truth about the wax. We have returned to the point from whence we departed and once again confirmed that the mind is a thinking thing and the only thing about which we cannot doubt. Even though the meditator claims that the turn to wax is a wandering, it is actually a crucial reworking of Descartes earlier arguments.

As this brief analysis of the wax passage has shown, Descartes' project was intended to be revolutionary and wax is an important component of that project. It offers the meditator a second path to think through the implications of the *cogito* and confirm the preeminence of the mind. Moreover, as Margreta de Grazia argues, Descartes' choice of wax symbolically represents his departure from scholasticism. It is a "choice of wax-without-signet. To feature wax alone was to dismantle the apparatus which... was key to those old opinions he determined to clear from his mind."[88] Where "[s]ignet and wax had represented the process by which objects in the world became objects of knowledge; wax by itself, however, suggests an autonomous consciousness, dependent on its own innate ideational resources."[89] It becomes the perfect model for Descartes' new understanding of the mind.

If de Grazia's work begins to suggest the symbolic implications of Descartes wax, it does not exhaust them. Its presence in the text also signals continuity. John Hollander suggests in *Melodious Guile*, that wax also stands as a topos for "sameness-under-apparent-change."[90] No matter how many shapes wax takes or whether a signet is involved in determining those shapes, it is, in Descartes' own words "the same wax."[91] While Descartes, of course, is literally talking about one piece of wax that is still "the same wax," even after it has been melted, we can take that statement more broadly as a comment on metaphysical philosophy.

Descartes' project might be radically different than Aristotle's, but it is still the same type of project. It is still a philosophy of the mind, and the mind is still understood to be fundamentally like wax, whether it shapes itself or is pressed into shape by the pressure of a signet. Thus, wax in Descartes' work not only signals change, but also his place within philosophical history. Indeed, the philosophical engagement with wax extends beyond the seventeenth century. In Freud's consideration of the mystic writing-pad and in Derrida's reading of Freud, the traditional association of wax with the mind continues to prove a compelling launching point for conceptualizing the mind.[92]

1.5   Working Wax

The brief survey we have just made of the nature, production, and uses of wax begins to suggest why it was an important material in the early modern period. However, something more needs to be said about what it means to write a book about wax. On the one hand, in writing about wax, I am contributing to a conversation about a specific material that is of interest to literary scholars, art historians, and philosophers working in a variety of periods, and one about which relatively little has been said.[93] In the introduction to *Ephemeral Bodies: Wax Sculptures and the Human Figure*, Roberta Panzanelli asks, "what is it about wax that has kept it anchored in artistic practice for millennia yet confined to the margins of art history?"[94] My questions are not her question, but they are similar, what does it mean to foreground wax and its literary, philosophical, and cultural uses? What can we learn about gender, the mind, the human, and the world by paying attention to wax?

My project takes the early modern period, and particularly the sixteenth and seventeenth centuries as its focus because, as we have already begun to see, wax was vitally important to philosophical and literary thought during that period. Just as wax is malleable and its forms are marked by an intrinsic instability, so too are our understandings of ourselves and our relations to others. The early modern period is one in which these understandings were changing. Indeed, wax could help model the period's relationship to both the classical age and the present one. In the classical era, wax was used to make death masks, and statuary and to serve as a mold for bronzes. Thus, when artists used wax in the sixteenth and seventeenth centuries, they were tapping into this artistic history, and bringing new life to a traditional form like a new impression on wax does for a signet ring. Similarly, as we have already seen wax was vitally important as a philosophical model for the mind in both classical philosophy and early modern philosophical thought, and thus, the latter period bears the print of the former. At the same time, since wax itself is an impermanent material, susceptible to decay and degradation, it insists always on engaging first and foremost with the present. It is, to an extent, a material that insists on its immediacy, that promises no future and offers up no past. As a material of art it aims at current viewers not future ones and thus anticipates a kind of modern mentality which Charles Baudelaire gives voice to in "The Painter of Modern Life" when he explains, "by 'modernity' I mean the ephemeral, the fugitive, the contingent."[95] Through its connection to Descartes, anatomical models, and global commerce, wax begins to model modernity. Wax is a material that can mediate between past and present and can represent simultaneously an insistence on both.

In taking up this project, I have adopted a series of methods and critical perspectives derived from new historicism, feminism, thing theory, posthumanism, and queer theory. My approach is new historicist insofar as I take seriously the relationship between texts and culture and seek to offer a "cultural poetics."[96] It is feminist insofar as it asks feminist questions about the association of women with wax. For example, I ask whether there is space for female agency when women are figured as perfectly malleable wax in Shakespeare's *A Rape of Lucrece*, and what we can learn from Spenser's wax Florimell's ability to pass as a woman. I ask, further, how Shakespeare's texts depict female friendship, whether Margaret Cavendish's physics advocates female rule, and how Webster presents female rule and female identity in *The Duchess of Malfi*. In asking these questions, I follow paths opened by Valerie Traub's work on material representations of gender, Laurie Shannon's treatment of female friendship, Eve Keller's feminist readings of science, and Dympna Callaghan's treatment of dramatic representations of female rule.[97] These scholars have offered me a framework and language with which to discuss the gendered questions that arise around wax.

I am also indebted to recent work on the role of things in literature and culture. In her introduction to a special issue of the *Journal of Medieval and Early Modern Studies*, Maureen Quilligan asks for a reconsideration of early modern objects and subjects that does not "insist that they mark early modernity" but instead "remain[s] embedded in a particular moment in time."[98] The essays contained in the volume respond to this challenge by tracing the histories of particular material objects and the ways they come to mediate the early modern subject. Beyond this collection, work by Ann Rosalind Jones, Peter Stallybrass, Maureen Quilligan, Margreta de Grazia, Juliet Fleming, Rayna Kalas, and others has sought to re-examine the importance of objects in early modern culture, seeking, in part, to recover the specific history of objects in the period and offer a more nuanced understanding of the relationships between subjects and objects.[99] The problem of focusing on subjects to the exclusion of "things, or objects, or beasts" extends beyond the early modern period, as Bruno Latour insists in *We Have Never Been Modern*.[100] There, Latour points to the proliferation of networks and hybrids and suggests that we have not and cannot succeed in fully separating objects from subjects, or fields of knowledge from each other, and that our "modernity" is illusory. Building on Latour's claims, my book suggests that wax is a hybrid material, one attached to both subjects and objects and one used to negotiate and think through the relationships between these categories. Perhaps more than any other object or material, tracing the paths offered by wax in the early modern period reveals the subject-object problem as a pressing concern of the early modern period, and one that was approached from a variety of angles and approaches.

In the last chapters of the book, I draw upon posthumanist theory in order to explore the way wax figures the human and challenges its limits. In particular, the work of Latour, Jane Bennett, Katherine N. Hayles, Rosa Briadotti, and Dona Haraway has influenced my thinking about posthumanism and theorizations of the human.[101] While early modern critics including Karen Raber, Joseph Campana, Scott Maisano, and Wendy Beth Hyman have helped me think through the early modern period's specific engagements with hybrids, machines, prosthetics, and automata.[102]

Finally, in conceptualizing my method, I have been heavily influenced by queer theory, which has illustrated, for me, the power of complexity and irresolvability. My debt to queer theory is to some measure topical. Questions of gender and sexuality recur throughout my work, and my approach to those questions is largely inflected by my reading of theorists such as Eve Kosofsky Sedgwick, Judith Butler, and Jonathan Goldberg.[103] Yet while questions of gender and sexuality are an important component of my project, queer theory has also inflected how I have come to understand wax itself as a material that is queer insofar as it embodies contradictory discourses and refuses to maintain one legible shape. The inherent instability of wax means that no matter what shape it takes, it speaks always of its own constructed nature and threatens always to take on new figurations. If as Annamarie Jagose suggests, "queer is always an identity under construction, a site of permanent becoming" then wax might be a productive figure through which to understand queerness, while the theoretical underpinnings of "queer" might provide a useful starting place for understanding how wax figures in early modern texts and cultural spaces.[104]

In the chapters that follow, I move thematically through some of the questions invited by wax. In doing so, I have allowed the project to take on a shape of its own, a shape determined not by chronology, but by connections that reach across time and space. I aim to offer a history of wax in early modern literature that can itself be modeled with wax. Wax, as we have seen is malleable and prone to taking new forms. Thus if history is comprised of moments that could be located on the body of wax, then as that piece of wax is molded and reshaped, previously noncontiguous moments can be brought together. In this project, I am tracing the connections that wax itself offers as its appearance in different cultural spaces and different discourses brings disparate texts and contexts into temporary alignment. Moments not explicitly connected by close proximity in time, or by direct influence, are brought together by their interest in a materiality figured through wax in various forms and situations.

NOTES

1. Tintoretto, *The Temptation of Saint Anthony*, 1577–1588, *San Trovaso, Venice*.
2. Carlo Ridolfi, "Delle Marviglie Dell'arte," in *Painters on Painting*, ed. Eric Protter (New York: Grosset & Dunlap, 1971), 54. In Italian, "Esercitauasi ancora nel far piccioli modelli di cera, e di creta, vestendoli di cenci, ricercandone accuratamente con le pieghe de'panni le parti delle membra, quali diuisaua ancora entro piccole case e prospettive composte di asse, e di cartoni, accomodandoui lumicini per le fenestre, recandoui in tale guisa i lumi, e le ombre. Sospendeua ancora alcuni modelli co'fili alle trauature, per osseruare gli effetti che faceuano veduti all'insù, per formar gli scorci posti ne'soffitti, componendo in tali modi bizzarre inuenzioni." *Le maraviglie dell' arte, ouero, Le vite de gl'illustri pittori veneti, e dello stato*, vol. 2 (Venice: Presso Gio. Battista Sgava, 1648), 6–7.

3. Marco Boschini, "Ricche Minere Della Pittura Veneziana," in *Italy and Spain, 1600–1750; Sources and Documents*, eds. Robert Enggass and Jonathan Brown (Englewood Cliffs, NJ, 1970), 52. In the Italian, "poiche sono ben si difficili gli scorcij, posti nel piano (come si è detto) ma di maggior difficoltà sono poi il formar scorzi nell'aria; mentre per l'aria non si possono far volar le statue: e pure questi nostri eruditi Pittori Veneziani fanno volare le figure Humane" *Le Ricche Minere Dell Pittura Venezia* (Venice, 1674), sig. e4r.

4. René Descartes, *Meditations on First Philosophy: With Selections from the Objections and Replies*, trans. and ed. John Cottingham, Cambridge Texts in the History of Philosophy, rev. ed. (Cambridge, UK: Cambridge University Press, 1997), 54. In the original Latin: "nuperrime ex favis fuit educta; nondum amisit omnem saporem sui mellis; nonnihil retinet odoris florum ex quibus collecta est; ejus color, figura, magnitudo, manifesta sunt; dura est, frigida est, facile tangitur." *Meditationes de Prima Philosophia*, vol. 7 of *Oeuvres de Descartes*, eds. Charles Adam and Paul Tannery (Paris: L. Cerf, 1897), 30. All subsequent references to the *Meditations* in Latin are to this volume. In the French: "qui vient d'estre tiré de la ruche: il n'a pas encore perdu la douceur du miel qu'il contenoit, il retient encore quelque chose de l'odeur des fleurs dont il a esté recueilly; sa couleur, sa figure, sa grandeur, sont apparentes; il est dur, il est froid, on le touche" *Meditations Touchant la Premiere Philosophie*, vol. 9 in *Oeuvres de Descartes* eds. Charles Adam and Paul Tannery (Paris: L. Cerf, 1897), 23. All subsequent references to *The Meditations* in French are to this volume.

5. Descartes, *Meditations on First Philosophy*, 54. In the Latin: "saporis reliquiae purgantur, odor expirat, color mutatur, figura tollitur, crescit magnitudo, fit liquida, fit calida, vix tangi potest, nec jam, si pulses, emittet sonum," 30. In the French: "ce qui y restoit de saveur s'exale, l'odeur s'évanoüit, sa couleur se change, sa figure se perd, sa grandeur augmente, il devient liquide, il s'échauffe, à peine le peut-on toucher, & quoy qu'on le frappe, il ne rendra plus aucun son," 23–24.

6. Descartes, *Meditations on First Philosophy*, 54. In the Latin: "remotis iis quae ad ceram non pertinent, videamus quid supersit: nempe nihil aliud quàm extensum quid, flexibile, mutabile," 31. In the French: "Considerons-le attentivement, & éloignant toutes les choses qui n'appartiennent point à la cire, voyons ce qui reste. Certes il ne demeure rien que quelque chose d'estendu, de flexible et de muable," 24.

7. Descartes, *Meditations on First Philosophy*, 54. In the Latin: "aliud quàm extensum quid, flexibile, mutabile," 31. In the French: "quelque chose d'estendu, de flexible et de muable," 24.

8. Descartes, *Meditations on First Philosophy*, 54. In the Latin: "nuperrime ex favis fuit educta; nondum amisit omnem saporem sui mellis; nonnihil retinet odoris florum ex quibus collecta est," 30. In the French: "qui vient d'estre tiré de la ruche: il n'a pas encore perdu la douceur du miel qu'il contenoit, il retient encore quelque chose de l'odeur des fleurs dont il a esté recueilly," 23.

9. Thomas William Cowan, *Wax Craft, All About Beeswax; Its History, Production, Adulteration, and Commercial Value* (London, 1908), 524.

10. Aristotle, "History of Animals," in *The Complete Works of Aristotle*, ed. Jonathan Barnes, 2 vols (Princeton, NJ, 1984), 553b28–554a11. All references to Aristotle are to Bekker numbers.

11. Aristotle, "History of Animals," 623b26–627b23.

12. Thomas Hill, *The Proffitable Arte of Gardening, Now the Third Tyme Set Fourth: To Whiche Is Added Muche Necessary Matter, and a Number of Secrettes with the Phisick Helpes Belonging to Eche Herbe, and That Easie Prepared. To This Annexed, Two Propre Treatises, the One Entituled the Marueilous Gouernment, Propertie, and Benefite of the Bées, with the Rare Secrets of the Honny and Waxe. And the Other, the Yerely Coniectures, Méete for Husbandme[N] to Knowe: Englished by Thomas Hill Londine* (London: Henry Bynneman, 1568), Sig. fol. 5.

13. Charles Butler, *The Feminine Monarchie or a Treatise Concerning Bees, and the Due Ordering of Them: Wherein the Truth, Found Out by Experience and Diligent Observation, Discovereth the Idle and Fond Conceipts, Which Many Haue Written Anent This Subiect. By Char: Butler Magd* (Oxford, 1609), Sig. G2v.

14. Ibid.

15. William Shakespeare, *The Second Part of Henry the Fourth*, *The Norton Shakespeare*, eds. Stephen Greenblatt, Walter Cohen, Jean E. Howard, and Katharine Eisaman Maus (New York: W. W. Norton, 1997), 4.3.204–206. Unless otherwise noted all Shakespeare references are to *The Norton Shakespeare*. References are to act, scene, and line.

16. Michael Drayton, "The Quest of Cynthia," in *Minor Poems of Michael Drayton*, ed. Cyril Brett (Oxford: Clarendon Press, 1907), 144–150. All references are by line number. Here, 182–184.

17. Drayton, "The Quest of Cynthia," 189–192.

18. Philip Sidney, *The Countess of Pembroke's Arcadia*, ed. Katherine Duncan-Jones (Oxford: Oxford University Press, 1985), 209.

19. Bartholomeus Anglicus, *Batman uppon Bartholome, his Booke De Proprietatibus Rerum, trans. John Trevisa and Stephen Batman* (London, 1582), Book 19, Chapter 61. In the Latin: "Cera autem quanto est recentior / tanto est odoratior / ductilior/ purior, et ad diversarum

impressionum et figurarum susceptionem aptior." Bartholomaei Anglici, *De Genuinis rerum coelestium, terrestrium, et inferarum Proprietabus, Libri XVIII*, edition secunda (Francofurt: Sumptibus N. Steinii, 1601), 1118.

20. Descartes, *Meditations*, 54. In the Latin, "fit liquida, fit calida," 30. In the French: "il devient liquide, il s'échauffe," 23.

21. Michael Tuck, "Everday Commodities, the Rivers of Guinea, and the Atlantic World: The Beeswax Export Trade, c. 1450–c.1800," in *Brokers of Change: Atlantic Commerce and Cultures in Pre-Colonial Western Africa*, ed. Toby Green (Oxford, 2012), 290–298.

22. Cadamosto, Alvise. *The Voyages of Cadamosto*, trans. G. R. Crone (London, 1937), 51.

23. Ibid., 51. The original Italian is available in Fracanzano da Montalboddo and Amerigo Vespucci, *Paesi Nouamente Retrovate & Novo Mundo da Alberico Vesputio Florentino intitulato 1508, In Facsimile* (Princeton, NJ: Princeton University Press, 1916). The Italian reads: "piuse marauegliauáo de uedere ardere una cádela de nocte i su uno candeliere perche in suo paese li no sanno far altra luce saluo quella del foco e non habiando mai piu uisto cádele ardere li parse una bella cosa e marauigliosa e perche in quel paese se troua mele: & lore zuzano el mele fora de la cera con la boccha e butala uta: unde hauendo Io comprato un poco de sauomelli li mostrai come se trazea el mel dala cera dapoi domandai se li saueano che cosa fosse quella: li resposeno che quella non era cosa da niente & in sua presentia li feci far alcune candele e seceli impiar," 42–43.

24. André Alvares de Almada, "Brief Treatise on the Rivers of Guinea, Part I, 1594," in *African Studies Collection* (1594, Department of History, University of Liverpool, 1984), 43, http://digital.library.wisc.edu/1711.dl/AfricanStudies.Almada01 (20 September 2015). The Portuguese reads: "He rio de grande trato d'escravos, roupa d'algodão branca e preta, e o mesmo algodão; muita cera, e posto que não façâo colmeias são tantas as abelhas, e o mato tanto, que por essa causa ha muito mel e cera." André Alvares d'Almada, *Tratado Brave dos Rios de Guine' Do Cabo-Verde, desde o Rio do Sanaga' Ate' aos baixos de Sant' Anna, 1594*. Facsimile, Porto: Typ. Commercial Portuense, 1841, 27.

25. Tuck, "Everday Commodities," 298.

26. For early modern accounts of maternal impression, see Michel de Montaigne, "Of the Power of the Imagination," in *The Complete Essays*, trans. Donald M. Frame (Stanford: Stanford University Press, 1958), 68–69 and Thomasso Buoni, "Problemes of beautie and all humane affections," trans. by Samson Leonard, in *Race in Early Modern England: A Documentary Companion*, eds. Ania Loomba and Jonathan Burton (New York, NY: Palgrave Macmillan, 2007), 163–165.

27. Pliny, *Natural History*, ed. and trans. H. Rackham, vol. 6 of 10, Loeb Classical Library (Cambridge, MA: Harvard University Press, 1968), 21.49. In the Latin: "cera fit expressis favis, sed ante purificatis aqua ac triduo in tenebris siccatis, quarto die liquatis igni in novo fictili, aqua favos tegente, tunc sporta colatis. rursus in eadem olla coquitur cera cum eadem aqua excipiturque alia frigida, vasis melle circumlitis."

28. Pliny, *Natural History*, 21.49. In Latin: "candidissima vero."

29. *The Statutes of the Realm*, vol. 4, part 1. Searchable text edition (Burlington, ON: TannerRitchie Publishing, 2007), 670.

30. Samuel H. Williamson, "Purchasing Power of Money in the United States from 1774 to 2010," Measuring Worth, 2009, http://www. measuringworth.com/ (29 May 2011).

31. See the conclusion for a brief discussion of the significance of wax and candles in England's religious history.

32. Shakespeare, *The True Tragedy of Richard Duke of York and the Good King Henry the Sixth*, 2.6.1–2.

33. Ibid., *The Tragedy of Macbeth*, 5.5.22–23.

34. If the candle's ability to light darkness lends it symbolic and poetic resonances, its complex mechanics also make it an object of physics, although not in the period under consideration. In his 1860 lecture, *The Chemical History of a Candle*, Michael Faraday commented, "there is not a law under which any part of the universe is governed which does not come into play and is touched upon in [the phenomena of burning a candle]. There is no better, there is no more open door by which you can enter into the study of natural philosophy than by considering the physical phenomena of a candle." Michael Faraday, "The Chemical History of a Candle," in *Scientific Papers: Physics, Chemistry, Astronomy, Geology*, ed. Charles W. Eliot (New York, 1910), 86.

35. Butler, *The Feminine Monarchie*, Sig. M5r–M5v.

36. Pliny, *Natural History*, 22.55. In Latin, "omnis autem mollit, calfaci, explet corpora, recens melior."

37. Butler, *The Feminine Monarchie*, Sig. M5v.

38. Cowan, *Wax Craft*, 18.

39. Bernhard Bischoff, *Latin Palaeography: Antiquity and the Middle Ages*, trans. Daibhm O. Cróinin and David Ganz, reprint edition (Cambridge, UK, 1990), 14.

40. See Juliet Fleming, *Graffiti and the Writing Arts of Early Modern England*, 2nd ed. (London: Reaktion Books, 2009), 73–76.

41. Ibid., 164.

42. Shakespeare, *Sonnet 122*, 1964.

43. Amanda Watson, "'Full Character'd': Competing Forms of Memory in Shakespeare's Sonnets," in *A Companion to Shakespeare's Sonnets*, ed. Michael Schoenfeldt (Oxford, 2007), 353.

44. Jonathan Goldberg, *Voice Terminal Echo: Postmodernism and English Renaissance Texts* (Abingdon, OX, 1986), 95.
45. The speaker's association of memory with wax inscription connects to the philosophical understanding of the mind as a block of wax upon which impressions can be made. Here, though, the speaker imagines that the memory works not through stamped images but inscribed words. Amanda Watson connects this image to a humanist pedagogy for memorization. "Full Character'd," 351–354.
46. Juliet Fleming argues in *Cultural Graphology: Writing after Derrida* that writing transforms other materials too: "Wood, fabric, canvas, or paper; think carefully and you will realize that the receptive surface is a membrane that changes and is changed by what it bears…. Writing becomes part of the material that supports it." Juliet Fleming, *Cultural Graphology: Writing After Derrida* (Chicago: University of Chicago Press, 2016), 141. Yet wax's transformation is different because it does not require one to "think carefully," and it does not require the addition of other substances.
47. Cowan, *Wax Craft*, 18.
48. Ovid, *Amores*, trans. in Raphael Lyne, "Lyrical Wax in Ovid, Marlowe, and Donne," *Ovid and the Renaissance Body*, ed. Goran V. Stanivukovic (Toronto, 2001), 193, 1.11.7–8, 1.11.13–14. In the Latin:

> accipe et ad dominam peraratas mane tabellas
> perfer et obstantes sedula pelle moras!
> …
> si quaeret quid agam, spe noctis vivere dices;
> cetera fert blanda cera notata manu.

Ovid, *Ovid's Amores, Book One: A Commentary*, eds. Maureen B. Ryan, and Caroline A. Perkins (Norman: University of Oklahoma Press, 2011), 112.
49. Lyne, "Lyrical Wax," 193.
50. Quintilian, *Institutes of Oratory or Education of an Orator*, trans. John Selby Watson (London: 1875), 10.3.31. In Latin: "scribi optime ceris, in quibus facillima est ratio delendi, nisi forte visus infirmior membranarum potius usum exiget, quae ut iuvant aciem, ita crebra relatione, quoad intinguntur calami, morantur manum et cogitationis impetum frangunt," in *Quintilian, Quintiliani Institutiones Oratoriae Liber X*, eds. W. Peterson (Oxford: Oxford University Press, 1892), 36.
51. Cowan, *Wax Craft*, 22.
52. Giorgio Vasari, *Lives of the Most Eminent Painters, Sculptors, & Architects*, vol. 6, trans. Gaston du C. de Vere (London: Macmillan,

1914), 87. In Italian, "Troppo sarei lungo se io avessi di questi che fanno ritratti di medaglie di cera a ragionare, perché oggi ogni orefice [ne] fa," *Le Vite de' Piu Eccellenti Pittori Scultori e Architettori*, edizione Giuntina, vol. 4 (1568) 630.

53. Michelangelo Buonarroti, "Michelangelo: Answer to Bendetto Varchi," trans. Robert W. Carden in Robert Klein and Henri Zerner, *Italian Art, 1500–1600: Sources and Documents* (Englewood Cliffs, NJ, 1966), 14. In the Italian, "io intendo scultura, quella che si fa per forza di levare: quella che si fa per via di porre, è simile alla pittura," *La Lettere di Michelangelo Buonarotti*, ed. Gaetano Milanesi (Florence, 1875), 522.

54. Vasari, *On Technique*, ed. Baldwin G. Brown, trans. Louisa Maclehouse (New York: Dover Publications, 1960), 143. In the Italian: "La Scultura è una Arte che levando il superfluo dalla materia suggetta, la riduce a quella forma di corpo che nella idea dello Artefice è disegnata," *Le Vite de' Piu Eccellenti Pittori Scultori e Architettori*, edizione Giuntina, vol. 1 (Florence, 1568) 82.

55. As Klein notes, the distinction between the two types of sculpture is classical in origin and can be found in Pliny (14n.3). Yet the clear preference for marble sculpture, or more generally sculpture "that is executed by cutting away from the block," in both Michelangelo and Vasari suggests that wax sculpture was not a privileged art form.

56. Vasari, *On Technique*, 148. In the Italian: "Sogliono gli scultori, quando vogliono lavorare una figura di marmo, fare per quella un modello -- che così si chiama --, cioè uno esemplo che è una figura di grandezza di mez[z]o braccio o meno o più secondo che gli torna comodo, o di terra o di cera o di stucco, perché e' possin mostrar in quella l'attitudine e la proporzione che ha da essere nella figura che e' voglion fare, cercando accomodarsi alla larghezza et alla altezza del sasso che hanno fatto cavare per farvela dentro" *Le Vite de' Piu Eccellenti Pittori Scultori e Architettori*, edizione Giuntina, vol. 1 (1568), 87.

57. Ibid., 149. In the Italian, "col giudicio e le mani lavorando," *Le Vite de' Piu Eccellenti Pittori Scultori e Architettori*, edizione Giuntina, vol. 1 (1568), 88.

58. Ibid. In the Italian, "crescendo la materia, con istecchi d'osso, di ferro o di legno si spinge indentro la cera, e con mettere dell'altra sopra si aggiugne e raffina, finché con le dita si dà a questo modello l'ultimo pulimento."

59. Ibid., 152. In the Italian, "e di qui nascono molti errori che sono nelle statue, ché, per la voglia ch'à l'artefice del vedere le figure tonde fuor del sasso a un tratto, spesso si gli scuopre un errore che non può rimediarvi se non vi si mettono pezzi commessi, come abbiamo visto costumare a molti artefici moderni; il quale rattoppamento è da ciabattini

e non da uomini eccellenti o maestri rari, et è cosa vilissima e brutta e di grandissimo biasimo" *Le Vite de' Piu Eccellenti Pittori Scultori e Architettori*, edizione Giuntina, vol. 1 (1568), 91.

60. Giovanni Battista Armenini, *On the True Precepts of the Art of Painting*, ed. Edward J. Olszewski (New York, 1977), 169. In the Italian, "Ma chi è che ancora non sappia che di una o di due figure di tondo rilievo, solamente col voltarle nel modo che sono per diverse vie, non se ne cavino molte in pittura e tutte tra sè diverse?" *De' Veri Precetti Della Pittura di M. Gio Battista Armenino Libri Tre*, ed. Stefano Ticozzi (Milan: Vincenzo Ferrario, 1820), 139.

61. Armenini, *True Precepts of the Art of Painting*, 169. In Italian, "poichè ciò pure si vede da chi punto considera nel Giudizio dipiuto da Michelangelo, lui essersi servito nel termine ch' io dico. Nè ei è mancato chi abbia detto quivi, ch' egli ne aveva alcune fatte di cera di mano sua, e che loro torceva le membra a modo suo, immollando prima le giunture nell' acqua calda, acciò quelle a rimorbidir si venissero; della qual via come forse riuscibile, io ne lascio la prova all' arbitrio di ognuno" *De' Veri Precetti Della Pittura*, 139.

62. *Armenini, True Precepts of the Art of Painting*, 170. In the Italian, "Io so bene che Leonardo Vinci, vedendo quello, e forse di ciò accorto, secondo ch'io intesi da un suo allievo in Milano, ebbe ardire di dire, che questo solo gli dispiaceva di quell' opera, che in troppi modi si era servito di poche figure, e che perciò tanto gli pareva veder muscoli nella figura di un giovane, quanto di un vecchio, ed il simile essere de contorni.la figura di un giovane, quanto di un vecchio, ed il simile essere de' contorni," *De' Veri Precetti Della Pittura*, 139–140.

63. Homer, *The Iliad*, trans. Richmond Lattimore (1951; repr. Chicago, 2011), 1.189. Citation is to book and line. In Greek, "στήθεσσιν λασίοισι" Homer, "Iliad, Books 1–12," in *Homeri Opera*, eds. David B. Munro and Thomas W. Allen, vol. 1 (Oxford University Press, 1920), 1.189.

64. Plato, "Theaetetus," *The Dialogues of Plato*, ed. and trans. Benjamin Jowett, vol. 4, 3rd ed. (London: Oxford University Press, 1892), 194e–195b. Plato objects to Homer's suggestion that the shaggy heart is positive. He writes, "but when the heart of anyone is shaggy — a quality which the all-wise poet commends …. then there is a corresponding defect in the mind... the shaggy and rugged and gritty... have the impressions indistinct" (194e–195b). Citation is to Stephanus number. In the Greek: "Οταν τοίνυν λάσιόν τὸ κέαρ ᾖ, ὃ δὴ ἐπήνεσεν ὁ πάντα σοθὸς ποιητής." *Plato VII, Theaetetus. Sophist*, ed. and trans. Harold North Fowler, Loeb Classical Library (Cambridge, MA: Harvard University Press, 1921). All Greek transcriptions of *The Theaetetus* that follow in the notes are from this edition.

65. Plato, "Theaetetus," 194c. In the Greek: "ψυχῆς 'κέαρ,' ὅ ἔφη Ὅμηρος αἰνιττόμενος τὴν τοῦ κηροῦ ὁμοιότητα, τότε μὲν καὶ τούτοις."
66. Plato, "Theaetetus," 191d. In Greek, "ὥσπερ δακτυλίων σημεῖα ἐνσημένους."
67. Plato, "Theaetetus," 191c. In Greek, "θὲς δή μοι λόγου ἕνεκα ἐν ταῖς ψυχαῖς ἡμῶν ἐνὸν κήρινον ἐκμαγεῖον, τῷ μὲν μεῖζον, τῷ δ' ἔλαττον, καὶ τῷ μὲν καθαρωτέρου κηροῦ, τῷ δὲ κοπρωδεστέρου, καὶ σκληροτέρου."
68. Plato, "Theaetetus," 196c. In the Greek: "ὁ γὰρ τοῦτο παθών, ὃ οἶδεν, ἕτεροναὐτὸ οἴεται εἶναι ὧν αὖ οἶδεν."
69. Plato, "Theaetetus," 197e. In Greek: "ὀρνίθωνἐπιστήμας νοῆσαι."
70. Plato, "Theaetetus," 197e. In Greek: "ἦν δ' ἂν ἐπιστήμην κτησάμενος καθείρξῃ εἰς τὸν περίβολον, φάναι αὐτὸν μεμαθηκέναι ἢ ηὑρηκέναι τὸ πρᾶγμα οὗ ἦν αὕτη ἡ ἐπιστήμη, καὶ τὸἐπίστασθαι τοῦτ' εἶναι."
71. Plato, "Theaetetus," 199b. In the Greek: "ὅταν θηρεύων τινά πού ποτ' ἐπιστήμην διαπετομένων ἀνθ' ἑτέρας ἑτέραν ἁμαρτὼν λάβῃ, τότε ἄρα τὰ ἕνδεκα δώδεκα ᾠήθη εἶναι, τὴν τῶν ἕνδεκα ἐπιστήμην ἀντὶ τῆς τῶν δώδεκα λαβὼν τὴν ἐν ἑαυτῷ οἷον φάτταν ἀντὶ περιστερᾶς."
72. Plato, "Theaetetus," 200b–200c. In the Greek: "ἣν οἶδεν ἡγεῖται; ἢ πάλιν αὖ μοι ἐρεῖτε ὅτι τῶν ἐπιστημῶν καὶ ἀνεπιστημοσυνῶν εἰσὶν αὖ ἐπιστῆμαι, ἃς ὁ κεκτημένος ἐν ἑτέροις τισὶ γελοίοις περιστερεῶσιν ἢ κηρίνοις πλάσμασι καθείρξας, ἔωσπερ ἂν κεκτῆται ἐπίσταται, καὶ ἐὰν μὴ προχείρους ἔχῃ ἐν τῇ ψυχῇ; καὶ οὕτω δὴ ἀναγκασθήσεσθε εἰς ταὐτὸν περιτρέχειν μυριάκις οὐδὲν πλέον ποιοῦντες."
73. Plato, "Theaetetus," 210b. In the Greek, Socrates asks: "ἦ οὖν ἔτι κυοῦμέν τι καὶ ὠδίνομεν, ὦ φίλε, περὶ ἐπιστήμης, ἢ πάντα ἐκτετόκαμεν" and Theaetetus agrees.
74. Still, there seems to be an implicit claim about the production of knowledge made throughout the piece by the trope of the midwife. From the very beginning of the dialogue, Socrates positions himself as a midwife attempting to aid Theaetetus in the birthing of his ideas and the determination of their worth.
75. Aristotle, "On the Soul," in *The Complete Works of Aristotle*, ed. Jonathan Barnes (Princeton, NJ: Princeton University Press, 1984), 424a18–424a23. Citations are to Bekker number. In the Greek: "Καθόλου δὲ περὶ πάσης αἰσθήσεως δεῖ λαβεῖν ὅτι ἡ μὲν αἴσθησίς ἐστι τὸ δεκτικὸν τῶν αἰσθητῶν εἰδῶν ἄνευ τῆς ὕλης, οἷον ὁ κηρὸς τοῦ δακτυλίου ἄνευ τοῦ σιδήρου καὶ τοῦ χρυσοῦ δέχεται τὸ σημεῖον." Aristotle, "On The Soul," in *Aristotle: On the Soul. Parva Naturalia. On Breath*, trans. Walter Stanley Hett, rev. edition, Loeb Classical Library (Cambridge, MA: Harvard University Press, 1957).
76. Aristotle, "On the Soul," 413a6–413a9. In Greek: "διὸ καὶ οὐ δεῖ ζητεῖν εἰ ἓν ἡ ψυχὴ καὶ τὸ σῶμα, ὥσπερ οὐδὲ τὸν κηρὸν καὶ τὸ σχῆμα, οὐδ'

ὅλως τὴν ἑκάστου ὕλην καὶ τὸ οὗ ὕλη· τὸ γὰρ ἓν καὶ τὸ εἶναι ἐπεὶ πλεοναχῶς λέγεται, τὸ κυρίως ἡ ἐντελέχειά ἐστιν."

77. Aristotle, "On the Soul," 413a3–413a9. In Greek: "κόρη καὶ ἡ ὄψις, κἀκεῖ ἡ ψυχὴ καὶ τὸ σῶμα τὸ ζῷον. Ὅτι μὲν οὖν οὐκ ἔστιν ἡ ψυχὴ χωριστὴ τοῦ σώματος, ἢ μέρη τινὰ αὐτῆς, εἰ μεριστὴ πέφυκεν, οὐκ ἄδηλον· ἐνίων γὰρ ἡ ἐντελέχεια τῶν μερῶν ἐστὶν αὐτῶν. Οὐ μὴν ἀλλ᾿ ἔνιά γε οὐθὲν κωλύει, διὰ τὸ μηθενὸς εἶναι σώματος ἐντελεχείας. Ἔτι δὲ ἄδηλον εἰ οὕτως ἐντελέχεια τοῦ σώματος ἡ ψυχὴ ὥσπερ πλωτὴρ πλοίου. Τύπῳ μὲν οὖν ταύτῃ διωρίσθω καὶ ὑπογεγράφθω περὶ ψυχῆς".

78. Marcus Tullius Cicero, "A Dialogue concerning Oratorical Partitions," *The Orations of Marcus Tullius Cicero*, trans. C.D. Yonge, 7 vols (London: G. Bell and Sons, 1852), vol. 4, 493. In Latin: "Nam ut illa constat ex notis litterarum et ex eo in quo imprimuntur illae notae, sic confectio memoriae tamquam cera locis utitur et in his imagines ut litteras collocate." *Cicero: On the Orator: Book 3. On Fate. Stoic Paradoxes. On the Division of Oratory: A Rhetorical Treatises*, trans. and ed. H. Rackham, Loeb Classical Library (Cambridge, MA: Harvard University Press, 1942), 330.

79. Ovid, *Metamorphoses*, ed. E. J. Kenney, trans. A. D. Melville (Oxford: Oxford University Press, 1986), 15.169–172. Citations are to book and line. In Latin:

> utque novis facilis signatur cera figuris
> nec manet ut fuerat nec formas servat easdem,
> sed tamen ipsa eadem est: animam sic semper eandem
> esse, sed in varias doceo migrare figuras.

Ovid. Metamorphoses. Hugo Magnus. Gotha (Germany): Friedr. Andr. Perthes. 1892.

80. Augustine relates the trinity to wax in *The Trinity*, trans. Edmund Hill, ed. John Rotelle, 5 vols (Brooklyn, NY: New City Press, 1991), vol. 1, 305–306. He figures the relationship of the Old Testament to the New Testament through wax in "Sermon 272b: On the Day of Pentecost," in *Sermons (230–272B) on the Liturgical Seasons*, trans. Edmund Hill, 7 vols (New Rochelle, NY: New City Press, 1993), vol. 3, 305.

81. Descartes, *Meditations on First Philosophy*, 53–54. In the Latin: "sed adhuc tamen videtur, nec possum abstinere quin putem, res corporeas, quarum imagines cogitatione formantur, & quas ipsi sensus explorant, multo distinctius agnosci quàm istud nescio quid meî, quod sub imaginationem non venit: quanquam profecto sit mirum, res quas animadverto esse dubias, ignotas, a me alienas, distinctius quàm quod verum

est, quod cognitum, quàm denique me ipsum, a me comprehendi. Sed video quid sit: gaudet aberrare mens mea, necdum se patitur intra veritatis limites cohiberi. Esto igitur, & adhuc semel laxissimas habe nas ei permittamus, ut, illis paulo post opportune reductis, facilius se regi patiatur" *Meditationes de Prima Philosophia*, 29–30. In the French: "Mais je ne me puis empescher de croire que les choses corporelles, dont les images se forment par ma penfée, & qui tombent sous les sens, ne soient plus distinctement connues que cette je ne sçay quelle partie de moy-mesme qui ne tombe point sous l'imagination: quoy qu'en effet ce soit une chose bien étrange, que des choses que je trouve douteuses & éloignées, soient plus clairement & plus facile-ment connues de moy, que celles qui sont véritables & certaines, & qui appartiennent à ma propre nature. Mais je voy bien ce que c'eft: mon esprit se plaist de s'égarer, & ne se peut encore contenir dans les justes bornes de la vérité. Relachons-luy donc encore une fois la bride, afin que, venant cy-apres à la retirer doucement & à propos, nous le puissions plus facilement régler & conduire" *Meditations Touchant la Premiere Philosophie*, 23.

82. Descartes, *Meditations on First Philosophy*, 55.

83. Descartes, *Meditations on First Philosophy*, 54. In the Latin: "Quid erat igitur in eâ quod tam distincte comprehendebatur?" *Meditationes de Prima Philosophia*, 30. In the French: "Qu'eft-ce donc que l'on connoidoit en ce morceau de cire auec tant de distinction?" *Meditations Touchant la Premiere Philosophie*, 24.

84. Descartes, *Meditations on First Philosophy*, 54. In the Latin: "Attenda mus, &, remotis iis quae ad ceram non pertinent, videamus quid supersit" *Meditationes de Prima Philosophia*, 30–31. In the French: "Considerons-le| attentivement, & éloignant toutes les choses qui n'appartiennent point à la cire, voyons ce qui refle" *Meditations Touchant la Premiere Philosophie*, 24.

85. Descartes, *Meditations on First Philosophy*, 54. In the Latin: "Quid verò est hoc flexibile, mutabile? An quod imaginor, hanc ceram ex figurâ rotundâ in quadratam, vel ex hac in triangularem verti posse? Nullo modo; nam innumerabilium ejusmodi mutationum capacem eam esse comprehendo, nec possum tamen innumerabiles imaginando percurrere; nec igitur comprehensio hacc ab imaginandi facultate perficitur" *Meditationes de Prima Philosophia*, 31. In the French: "Or qu'est-ce que cela: flexible & muable? N'est-ce pas que j'imagine que cette cire estant ronde est capable de devenir quarrée, & de passer du quarré en une figure triangulaire? Non certes, ce n'est pas cela, puisque je la conçoy capable de recevoir une infinité de semblables changemens, & je ne sçaurois neantmoins parcourir cette infinité par mon imagination, & par consequent cette conception que j'ai de la cire ne s'accomplit pas par la faculté d'imaginer" *Meditations Touchant la Premiere Philosophie*, 24.

86. Descartes, *Meditations on First Philosophy*, 54. In the Latin: "Superest igitur ut concedam, me nequidem imaginari quid sit haec cera, sed solâ mente percipere" *Meditationes de Prima Philosophia*, 31. In the French: "Il faut donc que je tombe d'accord, que je ne sçaurois pas mesme conceuoir par l'imagination ce que c'est que cette cire, & qu'il n'y a que mon entendement seul qui le conçoiue" *Meditations Touchant la Premiere Philosophie*, 24.

87. Descartes, *Meditations on First Philosophy*, 54. In the Latin: "Atqui, quod notandum est, ejus perceptio non visio, non tactio, non imaginatio est, nec unquam fuit, quamvis prius ita videretur, sed solius mentis inspectio" *Meditationes de Prima Philosophia*, 31. In the French: "Mais ce qui est à remarquer, sa perception, ou bien l'action par laquelle on l'aperçoit, n'est point une vision, ny un attouchement, ny une imagination, & ne l'a jamais esté, quoy qu'il le semblait ainsi auparavant, mais seulemente une inspection de l'esprit" *Meditations Touchant la Premiere Philosophie*, 24–25.

88. Margreta, de Grazia, "Imprints: Shakespeare, Gutenberg, and Descartes," *Printing and Parenting in Early Modern England*, eds. Douglas A. Brooks and Jennifer Wynne Hellwarth (Aldershot, UK: Routledge, 2005), 30.

89. Ibid., 31.

90. John Hollander, *Melodious Guile: Fictive Pattern in Poetic Language* (New Haven, CT: Yale University Press, 1988), 218.

91. Descartes, *Meditations*, 20. In the Latin, "remanet cera" *Meditationes de Prima Philosophia*, 30. In the French: "la mesme cire demeure" *Meditations Touchant la Premiere Philosophie*, 24.

92. Sigmund Freud, "A Note Upon the 'Mystic Writing Pad,'" in *General Psychological Theory: Papers on Metapsychology*, trans. Philip Rieff (New York: Touchstone, 1997); Jacques Derrida, "Freud and the Scene of Writing," trans. Jeffrey Mehlman. *Yale French Studies* 48 (1972): 74–117.

93. There are some key exceptions worth noting. Margreta de Grazia's "Imprints: Shakespeare, Gutenberg, Descartes" has been very influential to my work, as has Raphael Lyne's "Lyrical Wax in Ovid, Marlowe, and Donne." Jenny Mann argues that wax figures all of the most essential "inquiries of Ancient and early modern rhetoric and poetics." "Pygmalion's Wax: 'Fruitful Knowledge' in Bacon and Montaigne," *Journal of Medieval and Early Modern Studies* 45, no. 2 (2015): 374–375.

94. Roberta Panzanelli, "Introduction" in *Ephemeral Bodies: Wax Sculpture and the Human Figure*, ed. Roberta Panzanelli (Los Angeles: Getty Publications, 2008), 1.

95. Charles Baudelaire, *The Painter of Modern Life, and Other Essay*, trans. Jonathan Mayne (London: Phaidon Press, 1970), 13. The French reads, "La modernité, c'est, le transitoire, le fugitif, le contingent." "Le Peintre de la vie modern," *Ouvres Completes de Charles Baudelaire*, volume 3, 58–114 (Paris: Ancienne Maison Michel Lévy Frères, 1885), 69.

96. Stephen Greenblatt, *Renaissance Self-Fashioning: From More to Shakespeare* (Chicago: University of Chicago Press, 1980), 5.

97. See, for example, Valerie Traub's "Gendering Mortality in Early Modern Anatomies," *Feminist Readings of Early Modern Culture: Emerging Subjects*, eds. Valerie Traub, M. Lindsay Kaplan, and Dympna Callaghan (Cambridge, UK: Cambridge University Press, 1996), 44–92. Eve Keller's "Producing Petty Gods: Margaret Cavendish's Critique of Experimental Science," *Margaret Cavendish*, ed. Sara H. Mendelson (Farnham, UK: Ashgate, 2009), 171–195 and *Generating Bodies and Gendered Selves: The Rhetoric of Reproduction in Early Modern England* (Seattle: University of Washington Press, 2007), and Dympna Callaghan's *Women and Gender in Renaissance Tragedy: A Study of King Lear, Othello, the Duchess of Malfi, and the White Devil* (Atlantic Highlands, NJ: Humanities Press International, 1989).

98. Maureen Quilligan, "Renaissance Materialities: Introduction," *Journal of Medieval and Early Modern Studies* 32, no. 3 (2002): 427.

99. See, for example, Ann Rosalind Jones and Peter Stallybrass, eds., *Renaissance Clothing and the Materials of Memory*, Cambridge Studies in Renaissance Literature and Culture (Cambridge, UK: Cambridge University Press, 2001); Margreta de Grazia and Maureen Quilligan, eds. *Subject and Object in Renaissance Culture*, Cambridge Studies in Renaissance Literature and Culture (Cambridge, UK: Cambridge University Press, 1996); Juliet Fleming, *Graffiti and the Writing Arts*; Rayna Kalas, *Frame, Glass, Verse: The Technology of Poetic Invention in the English Renaissance* (Ithaca, NY: Cornell University Press, 2007).

100. Bruno Latour, *We Have Never Been Modern*, trans. Catherine Porter (Cambridge, MA: Harvard University Press, 1993), 13. In the original French, "celle de choses, ou des objets, ou de bêtes." *Nous n'Avons Jamais Ete Modernes: essai d'anthropologie symétrique* (Paris: La Decouverte, 1991), 23.

101. See Latour, *We Have Never Been Modern*; Jane Bennett, *Vibrant Matter: A Political Ecology of Things* (Durham: Duke University Press, 2010); Katherine N. Hayles, *How We Became Posthuman: Virtual Bodies in Cybernetics, Literature, and Informatics* (Chicago: University of Chicago Press), 1999; Rosa Braidotti, *The Posthuman* (Cambridge, UK: Polity Press, 2013); and Dona Haraway, *Simians, Cyborgs, and Women: The Reinvention of Nature* (New York: Routledge, 1991).

102. See Karen Raber, *Shakespeare and Posthumanist Theory*, Shakespeare and Theory (London: The Arden Shakespeare, 2018); Joseph Campana and Scott Maisano, eds. *Renaissance Posthumanism* (New York: Fordham University Press, 2016); and Wendy Beth Hyman, ed., *The Automaton in English Renaissance Literature*, Literary and Scientific Cultures of Early Modernity, reprint edition (Abingdon, OX: Routledge, 2016).

103. See, for example, Eve Kosofsky Sedgwick, *Epistemology of the Closet*, updated edition (Oakland: University of California Press, 2008); Judith Butler, *Gender Trouble*, reprint edition (New York, NY: Routledge, 2006); and Jonathan Goldberg, *The Seeds of Things: Theorizing Sexuality and Materiality in Renaissance Representations* (New York, NY: Fordham University Press, 2009).

104. Annemarie Jagose, *Queer Theory: An Introduction* (New York: New York University Press 1997), 131.

REFERENCES

Almada, Andre Alvares d'. *Tratado Brave Dos Rios de Guine' Do Cabo-Verde, Desde o Rio Do Sanaga' Ate' Aos Baixos de Sant' Anna, 1594.* Facsimile. Porto: Typ. Commercial Portuense, 1841.

———. *Brief Treatise on The Rivers of Guinea, Part I, 1594.* Edited and translated by P. E. H. Hair. Liverpool: Department of History, University of Liverpool, 1984. http://digital.library.wisc.edu/1711.dl/AfricanStudies.Almada01.

Aristotle. "History of Animals." In *The Complete Works of Aristotle: The Revised Oxford Translation*, edited by Jonathan Barnes, 1:774–993. Princeton, NJ: Princeton University Press, 1984.

———. "On The Soul." In *Aristotle: On the Soul. Parva Naturalia. On Breath*, translated by Walter Stanley Hett, rev. edition. Loeb Classical Library. Cambridge, MA: Harvard University Press, 1957.

———. *The Complete Works of Aristotle: The Revised Oxford Translation, One-Volume Digital Edition.* Princeton, NJ: Princeton University Press, 2014.

Armenini, Giovanni Battista. *De veri precetti della pittura.* Edited by Stefano Ticozzi. Milan: Vincenzo Ferrario, 1820.

———. *On the True Precepts of the Art of Painting.* Edited by Edward J. Olszewski and B. Franklin, 1977.

Augustine, Saint. *Sermons 230-272B on the Liturgical Seasons.* Translated by Edmund Hill. Vol. 3. 7 vols. New York: New City Press, 1994.

———. *The Trinity.* Edited by John Rotelle. Translated by Edmund Hill. Vol. 1. 5 vols. New York: New City Press, 1991.

Bartholomaei, Anglici. *De Genuinis Rerum Coelestium, Terrestrium, et Inferarum Proprietabus, Libri XVIII.* Editio secunda. Francofurti: Sumptibus N. Steinii, 1601.

————. *Batman Vppon Bartholome His Booke De Proprietatibus Rerum, Newly Corrected, Enlarged and Amended: With Such Additions as Are Requisite, Vnto Euery Seuerall Booke: Taken Foorth of the Most Approued Authors, the Like Heretofore Not Translated in English. Profitable for All Estates, as Well for the Benefite of the Mind as the Bodie. 1582.* Translated by John Trevisa and Stephen Batman. London: Imprinted by Thomas East, dwelling by Paules wharfe, 1582.

Baudelaire, Charles. "Le Peintre de la vie modern." In *Oeuvres complètes de Charles Baudelaire: L'art romantique. 1868,* 58–114. Paris: Michel Lévy frères, 1868.

————. *The Painters of Modern Life.* London: Phaidon Press, 1970.

Bennett, Jane. *Vibrant Matter: A Political Ecology of Things.* Durham: Duke University Press Books, 2010.

Bischoff, Bernhard. *Latin Palaeography: Antiquity and the Middle Ages.* Reprint edition. Cambridge, UK: Cambridge University Press, 1990.

Boschini, Marco. *Le Ricche Minere Dell Pittura Venezia.* Venice: Appresso Francisco Nicolini, 1674.

————. "Ricche Minere Della Pittura Veneziana." In *Italy and Spain, 1600–1750: Sources and Documents,* edited by Robert Enggass and Jonathan Brown, 51–54. Englewood Cliffs, NJ: Prentice-Hall, 1970.

Braidotti, Rosi. *The Posthuman.* 1st edition. Cambridge, UK and Malden, MA, USA: Polity2013.

Britain, Great. *The Statutes of the Realm.* Vol. 4. Burlington, ONT: TannerRitchie Publishing, 2007.

Buonarroti, Michelangelo. *La lettere di Michelangelo Buonarroti.* Edited by Gaetano Milanesi. Florence: Felice Le Monnier, 1875.

————. "Michelangelo: Answer to Bendetto Varchi." In *Italian Art, 1500–1600: Sources and Documents,* edited by Robert Klein and Henri Zerner, 13–14. Englewood Cliffs, NJ: Prentice-Hall, 1966.

Buoni, Thomasso. "Problemes of Beautie and All Humane Affections." In *Race in Early Modern England: A Documentary Companion,* edited by Jonathan Burton and Ania Loomba, translated by Samson Leonard. New York: Palgrave Macmillan, 2007.

Butler, Charles. *The Feminine Monarchie or a Treatise Concerning Bees, and the Due Ordering of Them: Wherein the Truth, Found Out by Experience and Diligent Observation, Discovereth the Idle and Fond Conceipts, Which Many Haue Written Anent This Subiect. By Char: Butler Magd.* Oxford, UK: Joseph Barnes, 1609.

Butler, Judith. *Gender Trouble: Feminism and the Subversion of Identity.* Reprint edition. New York: Routledge, 2006.

Callaghan, Dympna. *Woman and Gender in Renaissance Tragedy: A Study of King Lear, Othello, The Duchess of Malfi, and The White Devil.* Atlantic Highlands, NJ: Humanities Press International, 1989.

Campana, Joseph, and Scott Maisano, eds. *Renaissance Posthumanism*. 1st edition. New York, NY: Fordham University Press, 2016.

Cicero. *Cicero: On the Orator: Book 3. On Fate. Stoic Paradoxes. On the Divisions of Oratory: A. Rhetorical Treatises*. Translated by H. Rackham. Loeb Classical Library. Cambridge, MA: Harvard University Press, 1942.

———. "A Dialogue Concerning Oratorical Partitions." In *The Orations of Marcus Tullius Cicero*, translated by C. D. Yonge, Vol. 4. London: G. Bell and Sons, 1852.

Cowan, Thomas William. *Wax Craft, All About Beeswax: Its History, Production, Adulteration, and Commercial Value*. London: S. Low, Marston & Company, 1908.

Crone, G.R., ed. *The Voyages of Cadamosto and Other Documents on Western Africa in the Second Half of the Fifteenth Century*. London: Hakluyt Society, 1937.

De Grazia, Margreta. "Imprints: Shakespeare, Gutenberg, and Descartes." In *Printing and Parenting in Early Modern England*, edited by Douglas A. (ed. and introd.) Brooks and Jennifer Wynne (afterword) Hellwarth, 29–58. Women and Gender in the Early Modern World (Women and Gender in the Early Modern World). Aldershot, UK: Ashgate, 2005.

Derrida, Jacques. "Freud and the Scene of Writing." Translated by Jeffrey Mehlman. *Yale French Studies* 48 (1972): 74–117.

Descartes, René. "Meditationes de prima philosophia." In *Oeuvres de Descartes*, edited by Charles Adam and Paul Tannery, Vol. 7. Paris: L. Cerf, 1897. http://archive.org/details/oeuvresdedescar08desc.

———. *Meditations on First Philosophy: With Selections from the Objections and Replies*. Edited and translated by John Cottingham. Rev. edition. Cambridge, UK: Cambridge University Press, 1997.

———. "Meditations Touchant la Premiere Philosophie." In *Oeuvres de Descartes*, edited by Charles Adam and Paul Tannery, 9:13–123. Paris: L. Cerf, 1897. http://archive.org/details/oeuvresdedescar08desc.

Drayton, Michael. "The Quest of Cynthia." In *Minor Poems of Michael Drayton*, translated by Cyril Brett, 144–50. Oxford, UK: Clarendon Press, 1907.

Faraday, Michael. "The Chemical History of a Candle." In *Scientific Papers: Physics, Chemistry, Astronomy, Geology*, edited by Charles Eliot. New York: P F Collier & Son, 1910.

Fleming, Juliet. *Cultural Graphology: Writing After Derrida*. Chicago and London: University of Chicago Press, 2016.

———. *Graffiti and the Writing Arts of Early Modern England*. 2nd edition. Material Texts. London: Reaktion Books, 2009.

Fracanzano da Montalboddo, and Amerigo Vespucci. *Paesi Nouamente Retrovati & Novo Mondo Da Alberico Vesputio Florentino Intitulato <1508>*. Vespucci Reprints, Texts and Studies, 6. Princeton: Princeton University Press, 1916. https://catalog.hathitrust.org/Record/100329178.

Freud, Sigmund. "A Note Upon the 'Mystic Writing Pad.'" In *General Psychological Theory: Papers on Metapsychology*, translated by Philip Rieff, n.d.

Goldberg, Jonathan. *The Seeds of Things: Theorizing Sexuality and Materiality in Renaissance Representations.* 1st edition. New York: Fordham University Press, 2009.
———. *Voice Terminal Echo: Postmodernism and English Renaissance Texts.* Abingdon, OX: Routledge, 1986.
Grazia, Margreta de, Maureen Quilligan, and Peter Stallybrass, eds. *Subject and Object in Renaissance Culture.* 1st edition. Cambridge, UK and New York: Cambridge University Press, 1996.
Greenblatt, Stephen. *Renaissance Self-Fashioning: From More to Shakespeare.* Chicago: University of Chicago Press, 1980.
Haraway, Donna J. *Simians, Cyborgs and Women: The Reinvention of Nature.* London: Free Assn Books, 1996.
Hayles, N. Katherine. *How We Became Posthuman: Virtual Bodies in Cybernetics, Literature, and Informatics.* 1st edition. Chicago, IL: University of Chicago Press, 1999.
Hill, Thomas. *The Profitable Arte of Gardening: Now the Thirde Time Set Forth : To Which Is Added Much Necessarie Matter, and a Number of Secretes, with the Phisicke Helpes Belonging to Eche Herbe, and That Easily Prepared. To This Is Annexed Two Proper Treatises, the One Entituled, the Marvellous Government, Propertie, and Benefite of the Bees, with the Rare Secrets of the Honie and Waxe.* London: Henrie Bynneman, 1568.
Hollander, John. *Melodious Guile: Fictive Pattern in Poetic Language.* New Haven, CT: Yale University Press, 1990.
Homer. "Iliad, Books 1–12." In *Homeri Opera*, edited by David B. Munro and Thomas W. Allen, 3rd edition. Vol. 1. Abingdon, OX: Oxford University Press, 1920.
———. *The Iliad of Homer.* Translated by Richmond Lattimore. Reprint edition. Chicago: University Of Chicago Press, 2011.
Hyman, Wendy Beth, ed. *The Automaton in English Renaissance Literature.* 1st edition. London and New York: Routledge, 2016.
Jagose, Annamarie. *Queer Theory: An Introduction.* 1st edition. New York: New York University Press, 1997.
Jones, Ann Rosalind, and Peter Stallybrass. *Renaissance Clothing and the Materials of Memory.* Cambridge, UK and New York: Cambridge University Press, 2001.
Kalas, Rayna. *Frame, Glass, Verse: The Technology of Poetic Invention in the English Renaissance.* 1st edition. Ithaca: Cornell University Press, 2007.
Keller, Eve. *Generating Bodies and Gendered Selves: The Rhetoric of Reproduction in Early Modern England.* Seattle: University of Washington Press, 2011.
———. "Producing Petty Gods: Margaret Cavendish's Critique of Experimental Science." In *Margaret Cavendish*, edited by Sara Heller Mendelson. Farnham: Ashgate, 2009.
Klein, Robert and Henri Zerner, eds. *Italian Art, 1500–1600: Sources and Documents.* Englewood Cliffs, NJ: Prentice-Hall, 1966.

Latour, Bruno. *Nous n'avons jamais été modernes.* Paris: La Découverte, 1991.
———. *We Have Never Been Modern.* Translated by Catherine Porter. Cambridge, MA: Harvard University Press, 1993.
Lyne, Raphael. "Lyrical Wax in Ovid, Marlowe, and Donne." In *Ovid and the Renaissance Body,* edited by Goran V. Stanivukovic, 191–206. Toronto, ON: University of Toronto Press, 2001.
Mann, Jenny C. "Pygmalion's Wax: "Fruitful Knowledge" in Bacon and Montaigne." *Journal of Medieval and Early Modern Studies* 45, no. 2 (2015): 367–393.
Montaigne, Michel de. "Of the Power of the Imagination." In *The Complete Essays of Montaigne,* translated by Donald M. Frame. 1st edition, 68–76. Stanford, CA: Stanford University Press, 1958.
Ovid. *Metamorphoses.* Edited by Hugo Magnus. Gotha (Germany): Friedr. Andr. Perthes, 1892.
———. *Metamorphoses.* Edited by E. J. Kenney. Translated by A. D. Melville. Oxford: Oxford University Press, 1998.
———. *Ovid's Amores, Book One: A Commetary.* Edited by Maureen B. Ryan and Caroline A Perkins. Oklahoma Series in Classical Culture 41. Norman: University of Oklahoma Press, 2011.
Panzanelli, Roberta, ed. *Ephemeral Bodies: Wax Sculpture and the Human Figure.* Los Angeles: Getty Publications, 2008.
Plato. *Plato, VII, Theaetetus. Sophist.* Translated by Harold North Fowler. Loeb Classical Library edition. Cambridge, MA: Harvard University Press, 1921.
———. "Theaetetus." In *The Dialogues of Plato Translated into English,* edited and translated by Benjamin Jowett. 3rd edition, 109–281. Abingdon: Oxford University Press, 1892.
Pliny. *Natural History.* Edited and translated by H. Rackham. Vol. 6. 10 vols. Cambridge, MA: Harvard University Press, 1968.
Quilligan, Maureen. "Renaissance Materialities: Introduction." *Journal of Medieval and Early Modern Studies* 32, no. 3 (2002): 427–431.
Quintilian. *Quintilian's Institutes of Oratory; or, Education of an Orator.* Translated by John Selby Watson. London: G. Bell and sons, 1875.
Raber, Karen. *Shakespeare and Posthumanist Theory.* Shakespeare and Theory. London and New York: The Arden Shakespeare, 2018.
Ridolfi, Carlo. "Delle Marviglie Dell'arte." In *Painters on Painting,* edited by Eric Protter, 71–72. New York, NY: Grosset & Dunlap, 1971.
———. *Le maraviglie dell'arte, ouero, Le vite de gl'illvstri pittori veneti, e dello stato.* Vol. 2. Venice: Presso Gio, 1648.
Sedgwick, Eve Kosofsky. *Epistemology of the Closet, Updated with a New Preface.* 1st edition. Berkeley, Los Angeles, and London: University of California Press, 2008.
Shakespeare, William. "Sonnet 122." In *The Norton Shakespeare,* edited by Stephen Greenblatt, Walter Cohen, Jean E. Howard, and Katharine Eisaman Maus, 1964. New York: W. W. Norton, 1997.

———. "The Second Part of Henry the Fourth." In *The Norton Shakespeare*, edited by Stephen Greenblatt, Walter Cohen, Jean E. Howard, and Katharine Eisaman Maus, 1293–1380. New York: W. W. Norton, 1997.

———. "The Tragedy of Macbeth." In *The Norton Shakespeare*, edited by Stephen Greenblatt, Walter Cohen, Jean E. Howard, and Katharine Eisaman Maus, 2555–2618. New York: W. W. Norton, 1997.

———. "The True Tragedy of Richard Duke of York and the Good King Henry the Sixth." In *The Norton Shakespeare*, edited by Stephen Greenblatt, Walter Cohen, Jean E. Howard, and Katharine Eisaman Maus, 291–370. New York: W. W. Norton, 1997.

Sidney, Philip. *The Countess of Pembroke's Arcadia:* Edited by Katherine Duncan-Jones. 1st edition. Oxford and New York: Oxford University Press, 1985.

Tintoretto. *The Temptation of Saint Anthony.* c. 1577. Oil on canvas, 282 × 165 cm. Venice. San Trovaso.

Traub, Valerie. "Gendering Mortality in Early Modern Anatomies." In *Feminist Readings of Early Modern Culture: Emerging Subjects*, edited by Valerie Traub, M. Lindsay Kaplan, and Dympna Callaghan, 44–92. Cambridge: Cambridge University Press, 1996.

Tuck, Michael. "Everyday Commodities, the Rivers of Guinea, and the Atlantic World: The Beeswax Export Trade, c. 1450–c. 1800." In *Brokers of Change: Atlantic Commerce and Cultures in Pre-Colonial Western Africa*, edited by Toby Green. 1st edition, 285–304. Oxford and New York: British Academy, 2012.

Vasari, Giorgio. *Le Vite de' Piu Eccellenti Pittori Scultori e Architettori.* Vol. 4. 6 vols. Florence: Appresso i Giunti, 1568.

———. *Le Vite de' Piu Eccellenti Pittori Scultori e Architettori.* Vol. 1. 6 vols. Florence: Appresso i Giunti, 1568.

———. *Lives of the Most Eminent Painters, Sculptors & Architects.* Translated by Gaston du C. de Vere. Vol. 6. 10 vols. London: Macmillan, 1914. http://archive.org/details/livesofmostemine10vasauoft.

———. *Vasari on Technique. Being the Introduction to the Three Arts of Design, Architecture, Sculpture and Painting, Prefixed to the Lives of the Most Excellent Painters, Sculptors and Architects.* Edited by G. Baldwin Brown. Translated by Louisa Maclehose. New York: Dover Publications, 1960.

Watson, Amanda. "'Full Character'd': Competing Forms of Memory in Shakespeare's Sonnets." In *A Companion to Shakespeare's Sonnets*, edited by Michael Schoenfeldt, 343–60. Oxford and Malden, MA: Blackwell 2007.

Williamson, Samuel H. "Measuring Worth—Purchasing Power of Dollar." Purchasing Power of Money in the United States from 1774 to Present, 2015. http://www.measuringworth.com/ppowerus/.

CHAPTER 2

Wax Seals: Gendered Relations in Shakespeare

Wax is a material that can be imprinted and inscribed. It can hold a shape but also be softened and made malleable, melted and re-formed, transformed on every sensory level.[1] These material possibilities correlate with the uses that wax was put to in early modern England, many of which concern the practice of writing. As we saw in the introduction, wax was used to seal letters and, impressed with a signet stamp, a wax seal could indicate ownership, authorship, and speak to questions of privacy and authority. Wax tablets were used for school exercises and account books as they could be wiped of impressions and redeployed, retaining only traces of previous inscriptions. Perhaps most importantly, at least for the purpose of this chapter, wax was a material deployed within a wide range of early modern texts as an object and a trope, to speak about power, agency, and reproduction. As Margreta de Grazia details in "Imprints: Shakespeare, Gutenberg, and Descartes," the signet–seal trope was "repeatedly evoked to illustrate … how man penetrated woman to produce children" and both literary and artistic depictions of women relied upon the trope to figure the womb.[2]

The persistence of the trope undoubtedly owes something to early modern understandings of sexual difference and reproduction, which borrow heavily from Aristotelian and Galenic thoughts. For Aristotle, women are an imperfect version of men, as Ian Maclean summarizes, "[b]ecause of lack of heat in generation, her sexual organs have remained internal, she is incomplete, colder and moister in dominant humors."[3]

© The Author(s) 2019
L. M. Maxwell, *Wax Impressions, Figures, and Forms in Early
Modern Literature*, Early Modern Cultural Studies 1500–1700,
https://doi.org/10.1007/978-3-030-16932-9_2

These material differences translate into different roles in reproduction, thus in *On the Generation of Animals*, Aristotle declares: "the female always provides the material, the male that which fashions it."[4] While Aristotle does not explicitly attach women to wax here, elsewhere he employs the trope of signet–seal to describe how sense perception works and again to figure the relationship between body and soul. We would not be amiss to think wax in relation to Aristotle's receptive material. Galen likewise agrees on the humoral differences between men and women, although he suggests they play a more active role in reproduction, producing their own imperfect seed.[5] The Galenic idea of the person might, as Eve Keller argues, be "quietly evocative of the posthuman … embedded in the world, grounded in the body, and conceptualized as a unity in the distributed functioning of the psychosomatic system."[6] For such a person, there would be no clear divisions between body and mind—the constitution of one determines the other and humoral constitutions have physiological implications.[7] By the sixteenth century, Aristotelian and Galenic ideas were in competition not only with each other, but also with new theories of the body and sexual difference derived from experimental anatomy.[8]

Still, while there was no singular understanding about the nature or physiological import of sexual difference in the medical community, in the cultural imagination and literature of the period women are often figured via wax in ways that connect their bodies and minds. Recall Pyrocles's description of Philoclea's navel as "A dainty seal of virgin wax, / Where nothing but impression lacks" to make her a complete woman and presumably a mother.[9] Similarly, C. Estienne's anatomical engravings depict the female womb as a seal, showing it blank in one engraving, and imprinted in a second.[10] The persistent gendering of the trope and its association with acts of reproduction enable it to participate in a familiar narrative of binary power relations wherein the woman is rendered as passive while the man occupies a position of agency, a narrative that itself can be traced back to Aristotle.[11]

We can see the effect of such associations in *Swetnam the Woman-Hater Arraigned by Women*, a play of unknown authorship, which was first performed around 1618 and published in 1620. A response to Joseph Swetnam's anti-woman pamphlet *The arraignment of lewd, idle, froward, and unconstant women*, the play imagines that Swetnam has left England for Sicily because of the uproar his pamphlet has caused. There, under the name Misogynos, he continues in his woman-hating ways until he is forced to repent. The entire play is interested in gender difference and the action centers on a trial of the sexes for their moral fortitude and their culpability in matters of the heart. After the Spanish Prince Lisandro is caught with the Sicilian Princess, in violation of her father's edict, the King demands that his judges ascertain who is "The *Primus Motor.*"[12] Which is to say, the judges must decide who is ultimately responsible for the assignation and should suffer the penalty of death, since "the Lawes of Sicilie / Forbid to punish two for one offence."[13] Both lovers swear that they are at fault. Consequently, the King decides that the judges should hear testimony on the culpability of men and women more generally and decide which gender is to blame for initiating love in order to settle the case. The champion for women, Atlanta, who is really the princess's lost brother Lorenzo in disguise, and the champion for men, Misogynos, who is really Swetnam in disguise, each offers arguments to the court, and both use the association of wax with women as the basis of their arguments.

Atlanta/Lorenzo argues that blaming women is tantamount to holding:

> The supple wax, the courteous-natur'd woman,
> As blamefull for receiuing the impression
> Of Iron-hearted man.[14]

Here men and women are placed in binary opposition and mapped onto a trope of signet–seal. Women's "supple," wax hearts yield to the pressure of masculine iron hearts as inevitably as wax gives way to metal. Atlanta/Lorenzo goes on to amplify her point:

> Wou'd any man, once hauing fixt his Seale
> To any Deed, though after he repent
> The Fact so done, rayle at the supple Wax,
> As though that were the cause of his vndoing?
> O idle leuitie! Wax hath's vse,
> And woman easily beares the man's abuse.[15]

Atlanta/Lorenzo makes her case not simply through the material difference of metal and wax, but also through the particular use of signet and seal as a kind of signature. Here the application of the seal to a deed embeds it in an economy of exchange dominated by men. Wax is a material of patriarchy, and by extension, so too are women. Both are "vse[d]" by men and, Atlanta/Lorenzo argues, they should bear no responsibility for that use. Where women are the material on which such relations are negotiated, men both use the signet and embody it. They are, for Atlanta/Lorenzo "Iron-hearted" and their hearts are "grauen / With curious and deceiuing Art, [by] foule shapes / And stamps of much abhord impietie."[16] It is these forms, whose origins Atlanta/ Lorenzo does not consider, that they press onto yielding women.

Interestingly Misogynos/Swetnam does not directly engage with Atlanta/Lorenzo's argument. Instead, he latches onto the possibility of female wax, but pushes it in different directions. Where Atlanta uses wax to emphasize women's vulnerability and gentleness, Misogynos implies that female inconstancy, mutability, and moral weakness are the qualities that attend women's association with wax. According to Misogynos, a man cannot be responsible for a woman just because he has imprinted her with "the Seale of Armes of loue" since it is possible that:

> ...another
> Came after him and did adulterate
> The stampe imprinted on her.[17]

In such an instance, he claims that excusing the woman would itself be "weake, and fond, / And woman-like."[18] The scenario that Misogynos imagines here is of an inconstant woman who trades one lover for the next, and he implies that this is the norm by refusing to engage with Atlanta's depiction of male/female relations and offering instead this scenario of serial relations. Misogynos's argument is far from convincing since he does not refute Atlanta's premise that wax women are vulnerable material on which male desire is written. He also does not explain why it would be the woman's fault if one man "adulterate[d]" the stamp of another. Still, he ultimately wins the trial, perhaps, as Atlanta implies, because the judges are "all men, and in this weightie businesse, / Graue Women should have sate as Judges" too.[19]

The dispute between Atlanta/Lorenzo and Misogynos illuminates some of the implications of associating women with wax. On the one hand, as Atlanta argues, ascribing wax qualities to women might suggest that they are not responsible for the impressions wrought on them or in them, and that they lack agency in matters of the heart. At the same time, the implications of malleability also raise questions around female honesty and constancy. Yet both Atlanta/Lorenzo and Misogynos suggest that the association of women with wax offers truths about their nature, even as they disagree about what such an association connotes. Still the guise of the Amazonian warrior that Lorenzo adopts troubles the binary gender relations that the characters seem to buy into. As Valerie Traub has argued, "the mythical Amazons provided the prototype of female autonomy in this period. Their alleged military prowess, practice of male infanticide, and instrumental use of men for reproduction were considered the height of female insubordination."[20] Thus even as the disguised Lorenzo articulates a claim for female waxiness, his choice of disguise offers a counter-narrative about female strength that disrupts the narrative of gender difference he provides. At the same time, his own gender offers further complication since the strongest female voice of the play is not actually a female voice at all.

In Shakespeare's *The Rape of Lucrece* and *Twelfth Night*, the same trope is also used to explore gender relations and again the easy associations between women and wax are disrupted. Just as in *Swetnam the Woman-Hater*, in *The Rape of Lucrece* (1594) and *Twelfth Night* (c. 1602), women's waxiness is offered as a matter of truth, a representation of what they are rather than what they should be. At first, Shakespeare's attachment of wax materiality to female agential and affective locations in these works seems to endorse the binary system of sexual difference and feminine susceptibility to masculine influences that we have been discussing. Yet, in Shakespeare, these narratives of difference are complicated by the immediate contexts of their deployments and Shakespeare's engagement with questions of reading and writing in each work. In *The Rape of Lucrece*, the narrative of binary difference is offered as an explanation for the maid's tears and competes with other alternative possibilities for the source of those tears while participating in a larger conversation about Lucrece's relationship to authorship and text. Shakespeare raises similar issues in *Twelfth Night* when Maria copies her mistress's hand and steals her signature impressure, "her Lucrece," to trick the steward, Malvolio, into fashioning himself into a fool.[21] By staging a wax Lucrece, Shakespeare literalizes the metaphor, continuing to explore both the connection of female bodies with texts and the possibility of female authorship through the intersections of Lucrece, Olivia, Maria, and Malvolio. Finally, when the cross-dressed Viola laments Olivia's newfound desire for her alter ego, she offers up a new version of the original metaphor, once again narrating female weakness as a way of explaining feminine susceptibility to desire, even though there is no true masculine pressure to work on Olivia. In each case, relationships between women disrupt and challenge the narrative of sexual difference that the trope of signet–seal provides.

Further, Shakespeare applies wax materiality to men in a way that disrupts the easy reading of difference that the trope initially seems to endorse. In *Love's Labour's Lost*, the possibility of masculine impression begins to suggest that not only can both genders occupy either side of the trope, but also that there is value in both positions. Thus, even as the trope works to narrate difference, it also destabilizes the binaries of active and passive, dominant and submissive, hard and soft, and male and female that mobilize the trope, suggesting that the relations it describes are not as straightforward—or as straight—as they might appear. Indeed, the malleability of the wax itself seems to enter the trope and leave the relationships narrated by the metaphor of signet and seal open to renegotiation and multiple interpretations.

2.1   WRITING LUCRECE

In *The Rape of Lucrece*, the narrator declares that "men have marble, women waxen minds,"[22] as the basis of his apology for women. Building on that premise, he continues, employing the language of logical proof throughout:

> And therefore are they formed as marble will.
> The weak oppressed, th' impression of strange kinds
> Is formed in them by force, by fraud, or skill.
> Then call them not the authors of their ill,
> No more than wax shall be accounted evil
> Wherein is stamped the semblance of a devil.[23]

The original claim of material difference becomes the basis for the ultimate argument that women are "not the authors of their ill." Instead, men who shape the female mind "by force, by fraud, or skill" occupy that role. The narrative digression excuses Lucrece by explaining that both her body and her mind are vulnerable to rape—to violent, nonconsensual shaping pressures. Such an excuse might be necessary since early modern legal and medical texts understood conception on the part of the rape victim as a sign of consent because pregnancy was thought to require a female orgasm.[24] While Shakespeare never reveals whether Lucrece conceives after being raped, by offering the excuse the narrator implies that, in succumbing to Tarquin, Lucrece's body or mind has somehow betrayed her. At the same time, the apology works to excuse Lucrece for her suicide, an act that would need excuse for Shakespeare's Christian readership, if not for her compatriots. By suggesting that Tarquin's forceful act has the power to shape her womb and mind, affecting her emotions, desires, thoughts, and perceptions, the narrator renders her blameless for all the events that follow.

Further by making both women's weakness and the manipulation of that weakness by men material, Shakespeare lends violent impression a certain inevitability and naturalness. If Lucrece cannot be held responsible for her actions, is she capable of agential action? The problem of agency becomes more insidious when we consider, once again, the metaphor in play. The trope of signet–seal not only provides a model of the physical and mental impact of Tarquin's rape on Lucrece, but also seems to normalize that relationship. After all, the material interaction of wax and marble always proceeds along predictable and seemingly innocuous terms. Consider: When a signet ring is pressed into wax to form a seal, the wax always takes on the shape of the ring because of the material difference between them. Sealing letters is a daily, mechanical, and completely unobjectionable act. Even if we think of the philosophical connotations of imprinting wax, we are left with reproductive and epistemological reproduction, acts that are inextricably entwined in being human and intrinsically harmless. Thus when the trope of signet–seal is used to speak about rape, its association with everyday acts starts to suggest, as Katharine Maus argues, that "rape is hardly outrageous; it is almost the nature of things."[25] Not only does the vulnerability of women seem to be a matter of innate sexual difference here, but the exploitation of that vulnerability seems both expected and natural. So far, Shakespeare's use of the trope plays into the binaries we have been discussing. However, even as the signet–seal trope is narrated, Shakespeare critiques the abuse that might result. After all, the narrator declares that the "weak" are "oppressed" in the exchange, reminding us that the frequency of an act does not affect its morality.

More, Shakespeare destabilizes the trope by mapping it on to Lucrece and her maid, rather than Lucrece and Tarquin.[26] While the lines clearly are interested in questions of gender difference, they are occasioned by and offered as an explanation for Lucrece's maid's response to Lucrece's grief. The girl finds Lucrece crying and without knowing the cause of her sorrow, mirrors it. Her tears are "enforced by sympathy / Of those fair suns set in her mistress' sky."[27] According to the narrator, the maid cries because she is a woman:

> Their gentle sex to weep are often willing,
> Grieving themselves to guess at others' smarts,
> And then they drown their eyes or break their hearts.[28]

It is at this moment that the narrator offers up the stanza that begins, "for men have marble, women waxen minds." The effect of these lines is to underscore the maid's softness and position her, with Lucrece, as a victim of Tarquin's abuse. That positioning is, to a certain extent, apt. Without Tarquin's violation of Lucrece, there would be no reason for the maid's tears. Yet the poem does not rest on those possibilities, instead it suggests the competing possibilities that Lucrece authors her maid's grief, that the maid is responsible for her own tears, or that they are enforced by sympathy to which neither woman fully consents. Together these possibilities challenge the signet–seal trope and its attachment to gender difference by suggesting that women can occupy both the role of signet and seal and that their relations might be governed by other forms of power altogether.

If Lucrece authors her maid's sorrow, then she occupies the position of the signet. Since the two women share a gender, her position must be secured through another kind of difference that provides her with the power to impress: in this case, class. As lady of the house she is much more powerful than her maid, and that power difference could allow Lucrece to occupy the masculine position. Certainly, the narrator's use of cosmological metaphors to indicate the immense difference in magnitude between Lucrece's grief and her maid's suggests the kind of power difference that would allow Lucrece to work on her maid in this way. Prior to comparing men to marble and women to wax, the narrator compares Lucrece's eyes to two "suns...cloud-eclipsèd"[29] and then suggests that the maid's tears are like those of "the earth" when "the sun being set, / Each flower [is] moistened like a melting eye."[30] Here Lucrece seemingly takes on the vastness of the universe with suns symbolizing her eyes; in contrast, the maid's scope is limited and terrestrial. If Lucrece's eyes are suns, they form the center of the maid's universe just as her mistress's needs and desires form the center of the maid's life of service. Again, the difference in social status between the two women seems to have something to do with the metaphorical positions that they occupy. Lucrece's sorrow is not simply greater; Lucrece herself is greater, which causes her tears to impact the maid in a way that simply would not be true if their positions were reversed. While the narrator does not explicitly connect suns or flowers to gender here, those positions are typically gendered in Shakespeare. The sun is most often gendered male (as counterpart to the female moon or mother earth) and flowers are strongly gendered female in other Shakespeare texts (only women get deflowered). Thus by mapping both of these positions onto women, Shakespeare is further destabilizing the claims of gender difference offered by the signet–seal trope and once again suggesting that Lucrece has agency in her encounter with the maid and that she plays the marble to her maid's wax.

Yet Lucrece is explicit that she does not desire the maid's outpouring, admonishing her:

> If thou dost weep for grief of my sustaining,
> Know, gentle wench, it small avails my mood.
> If tears could help, mine own would do me good.[31]

Her discomfort with the maid's display invites us to reconsider the idea that she authors it. As mentioned above, the poem also provides another possibility for the source of the maid's tears, sympathy. As Amanda Bailey has argued, sympathy in the sixteenth and seventeenth centuries was not yet a "moral sentiment."[32] Instead, it was a term in flux, one that attached both to an understanding of the natural world as replete with sympathetic energies that could move subjects without their consent and which was also "increasingly invoked to describe the experience of fellow-feeling between and among human beings."[33] When the narrator declares that the maid's tears are "enforced by sympathy / Of those fair suns set in her mistress' sky"[34] he plays off of both definitions. The cosmological metaphors invoke the sympathetic model of nature and suggest that the maid's grief is a natural and inevitable effect of her connection to her mistress—a connection not necessarily dependent on feelings, but on shared affinities or natures, on a deeper link that might exist between flower and sun as much as between maid and mistress. Such a reading would suggest that neither Lucrece nor Tarquin directly author the maid's tears, but rather that she is acted upon by a force outside all of them.

At the same time, the narrator suggests that the maid's identification with Lucrece here is an act of will. He relays:

> Their gentle sex to weep are often willing,
> Grieving themselves to guess at others' smarts,
> And then they drown their eyes or break their hearts.[35]

This formulation comes much closer to a modern understanding of sympathy as an apprehending of the feelings of another and would be better understood in the early modern period as pity. As the narrator would have it, because she is a woman the maid, as an act of "will[ ]" imagines or "guess[es]" at the harm that has befallen her mistress, inflicting injury on herself as a result. If the maid's tears are a result of pity that she feels having imagined her mistress's grief, then she becomes author of her own ill. Whether the exchange is governed by external impression, sympathy, or pity does not change the result; the maid cries either way. However, if the maid's tears are the result of pity her relationship with Lucrece no longer seems to work according to the same violent oppression as Lucrece's encounter with Tarquin. Instead the narrative of pity introduces desire on the part of the maid to be reshaped. Both her desire and the display that result from that desire are predicated on possibilities of similarity rather than difference.

The possibilities of sympathy and pity further destabilize the trope of signet–seal by suggesting transformation on the basis of sympathetic energies and likeness rather than difference. Unfortunately for Lucrece, as powerful as these possibilities may be, they fail to prevent the rape in the first place. When Tarquin surprises Lucrece in her bedchamber, she attempts to influence him through a rhetoric of pity. She pleads,

> O, if no harder than a stone thou art
> Melt at my tears, and be compassionate.
> Soft pity enters at an iron gate.[36]

Lucrece's appeal to Tarquin depends on the fact that as hard as stone may be, it can be softened, worn down, and shaped by water. In Sonnet 55, Shakespeare capitalizes on the susceptibility of stone to erosion when he proclaims, "Not marble nor the gilded monuments / Of princes shall outlive this powerful rhyme."[37] Lucrece, playing off the same material qualities, suggests that Tarquin's hardness does not preclude the possibility for pity and that her verbal appeal should have the power to penetrate his will. Lucrece's plea also implies that Tarquin's hardness is in excess of his gender. Even if men's minds are marble, marble is only stone, and stone can still be moved by water. When her appeal fails, the fault seems to lie in Tarquin's impenetrability as an individual rather than as a man. He may indeed be "harder than a stone," harder than the "marble" of other men and thus not susceptible to the call of pity, especially since he is not swayed by his allegiance to any "holy human law" or "common troth."[38] While the maid's fellow feeling is of no use to Lucrece, Tarquin's pity would have prevented his crime and her violation. When the maid weeps, she has no power to lessen Lucrece's pain. Her softness does not ameliorate the situation. A softened Tarquin, on the other hand, would be incapable of performing rape both ethically and physically.

Thus while Shakespeare's use of the signet–seal trope disrupts the binaries of male/female, active/passive, and strong/weak by affording Lucrece the opportunity to occupy the position of the signet and by suggesting different mechanisms of power that do not attach to gender difference, such possibilities are undercut by the violence of Tarquin's actions. Lucrece may author the maid's tears, her letter to Collatine, and even her own suicide, but she experiences herself as a text written by Tarquin and only seems to be able to imagine changing the meaning of that text through her final act. When Lucrece drives the knife into her own heart, she makes an impression in her flesh and in the hearts and minds of her audience. For a moment, she occupies both halves of the signet–seal trope; she is simultaneously author and text and has the power of both positions. Unfortunately, that doubleness is momentary. Her death forecloses any future acts of authorship and leaves her only the position of text, a position which is weak insofar as it leaves her, like wax, malleable in the hands of her desiring readers. Yet Lucrece chooses to become a text not because it is a position of weakness but because of the power it offers her.[39] Her suicide makes Tarquin's crime legible and provides her with the possibility of influencing other minds. Certainly, the men who witness her death are galvanized by the sight, uniting in action over her bleeding body. The effectiveness of her display reminds us that despite their malleability, texts can make impressions, inspire sympathy, and circulate more widely than a virtuous Roman woman.

2.2   WRITING MARIA/WRITING OLIVIA

Lucrece as text reappears in Shakespeare's *Twelfth Night* to help frame, once again, the relation of women to acts of writing and reading. The figure of Lucrece enters *Twelfth Night* as Olivia's impressure, which her chambermaid Maria has pressed into service in order to seal a counterfeit letter. As a seal on a letter, Lucrece literally becomes a wax body and a text to be read—or, perhaps more accurately, misread. Through the deployment of her form, Shakespeare revisits the questions of gender, authorship, and textuality that reverberate through *The Rape of Lucrece* and again considers the relationship of authenticity and authorship in the context of a same-sex mistress–maid relationship. The complex interplay between Maria, Olivia, and Malvolio around questions of agency, authorship, reader, and text troubles the ideas that any of these relationships map onto binary positions. At the same time, the play returns to wax to work out the relation of desire to acts of gendered writing and the trope of signet–seal when Viola/Cesario declares, "How easy is it for the proper false / In women's waxen hearts to set their forms!" in order to explain Olivia's sudden infatuation for the disguised messenger.[40] Together, the physically staged wax seal and the metaphorical reconsideration of female waxiness and female desire work to further problematize the gender binaries that are explicitly mapped onto the trope of signet–seal in both *The Rape of Lucrece* and *Twelfth Night*, opening up more space both for female agency and desire and for complex networks of relationality by suggesting that relations and gender more broadly may not be governed by material difference.

In *Twelfth Night*, Lucrece is the image of both Olivia's signet and seal, chosen perhaps because she represents the ideals of chastity which Olivia desires to be associated with. However, as such she is merely object, pressed into service of another woman's writing, and when used by Maria to trick Malvolio, into another woman's act of counterfeiting. When Malvolio finds the letter, he notices the seal and recognizes it as Olivia's, exclaiming, "and the impressure her Lucrece, with which she uses to seal."[41] Reduced to an image on a stamp, Lucrece's form has been disconnected from her own narrative, co-opted into a project of mechanical reproduction, and used to testify to a false claim of authorship. The co-option of her form testifies to her usefulness as textual body and as material of wax to be manipulated at will. Further, her use as seal allows Shakespeare to once again highlight the vulnerability of the female body. As de Grazia has suggested, breaking the wax seal repeats and revisits the original act of rape, recreating Lucrece's tragedy in miniature.[42] In the context of the play, the invocation of Lucrece's narrative serves to dramatize Malvolio's foolishness and expose his transgressive desires. At the same time, it again invites us to associate rape with the kind of daily violence enacted on objects.

Yet since Maria authors this letter in order to write Malvolio into a position of ridicule, the relation of the wax seal to questions of authorship and gender is destabilized. As Karen Robertson has suggested, in wielding the pen as a weapon of revenge, Maria takes on "an oddly masculine position, while Malvolio, the reader of a love letter, is feminized in his exposure."[43] Certainly, Maria uses the letter to shape Malvolio into exactly the suitor that would most displease her lady. She tricks him into wearing "a color she abhors," sporting "a fashion she detests," and appearing before her with an "unsuitable … disposition."[44] Maria's usurpation of Olivia's seal allows her to write Malvolio doubly; he becomes both the reader of her text and a second text that Olivia will read with disapprobation. While Maria never uses the metaphor of stamping and impressing, the end result is akin to a printed image. As she gleefully informs Sir Toby, "he does smile his face into more lines than is in the new map with the augmentation of the Indies."[45] Like Lucrece, whose face is figured as "that map which deep impression bears," Malvolio is transformed by his encounter.[46]

Still, that transformation is once again, not strictly mechanical. It does not work like the pressure of hard upon soft, marble on wax, or signet on seal. As Maria's description reveals, Malvolio transforms himself: he "*smiles* his face" into the image that Olivia will read (emphasis added). Malvolio's new shape requires his active participation in the act of reading and Maria's knowledge of both his desires and their mistress's. He sees what he wants to see in the text, creating its meaning through acts of volition:

> *Jove knows I love,*
> *But who?*
> *Lips do move;*
> *No man must know.*
> 'No man must know.' What follows? The numbers
> altered. 'No man must know.' If this should be
> thee, Malvolio?[47]

The gap between what Maria writes—a line at odds with the meter and that rhymes with Malvolio—and what Malvolio reads—proof of Olivia's desire for him—is key to Maria's project. Maria's revenge requires Malvolio's active participation in his own ruin because her revenge depends on exposing his desires as not only transgressive, but also as initiating within him. Any steward could be excused for responding positively to explicit protestations of love from his wealthy aristocratic mistress, but Malvolio's projection of himself into Maria's text reveals desires that go beyond mere opportunistic ambition. Thus importantly, Malvolio becomes both reader and author of the text that he reads and, like Lucrece's maid, can be understood simultaneously as the product of another's authoring act and his own desiring will.

If Malvolio's participation in his own ridicule raises questions about the extent to which he might be understood through wax, Maria's position as counterfeiter also complicates her relation to the authorship and thus to the signet she uses to seal the letter. Throughout the play, Maria's power derives from Olivia's, and she frequently serves as Olivia's voice in the play—chiding Sir Toby, positioning herself between the clown, Feste, and her mistress's ire, and serving as the gatekeeper responsible for bringing Viola/Cesario to her mistress's attention.[48] Thus, as Jessica Tvordi notes, Maria legitimately "acts as Olivia's proxy, frequently regulating male discourse in Olivia's absence."[49] When she wields Olivia's signet metaphorically or literally, Maria acts as author, but her authorship is constrained by the need to act for her mistress and emulate her hand—she bears to some extent Olivia's imprint. Perhaps that is why when Malvolio complains about the letter to Olivia, Olivia does not seem particularly affronted by the usurpation and defers any potential punishment beyond the curtain's fall. Olivia may see herself as partially responsible for Maria's writing, and the gulling of Malvolio, while not authored or authorized by Olivia, may be in line with her desires.

The comic subplot that revolves around Maria and Malvolio revisits the questions surrounding women's relationships to writing that we saw in *The Rape of Lucrece*. As in the narrative poem, Shakespeare uses a wax signet to think through the relation of author and text to desire, destabilize traditional gender roles, and challenge the boundaries of class. Maria's position as writing woman and maid complicates her relation to the signet–seal trope. She is wax in relation to Olivia, and decidedly not in relation to Malvolio and these relationships are governed by her relative class status as much as her gender. At the same time, Malvolio's reading of Maria's letter suggests his own softness, vulnerability, and malleability—aligning him with wax; while his interpretive leaps infuse that position with active possibilities. Reading the subplot with wax reveals how both Maria and Malvolio fail to conform to gender binaries and the extent to which positions of writing and reading can also have a complicated relationship to agency and passivity.

The wax seal that Maria affixes to the letter is not the only wax seal of the play. Olivia's heart is also imagined as wax by the chameleon-like figure, Viola/Cesario, in order to explain how the lady has fallen for the cross-dressed Viola. This metaphoric deployment of the trope of signet–seal to explain the erotic desire of one woman for another, albeit another disguised as a man, destabilizes the association of women with wax even further by attaching the trope of signet–seal to a relationship in which gender difference is only illusory.

After Maria describes Viola/Cesario as a "fair young man," Olivia decides to admit the seeming page, who has been sent to woo Olivia on behalf of Duke Orsino. Viola/Cesario's attempts to seduce Olivia prove successful, but not in the way that she intends. Instead of winning Olivia's heart for Orsino, she wins it for herself, which she discovers when Malvolio, who has been sent to return a ring that Viola never left, overcomes her on the road. On receiving the falsely returned ring, Viola exclaims,

> Disguise, I see thou art a wickedness
> Wherein the pregnant enemy does much.
> How easy is it for the proper false
> In women's waxen hearts to set their forms!
> Alas, our frailty is the cause, not we,
> For such as we are made of, such we be.[50]

In this speech, the questions of falseness and gendered relationships that we have been exploring are revisited. Just as Maria's use of the seal represents a false authority, here both the speech and Olivia's desire have been occasioned by lies, the former by the returned ring and the latter by Viola's disguise. Whereas Olivia downplays Maria's usurping authorship, Viola sees her own disguise as "a wickedness," one that allows space for "the pregnant enemy" to work.

When Viola chooses the metaphor of "women's waxen hearts," she attempts to rhetorically erase possibilities of female–female desire by rewriting those desires in terms of male–female relations, suggesting that a woman could not imprint another woman's heart because women do not possess the shaping force of men. Instead, Viola imagines some active force has worked through her to spark Olivia's desire. She names that active force alternatively as "disguise," "the pregnant enemy," and "the proper false." While none of these subjects are explicitly gendered male, they are offered up as the material oppositions of "women's waxen hearts," suggesting they are both masculine and hard. Certainly, we can see how the masculine gender could attach to each impressing subject. Viola's disguise is men's clothing, or more broadly, her masculine appearance. Similarly, "the pregnant enemy" seems to allude to Satan, who is typically gendered male, while the "proper false" refers to both of these deceptively appealing, already masculinized forms. These pressures find it "easy" to "set their forms" in women's hearts, shaping desire through an application of force that is derived from their gender and perhaps also through their connection to deceit. Despite her position as the object of Olivia's desires, Viola takes great pains to separate herself from these impressing forces. She locates wickedness in the disguise itself, in removable clothing rather than in the act of disguising for which she would bear responsibility. Moreover, she adopts the plural "we" to locate herself with Olivia as desiring women free from blame for those desires. Instead of accepting responsibility for the imprint of Olivia's heart, she casts herself as fellow victim, as another wax woman.

Yet the narrative of masculine impression fails to explain Olivia's desire either rhetorically or substantively. Neither "disguise" nor the "pregnant enemy" seems to line up with the cold, hard, impervious masculinity that we saw in *The Rape of Lucrece*. "Disguise" simply covers over Viola's female body or, alternatively, reveals the boy actor underneath the female costume.[51] Viola/Cesario's masculinity is performed, its power derived from disguise, which suggests a certain malleability. Viola/Cesario does not materially shift from wax to marble on donning male clothing. She is "made of" the same stuff as always and a different disguise would be more or less effective in making her appear a convincing man. Similarly, the "pregnant enemy" could be "pregnant" in the sense of "easily influenced, receptive, inclined, ready" or, perhaps, in the same way as an expectant mother.[52] Both senses of "pregnant" suggest malleability, an openness to change already inherent in "disguise," which belies the material opposition that Viola attempts to narrate. Just as she is doubly gendered, these "masculine" positions are not hard and rigid but share in the malleability of wax and the malleability of gender that runs through the play. They do not seem to possess the material qualities required to force Olivia's desire, indicating that her desire may not be forced or may proceed along different terms that are not rooted in material gender difference.

If we look at the wooing scene, we see how the trope fails to represent the desires in play. First, to the extent that Viola/Cesario writes herself out of the position of the signet, the trope does not accommodate her desire for Olivia and her role in seducing her. As Valerie Traub has argued, Viola is not simply Orsino's agent, passively delivering his message. Instead, she woos, as Traub notes, "with a fervor that exceeds her 'text.'"[53] Armed with Orsino's "excellently well penned" script, she at first sees that text as her limit.[54] When Olivia asks her about herself, she claims that she "can say little more than I have studied, and that question's out of my part."[55] As the conversation proceeds, however, Viola moves beyond the text, asking to see Olivia's face and then imagining herself in Orsino's place. By the time Viola/Cesario proclaims,

> If I did love you in my master's flame,
> With such a suff'ring, such a deadly life,
> In your denial I would find no sense,

she has moved far beyond Orsino's text and generated a new narrative of wooing.[56] She not only uses language that is her own, but enthusiastically pursues the role of suitor and Olivia's desires. Orsino seems to anticipate and authorize Viola/Cesario's departure from the script, commanding her to "be clamorous and leap all civil bounds / Rather than make unprofited return."[57] Yet there is a gap between what Orsino imagines and what Viola/Cesario performs. Where Orsino acknowledges that she might have to go off script in order to gain access to Olivia, Viola/Cesario's success in wooing Olivia depends on her articulation of her own desires after she has been admitted to Olivia's presence. Her attempts at seduction fail until she improvises, occupies the role of author, and projects herself into a scene of hypothetical wooing. While scholars have often read Viola/Cesario as actor here rather than author, Mary Jo Kietzman makes the compelling argument that she is both, describing her as an actor–author to "suggest both the nature of Shakespeare's own authorship—a collaboration with… talented actors…—as well as the measure of agency actors possessed in the interpretation and performance of their parts in dialogue with the script, the other actors, and the audience."[58] At this moment, as actor, author, and suitor she occupies positions that Shakespeare attaches elsewhere to the masculine possibilities of the signet.

While the trope of signet–seal fails to represent what has transpired between Viola/Cesario and Olivia in part because Viola refuses to claim the position of the signet, it also fails because it operates only through difference. Viola/Cesario's success as author does not erase her feminine body and feminine qualities, which also play a role in seducing Olivia. In fact, Orsino chooses her as his emissary because she resembles a woman, as he explains:

> For they shall yet belie thy happy years
> That say thou art a man. Diana's lip
> Is not more smooth and rubious; thy small pipe
> Is as the maiden's organ, shrill and sound,
> And all is semblative a woman's part.
> I know thy constellation is right apt
> For this affair….[59]

These much-commented lines reveal how feminine Viola/Cesario is, even in disguise. They also reveal a theory of desire in which femininity is the quality that would make a man "right apt" for the seduction of a woman. Viola/Cesario is a good agent to transmit Orsino's desires explicitly because "all is semblative a woman's part."[60] Indeed, when Olivia reflects on her newfound desire for Viola/Cesario, she describes a subtle seduction that relies primarily on the visual. She explains:

> Methinks I feel this youth's perfections
> With an invisible and subtle stealth
> To creep in at mine eyes.[61]

Viola/Cesario's perfections are located in her girlish appearance and while Olivia attributes agency to these perfections, their "subtle stealth" seems far removed from the metaphor of "easy" impression narrated by the signet–seal trope. Thus Viola/Cesario's effect on Olivia does not seem to be simply a matter of masculine impression. Instead, women also seem to be able to impress women—or at least to attract women through possibilities of sameness. While Viola allies herself to Olivia by claiming to also possess a waxen heart, her choice of the signet–seal trope fails to explain how they might act on each other on the basis of those similarities.

Ultimately, the gendered narrative that Viola/Cesario provides does not satisfactorily explain what has transpired in the preceding scene. Moreover, it does not account for Olivia's decision to send Cesario her ring. Viola/Cesario reads the ring as a sign of Olivia's desire, and of her waxen heart. However, the ring, while most likely not a signet ring itself, recalls the male half of the trope. It is the only ring verbally or visually staged during Viola/Cesario's speech and thus provides a visual counterpart to the waxen heart, even as it might also suggest the female vagina on the basis of its shape.[62] Moreover, if we consider how Olivia maps onto our binary categories during this scene, we see that her decision to send the ring is an active choice, an attempt to woo, to arouse Cesario's desire and imprint his heart. She uses her ring to perform what the trope names the male act of impression, or, perhaps, she uses her ring to perform the aristocratic act of impression. She believes that Viola/Cesario is a servant and as such, should be easily seduced. While her attempt ultimately proves unsuccessful with the disguised Viola, her success with Viola's twin, Sebastian, suggests that her failure is not rooted in her gender.[63] With Sebastian she is able to take on the active role suggesting that the narrative inscribed in the trope of signet–seal is either false or far more flexible than might be readily apparent.

The trope of signet–seal does not adequately explain how desire works in *Twelfth Night* because any character can occupy the position of signet and any character's heart can be wax. Despite Viola's attempt to map desire onto questions of gender, the multiple locations of desire in the play suggest that desire cannot be reduced to a simple narrative of impression. Instead, every character seems to possess a heart that too easily adopts the image of a beloved and forfeits a measure of agency in doing so. While the end of the play contains some of the subversive possibilities, offering as Jonathan Goldberg has argued, "not merely heterosexual resolution… but the preservation of the aristocracy from lower-class incursion," none of these closures are complete.[64] Goldberg reminds us that Sebastian and Viola's class appropriateness for Olivia and Orsino "does not dispose of the fact that both [Orsino] and Olivia fell in love with their servants, or that Toby has married Maria, the servant who can simulate Olivia's hand."[65]

Further, marriage does not foreclose the possibility of continued desires or erotic relationships between Sebastian and Antonio, the captain who rescues him, or Olivia and Viola. For Traub, "*Twelfth Night's* conclusion seems only ambivalently invested in the 'natural' heterosexuality it imposes."[66] Sebastian equivocates on his gender, naming himself a maid, and Viola remains dressed as Cesario even though engaged to Orsino. Indeed, as Laurie Shannon has argued, the very naturalness of heterosexuality is called into question when Sebastian tells Olivia, "So comes it, lady, you have been mistook. / But nature to her bias drew in that."[67] Drawing on discourses of likeness in the period, Shannon reads these lines to mean that "'nature' only drew to, not from, its bias, reflecting the principle that 'like seeks like' that structures Renaissance ideas of attraction and repulsion."[68] Which is to say, that Olivia's attraction to Viola is in line with nature's bias, and that she is "mistook" when she marries Sebastian. Thus the malleability of desire together with the malleability of gender in the play leaves open the possibility of queer exchanges, even as the curtain closes.[69] While *Twelfth Night* voices the possibility of feminine weakness and vulnerability, the play refuses to settle on that vision of women or male–female relations.

2.3   Writing Gender

If women are not as similar to wax in Shakespeare as the signet–seal trope would suggest, men might be more so. We have already seen that Tarquin is more monster than man when he fails to soften and pity Lucrece. Looking more broadly, we might notice other such moments in Shakespeare. For example, in *Titus Andronicus*, Titus begs for mercy for his sons by way of wax, exclaiming:

> A stone is soft as wax, tribunes more hard than stones.
> A stone is silent, and offendeth not,
> And tribunes with their tongues doom men to death.[70]

Here, being like wax is not incompatible with manhood. Instead, wax again offers a model for pity that would secure the tribunes' claim to humanity, or at least bring them as near to it as the stones upon which Titus casts his gaze. The possibilities of pity, mercy, and compassion become one place where softness is valorized and available to both men and women in Shakespeare.

Another such location is love, as we saw in *Twelfth Night*. Malvolio, while not exactly a man to be emulated, proves more malleable than Maria. Similarly, in *Love's Labour's Lost*, the King of Navarre proves softer and more malleable than the binary of signet–seal suggests. Despite his vow to defeat our "own affections / And the huge army of the world's desires" by forswearing appetitive pleasures for three years, he falls in love with the princess.[71] Boyet regales the princess with Navarre's symptoms:

> Why, all his behaviours did make their retire
> To the court of his eye, peeping through desire.
> His heart like an agate with your print impressed,
> Proud with his form, in his eye pride expressed.[72]

Again, we find a trope of impression, but now the Princess is the stamp and the King's heart is the location of impression. He has been rendered vulnerable to her form.

Meanwhile, wax has been replaced by agate, a material that can be carved and inscribed like wax but is not nearly so soft. Indeed, agate was a material commonly used to fashion signets. Thus Navarre's softness is only relative. His heart is vulnerable to the shaping pressures of love, but still hard enough to make impressions on wax. Further, his heart's pleasure in its new shape is generative: "Proud with his form, in his eye pride expressed."[73] Impression leads to expression and sparks a chain of subsequent impressions and expressions first in Boyet, who observes the King's transformation, and then in the princess who hears about it from him.[74] Just as a carved agate stone can imprint countless wax seals, so too the transformed masculine heart becomes a vehicle for textual production.[75] Shakespeare's use of agate to figure Navarre's vulnerable masculine heart reveals a complex network of relationships and suggests how impression can become a source of power and pride. Navarre's heart is soft, but not too soft, written but also capable of writing. Agate's material, functional, and metaphorical relationship to wax allows it to testify compellingly about how Navarre might relate to the Princess and to other characters within the play. Further, Shakespeare's substitution of agate for wax here might suggest that there is still something materially different about men and how they experience desire.

Although such a reading is possible, it threatens to obscure the extent to which Shakespeare's men are vulnerable to desire and can be shaped by both feminine and masculine pressures. Shakespeare's emphasis here is on the ease with which Navarre's heart is written, and his invocation of agate complicates but does not erase Navarre's relation to the signet–seal trope and to possibilities of masculine waxiness. Taken together, Shakespeare's many deployments of the signet–seal trope suggest that any person can occupy any part of the trope and that all sorts of relationships between various subject positions are possible. Further, it suggests that to be impressible, to be vulnerable to the shaping pressures of others, is fundamental to the human condition and even desirable. Thus while Shakespeare uses the trope to narrate gender difference, that narration often undoes itself, which suggests that the difference being narrated is neither absolute nor always maintained and that gender difference itself is a construction perilously maintained. Indeed, this seems true not just in Shakespeare but also in other early modern deployments of the signet–seal trope, as we saw in *Swetnam the Woman-Hater*. Wax might often be attached to femininity and to the female possibilities of reproduction, but that attachment proves unstable in just the same ways that gender itself proves unstable.

The malleability of wax makes gender difference provisional and thus renders desire based on difference contingent. If women and men can both be like wax be moved by possibilities of sameness as well as difference then neither gender difference nor cross-sex desire seems to govern the relations between subjects, or offer insight into the nature of subjectivity. Instead, we might again turn to wax to better understand both the complex mechanisms of relationality and subjectivity. As I mentioned in the introduction, wax offers a model of queer subjectivity insofar as it refuses to take on stable forms and continuously offers itself up for renegotiation. Yet here, we could argue that model applies to all subject positions. Paying attention to the instability of wax around gender reveals not only the shaping power of difference but also that afforded by sameness. Thus reading the wax self allows us to recognize the instability of selfhood at the same time that we acknowledge its constructed nature and see the flexibility of desire at the same time that we become aware of its relation to power.

Notes

1. René Descartes famously elaborates on wax's capacity to change on every sensory register in *Meditations on First Philosophy: With Selections from the Objections and Replies*, ed. John Cottingham (Cambridge, UK: Cambridge University Press, 1996), 20. See discussion in the introduction to this book.
2. Margreta De Grazia, "Imprints: Shakespeare, Gutenberg, and Descartes," in *Printing and Parenting in Early Modern England*, eds. Douglas A. Brooks and Jennifer Wynne Hellwarth, Women and Gender in the Early Modern World (Aldershot, UK: Ashgate, 2005), 32.
3. Ian Maclean, *Renaissance Notion of Woman: A Study in the Fortunes of Scholasticism and Medical Science in European Intellectual Life* (Cambridge, UK: Cambridge University Press 1980), 31.
4. Aristotle, Generation of Animals in *The Complete Works of Aristotle: The Revised Oxford Translation*, ed. Jonathan Barnes, Vol. 1 (Princeton, NJ: Princeton University Press), 2.4.738b20–23. In Greek: "ἀεὶ δὲ παρέχει τὸ μὲν θῆλυ τὴν ὕλην, τὸ δ᾽ ἄρρεν τὸ δημιουργοῦν." Greek transcribed from Aristotle, *Generation of Animals*, trans. by A. L. Peck (Cambridge, MA: Harvard University Press, 1942). All Greek transcriptions of *Generation of Animals* are from the same.
5. See Maclean 30, 35–36.
6. Eve Keller, *Generating Bodies and Gendered Selves: The Rhetoric of Reproduction in Early Modern England* (Seattle, WA: University of Washington Press, 2007), 32.
7. See Maclean, 42. See also Gail Kern Paster, *Humoring the Body: Emotions and the Shakespearean Stage* (Chicago: University of Chicago Press, 2004), 78–79 for a discussion on how women's humoral composition might impinge on their agency. See also Keller, 19–46, for a reading that connects the Galenic body to posthuman understandings of the body.
8. See Maclean for a discussion of Gabriele Falloppio and his work on female genitalia, for example, 33.
9. Philip Sidney, *The Countess of Pembroke's Arcadia*, ed. Katherine Duncan-Jones (Oxford: Oxford University Press, 1985), 209. See introduction and Chapter 6 for further discussion of this moment in the *Arcadia*.
10. Charles Estienne, *De Dissectione partium corporis humani libri tres* (Paris: Apud Simonem Colinaeum 1545), 271, 275.
11. Wax is associated with reproduction from Aristotle onwards because of Aristotle's assertion that men provide the form of offspring and women provide their material. See de Grazia for more discussion, especially 34.
12. *Swetnam the Woman Hater: The Controversy and the Play*, ed. Cory Crandall (Lafayette, IN: Purdue University Studies, 1969), 3.1.39. References are to act, scene, and line.

13. Ibid., 3.1.36–37.
14. Ibid., 3.3.70–73.
15. Ibid., 3.3.75–80.
16. Ibid., 3.3.72–74.
17. Ibid., 3.3.84, 86–88.
18. Ibid., 3.3.88–89.
19. Ibid., 3.3.264–65.
20. Valerie Traub, *The Renaissance of Lesbianism* (Cambridge: Cambridge University Press, 2002), 65.
21. William Shakespeare, *Twelfth Night* in *The Norton Shakespeare: Based on the Oxford Edition*, eds. Stephen Greenblatt et al. (New York: W. W. Norton, 1997), 2.5.84. References are to act, line, and scene.
22. Shakespeare, *The Rape of Lucrece*, 1240. All citations of *The Rape of Lucrece* follow *The Norton Shakespeare* and are to line number.
23. Ibid., 1241–1246.
24. Barbara Baines, "Effacing Rape in Early Modern Representation," *English Literary History* 65, no. 1 (1998): 88.
25. Katharine Eisaman Maus, "Taking Tropes Seriously: Language and Violence in Shakespeare's Rape of Lucrece," *Shakespeare Quarterly* 37, no. 1 (1986): 75.
26. Jonathan Crewe has argued that Shakespeare deploys a strategy of "shifting reified antitheses and fixed alignments" throughout the poem. See Jonathan Crewe, *Trials of Authorship: Anterior Forms and Poetic Reconstruction from Wyatt to Shakespeare* (Berkeley, CA: Berkeley University Press, 1990), 140.
27. Shakespeare, *Rape of Lucrece*, 1229–1230.
28. Ibid., 1238–1240.
29. Ibid., 1224.
30. Ibid., 1226–1227.
31. Ibid., 1272–1274.
32. Amanda Bailey, "Speak What We Feel: Sympathy and Statecraft," in *Affect Theory and Early Modern Texts: Politics, Ecologies, and Form*, eds. Amanda Bailey and Mario DiGangi (Basingstoke: Palgrave Macmillan, 2017), 30.
33. Ibid.
34. Shakespeare, *Rape of Lucrece*, 1229–1230.
35. Ibid., 1237–1239.
36. Ibid., 593–95.
37. "The Sonnets and 'A Lover's Complaint,'" in *The Norton Shakespeare: Based on the Oxford Edition*, eds. Stephen Greenblatt et al. (New York: W. W. Norton, 1997), Sonnet 55, 1–2. References are to line numbers.
38. Shakespeare, *The Rape of Lucrece*, 571.
39. For more on Lucrece as text see Crewe, *Trials of Authorship*, 162.
40. Shakespeare, *Twelfth Night*, 2.2.27–28.

41. Ibid., *Twelfth Night*, 2.5.84–85.
42. de Grazia, "Imprints," 42. See also Karen Robertson, "A Revenging Feminine Hand in *Twelfth Night*," in *Reading and Writing in Shakespeare*, ed. David Bergeron (London, 1996), 122.
43. Robertson, "Revenging Feminine Hand," 121, 126.
44. Shakespeare, *Twelfth Night*, 2.5.174–176.
45. Ibid., 3.2.66–68.
46. Shakespeare, *Rape of Lucrece*, 1712.
47. Shakespeare, *Twelfth Night*, 2.5.87–92.
48. Ibid., 1.3.6–7, 1.5.85–86.
49. Jessica Tvordi, "Female Alliance and the Construction of Homoeroticism in *As You Like It* and *Twelfth Night*" in *Maids and Mistresses, Cousins and Queens: Women's Alliances in Early Modern Europe*, eds. Susan Frye and Karen Robertson (Oxford: Oxford University Press, 1999), 123.
50. Shakespeare, *Twelfth Night*, 2.2.25–30.
51. Since Viola would have been played by a boy actor on the Shakespearean stage, her status as "woman" is also construction, and arguably more so. See Stephen Orgel's *Impersonations: The Performance of Gender in Shakespeare's England* (Cambridge: Cambridge University Press, 1996), for more on the implications of portrayal of Viola/Cesario by a boy actor.
52. *Oxford English Dictionary*, 2nd ed., s.v. "pregnant." Shakespeare uses this meaning of "pregnant" in *Hamlet, Pericles*, and elsewhere in *Twelfth Night*, making it highly plausible that he has it in mind here as well.
53. Valerie Traub, *Desire and Anxiety: Circulations of Sexuality in Shakespearean Drama* (London: Routledge, 1992), 130.
54. Shakespeare, *Twelfth Night*, 1.5.154.
55. Ibid., 1.5.158–159.
56. Ibid., 1.5.233–235.
57. Ibid., 1.4.20–21.
58. Mary Jo Kietzman, "Will Personified: Viola as Actor-Author in Twelfth Night," *Criticism: A Quarterly for Literature and the Arts* 54, no. 2 (Spring 2012): 259–60.
59. Shakespeare, *Twelfth Night*, 1.4.29–35.
60. See Laurie Shannon, "Nature's Bias: Renaissance Homonormativity and Elizabethan Comic Likeness," *Modern Philology: A Journal Devoted to Research in Medieval and Modern Literature* 98, no. 2 (November 2000), 207–208 for another reading of this discourse of likeness.
61. Shakespeare, *Twelfth Night*, 1.5.266–268.
62. For the connection of rings to vaginas see Allison Findlay, *Women in Shakespeare: A Dictionary* (London and New York: Bloomsbury Arden Shakespeare, 2010), 348.
63. Although her success with Sebastian also does not seem to be located in class difference.

64. Jonathan Goldberg, *Shakespeare's Hand* (Minneapolis: University of Minnesota Press, 2003), 100.
65. Ibid., 100.
66. Traub, *Desire and Anxiety*, 138.
67. Shakespeare, *Twelfth Night*, 5.1.252–53.
68. Shannon, "Nature's Bias," 210.
69. See Julie Crawford, "The Homoerotic of Shakespeare's Elizabethan Comedies," in *A Companion to Shakespeare's Works, Vol. III: The Comedies*, eds. Richard Dutton and Jean E. Howard, 137–138 for another reading of how marriage might not resolve the queerness of the play.
70. Shakespeare, *Titus Andronicus*, 3.1.44–46. Reference is to act, scene, and line.
71. Shakespeare, *Love's Labour's Lost*, 1.1.9–10. References are to act, scene, and line.
72. Ibid., 2.1.233–236.
73. Ibid., 2.1.236.
74. The doubleness of impression and expression at this moment is also the doubleness of the eye, especially in the early modern period, when competing theories of vision offered the possibility that vision worked via emission. For Navarre, the eye is both the organ that receives the image of the beloved and also the organ that conveys his new feelings. In fact, it is the organ that dominates the transmission of desire. Within Boyet "all senses to that sense did make their repair" so only the eye manages either to "feel" or to "speak." Moreover, this communication proceeds from one set of eyes to another, such that Boyet claims "all eyes saw his eyes enchanted with gazes." Eyes thus become the subject and object of vision, receiving and expressing the totality of desire.
75. The impression of Lucrece is also textually generative. However, she experiences no similar pleasure in the proliferation of texts and the transition from text to author seems more perilous.

References

Aristotle. *Generation of Animals*. Translated by A. L. Peck. Loeb Classical Library 366. Cambridge, MA: Harvard University Press, 1942.

Aristotle. "Generation of Animals." In *The Complete Works of Aristotle: The Revised Oxford Translation*, edited by Jonathan Barnes, 1111–1218. Princeton, NJ: Princeton University Press, 1984.

Bailey, Amanda. "Speak What We Feel: Sympathy and Statecraft." In *Affect Theory and Early Modern Texts: Politics, Ecologies, and Form*, edited by

Amanda Bailey and Mario DiGangi, 27–46. Basingstoke: Palgrave Macmillan, 2017.

Baines, Barbara J. "Effacing Rape in Early Modern Representation." *English Literary History* 65, no. 1 (Spring 1998): 69–98.

Crandall, Coryl, ed. "Swetnam, the Women Hater." In *Swetnam, the Women Hater: The Controversy and the Play*, Critical edition. Lafayette, IN: Purdue University Press, 1969.

Crawford, Julie. "The Homoerotics of Shakespeare's Elizabethan Comedies." In *A Companion to Shakespeare's Works, Volume III: The Comedies*, edited by Richard Dutton and Jean E. Howard, 137–58. Blackwell Companions to Literature and Culture: 17–20. Malden, MA: Blackwell, 2006.

Crewe, Jonathan V. *Trials of Authorship: Anterior Forms and Poetic Reconstruction from Wyatt to Shakespeare*. Berkeley: University of California Press, 1990.

De Grazia, Margreta. "Imprints: Shakespeare, Gutenberg, and Descartes." In *Printing and Parenting in Early Modern England*, edited by Douglas A. Brooks and Jennifer Wynne Hellwarth, 29–58. Women and Gender in the Early Modern World. Aldershot, UK: Ashgate, 2005.

Descartes, Rene. *Meditations on First Philosophy: With Selections from the Objections and Replies*. Edited and translated by John Cottingham. Rev. ed. Cambridge, UK: Cambridge University Press, 1997.

Estienne, Charles. *De Dissectione Partium Corporis Humani Libri Tres*. Paris: Apud Simonem Colinaeum, 1545.

Findlay, Alison. *Women in Shakespeare: A Dictionary*. Reprint edition. London: The Arden Shakespeare, 2014.

Goldberg, Jonathan. *Shakespeare's Hand*. Minneapolis: University of Minnesota Press, 2003.

Keller, Eve. *Generating Bodies and Gendered Selves: The Rhetoric of Reproduction in Early Modern England*. Seattle: University of Washington Press, 2011.

Kietzman, Mary Jo. "Will Personified: Viola as Actor-Author in Twelfth Night." *Criticism: A Quarterly for Literature and the Arts* 54, no. 2 (Spring 2012): 257–89.

Maclean, Ian. *The Renaissance Notion of Woman: A Study in the Fortunes of Scholasticism and Medical Science in European Intellectual Life*. Cambridge, UK: Cambridge University Press, 1980.

Maus, Katharine Eisaman. "Taking Tropes Seriously: Language and Violence in Shakespeare's Rape of Lucrece." *Shakespeare Quarterly* 37, no. 1 (1986): 66–82.

Orgel, Stephen. *Impersonations: The Performance of Gender in Shakespeare's England*. Cambridge, UK: Cambridge University Press, 1996.

Paster, Gail Kern. *Humoring the Body: Emotions and the Shakespearean Stage*. Chicago: University of Chicago Press, 2004.

Robertson, Karen. "A Revenging Female Hand in Twelfth Night." In *Reading and Writing in Shakespeare*, edited by David Bergeron. London: Associated University Presses, 1996.

Shakespeare, William. "Love's Labour's Lost." In *The Norton Shakespeare*, edited by Stephen Greenblatt, Walter Cohen, Jean E. Howard, and Katharine Eisaman Maus, 733–802. New York: W. W. Norton, 1997.

———. "Rape of Lucrece." In *The Norton Shakespeare*, edited by Stephen Greenblatt, Walter Cohen, Jean E. Howard, and Katharine Eisaman Maus, 635–82. New York: W. W. Norton, 1997.

———. "The Most Lamentable Tragedy of Titus Andronicus." In *The Norton Shakespeare*, edited by Stephen Greenblatt, Walter Cohen, Jean E. Howard, and Katharine Eisaman Maus, 371–434. New York: W. W. Norton, 1997.

———. "The Sonnets and 'A Lover's Complaint.'" In *The Norton Shakespeare*, edited by Stephen Greenblatt, Walter Cohen, Jean E. Howard, and Katharine Eisaman Maus, 1915–90. New York: W. W. Norton, 1997.

———. "Twelfth Night." In *The Norton Shakespeare*, edited by Stephen Greenblatt, Walter Cohen, Jean E. Howard, and Katharine Eisaman Maus, 1761–1822. New York: W. W. Norton, 1997.

Shannon, Laurie. "Nature's Bias: Renaissance Homonormativity and Elizabethan Comic Likeness." *Modern Philology: A Journal Devoted to Research in Medieval and Modern Literature* 98, no. 2 (November 11, 2000): 183–210.

Sidney, Philip. *The Countess of Pembroke's Arcadia:* Edited by Katherine Duncan-Jones. 1st edition. Oxford and New York: Oxford University Press, 1985.

Traub, Valerie. *Desire and Anxiety: Circulations of Sexuality in Shakespearean Drama*. London and New York: Routledge, 1992.

———. *The Renaissance of Lesbianism in Early Modern England*. Cambridge Studies in Renaissance Literature and Culture 42. Cambridge, UK: Cambridge University Press, 2002.

Tvordi, Jessica. "Female Alliance and the Construction of Homoeroticism in As You Like It and Twelfth Night." In *Maids and Mistresses, Cousins and Queens : Women's Alliances in Early Modern England*, edited by Susan Frye and Karen Robertson, 114–30. Oxford: Oxford University Press, 1999.

CHAPTER 3

Wax Minds: Writing Subjectivity and Agency in *Hamlet* and *The Atheist's Tragedy*

In this chapter, I turn from wax women to wax minds. Wax is a material that figures the mind in countless early modern works of literature and philosophy. While deployments of the trope vary, generally the wax mind is imagined as a textual space that might be subject to erasure and reinscription. A wax subjectivity, like a wax sculpture, is provisional: simultaneously laden with potentiality and vulnerable; capable of new forms, while haunted by the prints and palimpsests of "pressures past."[1] Wax, we shall see, is an apt metaphor for the mind, and one with a long history in Western thought, reaching back to Plato. Yet from these earliest articulations, the association of the mind with wax has raised questions around agency and ethics. Who authors the mind and when? Who bears responsibility for the nature and efficacy of those impressions? To what extent might we understand ourselves as texts already written, and to what extent might we have the capacity to write and rewrite ourselves? How do authoring figures like fathers or schoolmasters enter into this conversation? And what of gender? Do the associations between women and wax that we explored in Chapter 1 matter when poets, philosophers, and playwrights think the mind as wax? While there are no singular answers to these questions, paying attention to the deployments of the signet–seal trope around the mind in a wide variety of texts reveals that wax was being used in this period to work out or at least attempt to work out the nature of subjectivity and the limits of agency.

© The Author(s) 2019
L. M. Maxwell, *Wax Impressions, Figures, and Forms in Early Modern Literature*, Early Modern Cultural Studies 1500–1700, https://doi.org/10.1007/978-3-030-16932-9_3

As I briefly sketched in the introduction, wax is an important philosophical model of the mind with roots in Plato and Aristotle. Famously, in the *Theaetetus*, Plato's Socrates asks Theaetetus to "imagine … that there exists in the mind of man a block of wax, which is of different sizes in different men; harder, moister, and having more or less purity in one than another, and in some of an intermediate quality."[2] This block of wax functions as a tablet on which memories can be imprinted, "as from the seal of a ring."[3] By figuring the mind as wax and treating all external stimuli as "the seal of the ring," Plato's Socrates provides a model for how the outside world is internalized. In this model, the mind is passive and acted upon by outside forces, but not all minds are the same. The quality of the wax, its purity, affects the ability of the mind to take a print: "the shaggy and rugged and gritty, or those who have an admixture of earth or dung in their composition, have the impressions indistinct, as also the hard, for there is no depth in them."[4] Thus even as the mind serves as a passive location for inscription, not all minds are the same, just as not all men are equally wise. As compelling as this model is, Socrates discards it because it cannot explain simple mathematical errors such as claiming that seven plus five is eleven. If the mind was truly like wax, then such errors could not occur because knowledge of arithmetic would either be there or it would not. Consequently, Socrates moves on to consider other models that might better account for the kinds of errors made by the mind, ultimately failing to settle on any of them.

In *The Theaetetus*, Plato does not explicitly raise questions of agency, but his discussion of the wax mind and the range of compositions possible in such a mind invites such considerations. To what extent can one condition one's mind and make it apt to receive prints? To what extent is the quality of the mind a matter of nature? Is there a relation between virtue and pliability? Might there be an ethical imperative to maintain a printable mind or to seek out virtuous prints? Plato's *Meno*, a dialogue focused on discovering the nature of virtue, suggests that the writing of the mind lies beyond human agency.

In the *Meno*, Plato suggests that the mind may be pre-imprinted and "that there is no teaching, but only recollection."[5] Again, his proof lies in mathematics. He asks Meno to call in an uneducated slave boy and proceeds to ask him questions about geometry, eventually getting the boy to assert that given a square, you can form a new square that is double the area of the original if you set the side length equal to the length of the diagonal of the initial square. While the boy makes several errors along the way, Socrates suggests that his ultimate success reveals an innate knowledge of geometry—knowledge that he only discovered in the practice of answering Socrates' questions. When carried back to the initial question of the nature of virtue, the geometry lesson suggests that even if virtue is a kind of knowledge it would not be teachable, as knowledge is a matter of memory rather than learning.[6] This theory casts serious doubt on the efficacy of education and limits an individual's agency by suggesting that one can only realize the knowledge or virtue that is pre-imprinted on the mind. Of course, like all of Plato's dialogues, *The Meno* leaves open many questions including what the actual difference between learning and discovery might be, how experience might figure into the idea of a pre-imprinted mind, and whether this pre-imprinted mind, might also be best understood through wax. Plato's Socrates also ultimately decides that virtue is not a form of knowledge, and is instead a gift of the God, further divorcing the living of a virtuous life from possibilities of will or agency, and also perhaps from the model of the wax mind.

While Plato does not fully settle on the mind as wax, it becomes, as Mary Carruthers has argued, a "governing model, or 'cognitive archetype'" for memory within Western cultures.[7] This occurs, at least in part, because Aristotle embraces the model of the wax mind. In his *On the Soul*, Aristotle explains that sense perception proceeds in precisely the same way as imprinting a seal, "a sense is what has the power of receiving into itself the sensible forms of things without the matter, in the way in which a piece of wax takes on the impress of a signet-ring without the iron or gold."[8] Gone is any hesitation over the aptness of the model, instead Aristotle insists that perception works just as impression does. Further, he holds that memory is intimately related to sense perception. In "On Memory," he explains, "it is clear that cognition of these objects is effected by the primary faculty of perception, and memory even of intellectual objects involves an image and the image is an affection of the common sense."[9] Since memory works through images, it is like sense perception: "It is clear that we must conceive that which is generated through sense-perception in the soul, and in the part of the body which is its seat, — viz. that affection the state whereof we call memory — to be some such thing as a picture. The process of movement stamps in, as it were, a sort of impression of the precept, just as persons do who make an impression with a seal."[10] While memory differs from sense perception—working through affection and concerned with the past rather than the present, it proceeds on many of the same terms.

Further, just as we saw in Plato, minds differ in their capacity to make memories:

> [I]n those strongly moved owing to passion, or time of life, no memory is formed; just as no impression would be formed if the movement of the seal were to impinge on running water; while there are others in whom, owing to the receiving surface being frayed, as happens to old walls, or owing to the hardness of the receiving surface, the requisite impression is not implanted at all. Hence both very young and very old persons are defective in memory; they are in a state of flux.[11]

The state of the wax mind explains why some minds have a greater capacity for memory than others. Again, Aristotle is more interested in explaining why memory sometimes fails and is more prone to failure in certain types of people—i.e., the young and old than he is in exploring questions of agency and virtue. Yet just as in Plato, the observation that all minds are not equally retentive begins to raise questions about how one might optimize the mind to promote memory, learning, and perhaps even virtue.

Following Aristotle, the trope of the wax mind, appears and reappears in classical texts, medieval treatises, and early modern books. As a trope, it succeeds in modeling both the immense capacity of the human mind, and some of its major limitations, since, depending on the age and quality of the mind the process of inscription and recollection could be more or less successful. In these later articulations, the questions of virtue, learning, and agency that I have been raising rise more explicitly to the surface and are once again modeled through wax.

3.1   Learning Wax Virtues

While Christian thought is far from monolithic, in both Catholic and Protestant texts, the idea that the mind, soul, or self might be impressible becomes a question of virtue. Where Plato and Aristotle arrive at the idea of the wax mind through inquiries into sense perception and memory, the metaphoric of wax, signet, seal, and impression enter religious discourse through the Bible. According to Genesis, God "created man in his own Image, in the Image of God created hee him; male and female created hee them" and man in turn transmits his image to his offspring: "Adam liued an hundred and thirtie years, and begate a sonne in his own likenesse, after his image."[12] While these passages might not seem to explicitly engage wax, the idea of transmitting a likeness is caught up in the possibilities of printing and stamping and the active formation of a passive substance. Further if the likeness being transmitted is ultimately God's likeness, then what is at stake is not simply biological reproduction, instead it is the reproduction of goodness.

Perhaps then it is not surprising that other parts of the Bible invoke wax tropes to explicitly discuss virtue. In Proverbs, the self is figured as inscribable: "Let not mercy and truth forsake thee: bind them about thy necke, write them vpon the table of thine heart."[13] Here virtue becomes a state to be actively sought and a matter of self-inscription. Similarly, in the Song of Solomon, the bride exhorts: "Set mee as a seal vpon thine heart, as a seale vpon thine arm; for loue is strong as death, iealousie is cruel as the graue: the coales thereof are coals of fire, which has a most vehement flame."[14] Blending the sacred and the erotic, the bride uses the trope of signet–seal to figure the relationship between the bride and husband together with the formative nature of their union. These passages differ from those of Aristotle and Plato in part by focusing on the heart, perhaps to emphasize an affective basis for virtue.

Medieval and early modern Christian thinkers could draw on both classical theories about memory and the wax mind and Biblical ideas about impressibility to consider the best means to cultivate a soul. In both Catholic and Protestant writings, the possibility that the self might be a site of impression becomes invested with ethical implications. For example, in the twelfth-century Catholic treatise, *The Moral Education of Novices*, Hugh of St. Victor suggests that the examples of Saints can be used to craft the self through practices of imitation and tempering:

Why do you think, brothers, that we are instructed to imitate the life and conduct of good men, unless so that through imitation of them we may be re-formed to the likeness of a new life? In fact in them the form of the likeness of God is clear and therefore when we are imprinted by these things through imitation, we are also shaped in the image of the same similitude. But it should be known that unless wax is first softened, it does not receive the form, so indeed a man is not bent to the form of virtue through the power of another's actions unless first through humility he is softened away from the hardness of all pride and contradiction.[15]

Here the model of signet and seal is deployed to explain how the imitation of virtue can aid in the reformation of that good Christian, and to insist on the responsibility of the supplicant to ready himself for virtuous impressions. According to Hugh, when we imitate the goodness of other men, we are emulating the form of God, and both the raised figure of the seal and its depressions reveal that form: "what else is indicated for us in this, except that we, who desire to be reformed through examples of the good as if by a certain seal that is very well sculptured out, discover in them certain lofty vestiges of works like projections and certain humble ones like depressions."[16] Hugh's instruction depends upon both the truth of divine impression and also the active participation of the subject being molded, who has some amount of agency here. He is responsible for inscribing the virtues of mercy and truth upon his own heart and for seeking out "examples of the good" that contain appropriate "lofty vestiges" and "humble ones."

Moreover, the good Christian is also responsible for conditioning the soul in order to make it ready for virtuous impression. Plato and Aristotle insist that impression can only occur on a certain kind of mind—one neither too hard, nor too soft, nor too much in flux—but devote little attention to how one might insure that kind of mind. Hugh however suggests that the supplicant must be humble, as "through humility he is softened away from the harness of all pride and contradiction." Thus the onus is on the soul seeking virtue. Becoming virtuous, while it depends on malleability, also requires acts of binding, writing, desiring, softening, and discovery.

With Hugh, we might understand wax virtue not as a singular act of impression, but as an iterative process, perhaps even as the result of *askesis*, which Pierre Hadot defines as spiritual exercises.[17] These exercises, which Hadot traces through classical philosophy and early Christian thought, condition the mind to respond appropriately to the contingencies of life, by repeated meditation and self-reflection. Through *askesis*, philosophy becomes "the art of living" rather than an abstract intellectual pursuit. While the exact nature of the practice varies from one philosophy to the next, Hadot suggests that they all focus on the present moment as a way of freeing the self from its passions and thus amount "to a transformation of our vision of the world, and to a metamorphosis of our personality."[18] Hugh's recommendation to novices to seek out examples of goodness and internalize those examples amounts to a prescription for transformative meditation, and wax models both the malleability of the self that enables the success of such practices and its ability to hold virtuous prints.[19]

Similarly, the sixteenth-century Protestant collection of women's sacred writing, *The Monument of Matrones* (1582), attaches virtue to the carefully cultivated wax self. *The Monument of Matrones* suggests that the divine imprint manifests in man's "reason, and delight in knowledge" which serve "as a signature and impression of the diuine Maiestie."[20] The anonymous meditation explains that this too should elicit virtuous action: "Esteeme therefore of thy selfe, as of the temple of God; seeing it pleased him to impart his likenesse to thee, as a high renowne, to adore and imitate God. Thou dooest imitate him, if thou be holie, as he is holie."[21] The emphasis here is slightly different than it was in the Catholic text. The seeker is directed to look inward and to God, rather than to other earthly models of virtue. Yet by locating the evidence of God's imprint in reason and a hunger for knowledge, it again suggests that honoring the divine imprint requires an individual to actively pursue truth as a way of honoring and adoring God.[22] Further, by embedding these ideas within a meditation, we again encounter the idea that emulating virtuous forms might be a spiritual exercise founded in repetition.

If Christian thought introduces virtue into the possibility of the wax mind, soul, and heart, early modern pedagogical texts also insist that the cultivation of the mind requires a certain level of receptivity, which depends on the age of the student, his past experiences, and matters of temperament. In Roger Ascham's *The Scholemaster* (1570), for example, he writes:

> if euer the nature of man be giuen at any tyme, more than other, to receiue goodnes, it is in innocencie of yong yeares, before, that experience of euill, haue taken roote in hym. For, the pure cleane witte of a sweete yong babe, is like the newest wax, most hable to receiue the best and fayrest printing: and like a new bright siluer dishe neuer occupied, to receiue and kepe cleane, anie good thyng that is put into it.[23]

Here Ascham suggests that the mind of the youth is most suited to inscription. Such a mind is like the "newest wax," and thus is "most hable to receiue the best and fairest printing." The schoolmaster is responsible for putting "good thyng[s]" into the mind, but the success of that endeavor depends on the state of the mind he encounters, and particularly here, on the unadulterated state of the mind.

While Ascham's discussion of wax impression might suggest that the ideal mind is also soft, or at least sufficiently soft to easily take impression, that turns out not to be the case. Elsewhere Ascham turns to other material metaphors in order to further describe the ideal student and insists that the best mind for learning is actually one that might initially seem overly hard. Indeed, a hard mind is preferable to an overly soft one, so long as "it be first well handled by the mother, and rightlie smothed and wrougth as it should."[24] This conditioning will make a mind suited for education, for:

> In woode and stone, not the softest, but hardest, be alwaies aptest for portrature, both fairest for pleasure, and most durable for proffit. Hard wittes be hard to receiue, but sure to keepe: painefull without werinesse, hedefull without wauering, constant without newfanglenes: bearing heauie thinges, thoughe not lightlie, yet willinglie: entring hard thinges, though not easelie, yet depelie, and so cum to that perfitnes of learning in the ende, that quicke wittes, seeme in hope, but do not in deede, or else verie seldome, euer attaine vnto.[25]

The wood and stone analogy here seems at odds with the wax one, but both depend on the same idea that education is itself a craft in which the schoolmaster serves as the artist, forming his students into his masterwork. As we saw in the introduction and will further explore in Chapter 5, wax is an apt material for sculpture because it is easily manipulated, but that same quality also renders wax vulnerable to change. Thus most finished sculptures in the period were wrought in marble or other hard materials after first being worked out in wax. These materials require more skill and effort to mold, but ultimately withstand the pressure of time more fully. Ascham explicitly invokes the art of portraiture in part to elevate the role of the educator, placing him on par with a consummate artist and suggesting that his products—well-molded minds—are valuable and durable goods. At the same time, the crafting of a young mind here comes to require a community effort. The hard mind is only preferable if it has been primed by the student's mother and made ready for inscription. While Ascham imagines that his students' minds might be hard like "woode and stone," his conception of the mind is still deeply informed by the idea of mind as wax. Teaching might be like impression, or engraving, but it is always a matter of fashioning images onto the surface of the mind that the student can than use and recall.

Ascham's insistence on modeling the mind might suggest that education is a process that happens to a student. However, throughout the treatise Ascham insists that the students must be treated gently to encourage their love of learning, as their affections impact the success of the endeavor. For example, he describes the Lady Jane Grey as a particularly exceptional student whose love of books was brought on by severe parents and a gentle schoolmaster, a combination that she tells Ascham is "one of the greatest benefites, that euer God gaue me."[26] Since lessons were such a pleasurable part of her life, she valued them and the knowledge they brought, and as a result, "my booke, hath bene so moch my pleasure, & bringeth dayly to me more pleasure & more, that in respect of it, all other pleasures, in very deede, be but trifles and troubles vnto me."[27] Even here, where Ascham is intent on praising Lady Jane Grey and also of advocating for a pedagogy of gentle correction, the primary responsibility for forming a mind rests on the schoolmaster, and not the student.

The end of education, for Ascham, is to instill forms of "goodnes."[28] Teaching knowledge and crafting virtue are intimately connected in the text, and Ascham is not alone in believing that character formation has something to do with impression or inscription. The idea is widespread in the period, For example, in his *Characters*, Sir Thomas Overbury writes "Character comes of this infinitive moode χαράξω which signifieth to ingrave, or to make a deep Impression. And for that cause, a letter (as A. B.) is called a character."[29] Writing letters and writing characters are both a matter of "deep Impression."

3.2   Writing Hamlet's Tables

When Hamlet encounters the ghost in the form of his father, he finds his mind unsuitable for the demands made upon it.[30] After the ghost departs, he exclaims:

> ...Remember thee?
> Ay, thou poor ghost, while memory holds a seat
> In this distracted globe. Remember thee?
> Yea, from the table of my memory
> I'll wipe away all trivial fond records,
> All saws of books, all forms, all pressures past,
> That youth and observation copied there,
> And thy commandment all alone shall live
> Within the book and volume of my brain,
> Unmixed with baser matter. Yes, yes, by heaven![31]

Here, the metaphor of the wax mind is pivotal to Hamlet's under-standing of himself and his attempt to remold his own interiority to better suit the project of revenge. While Hamlet never explicitly states that the material of his mind is wax, he invokes it through his discus-sion of "pressures past."[32] Still his preoccupation here is not the careful construction and refining of impressions, or the cultivation of knowl-edge, as we saw in Ascham, nor with the transformation of the self through repeated acts of meditation, as we saw in Hugh of St. Victor. Instead, Hamlet wants to wipe his mind clean and reinscribe it with only his father's commandment, reforming himself into the instrument of revenge. As Jonathan Goldberg has argued, "Hamlet receives the Ghost's *words* as a scriptive command, one that re-marks his haunted memory as a locus of inscription, erasure, and reinscription."[33] It is a moment in which "subjectivity is a scene of writing" and specifically a scene of writing wax—with all the malleability that entails.[34] It is also a moment that imagines the possibility—as Garret Sullivan has noted—of the "annihilation and reformation of the self."[35] As much as this scene is a scene of writing, it is also one of erasure. Despite Hamlet's insistence that the matter that currently occupies his mind is trivial and base, this very collection of knowledge and experience shapes him and rewriting his mind according to the ghost's command would be radical act, one that would align with his suicidal impulses—his conflict over whether "to be, or not to be"[36]—and echo the spiritual peril implicit in his mission of revenge.[37]

Hamlet desires this radical reinscription of the self because he finds his mind unprepared to respond to the ghost adequately, either by refusing or accepting the command for revenge. Presumably, the inadequacy is the result of a disconnect between what is written on Hamlet's mind, the "saws of books" and "pressures past" and the task of revenging. This is true whether Hamlet's mind has been written by his scholastic experi-ences or by religious teachings, as revenge is not a mission compatible with scripture. Romans 12, after all, exhorts, "auenge not your selues, but rather giue place vnto wrath: for it is written, Uengeance is mine; I will repay, saith the Lord."[38] Within the revenge tragedy genre, this passage is often referenced, and while Hamlet never explicitly refers to it, his awareness that he risks "coupl[ing] hell" when he discourses with the ghost suggests that he knows vengeance is not compatible with scripture and also, it seems, not compatible with who he is prior to meeting the ghost. We can imagine Hamlet as one of Ascham's students, shaped by life and schooling toward virtue. For such a mind, the call to revenge would demand a rewriting of the self.

By promising to "wipe away all trivial fond records" and let his father's stamp live "all alone ... / Within the book and volume of my brain." Hamlet also seems to be fantasizing a return to an idealized relationship with his father. After all, the trope of signet–seal models conception, as we saw in Chapter 1, and that model imagines that a child, and especially a son, comes into the world bearing his father's print. This encounter then seems to be a repetition of that initiatory act of impression, a reassertion of his father's authority and authoring power, and one that might free Hamlet of the responsibility of his own agency and selfhood while perhaps righting the damage that may have been done by Hamlet's political disinheritance. In Margreta de Grazia's, *'Hamlet' Without Hamlet*, she argues that critics have not paid sufficient attention to Hamlet's political dispossession as the source of (or solution to) his seemingly complex interiority. She asks whether "the cause of Hamlet's distraction" might not "like an open secret, be obvious to all?"[39] Certainly here, realigning himself with his father's signet might restore his relationship to Hamlet senior as both son and heir.

Later in the play, when Hamlet uses his father's signet to doom Rosencrantz and Guildenstern, he realizes his fantasy of claiming his father's authority as his own:

> I had my father's signet in my purse,
> Which was the model of that Danish seal;
> Folded the writ up in form of th'other,
> Subscribed it, gave't th'impression, placed it safely,
> The changeling never known.[40]

Here Hamlet, who fails to assume his father's place as King, gains that power temporarily through the signet ring. "[T]hat Danish seal" carries the weight of the crown's authority and by employing it, Hamlet is able to write Rosencrantz's and Guildenstern's execution and escape his own. This easy act of writing, which may, as Hamlet claims, be ordained by heaven, stands in contrast to Hamlet's earlier attempt to inscribe his mind with the edict of revenge or carry out his revenge on Claudius. The rhetoric of the "changeling" insists on the inauthenticity of Hamlet's usurpation, while also suggesting that the act of writing is an act of parenthood and carries the same risks of falsehood as biological reproduction. Hamlet's seal substitutes undetected for Claudius's own. Yet that substitution is unstable, as de Grazia notes "the revised command gives him only as much time as it takes for Rosencrantz and Guildenstern to sale to Enlgand, be executed, and then word of the execution to reach Denmark."[41] His father's signet alone is not enough to permanently restore his political power, nor does his command prove sufficient to entirely remake Hamlet.

The metaphor of the wax mind in *Hamlet* raises questions of agency—What range of choices is available to Hamlet, given the state of his mind? To what extent can the self be rewritten to afford new choices? To what extent can others rewrite us? Hamlet does not, of course, succeed in erasing all previously acquired knowledge or experience from his mind, and while the ghost's command certainly makes an impression, it does not come to live "all alone / within the book and volume of [his] brain." After all, if Hamlet's mind could be rewritten in service of revenge, he would be able to erase all possibilities for inner conflict, which would dramatically shorten the play. The failure is already implicit in the metaphor. Wax tablets can be erased with the application of heat, but that erasure is never complete. Remnants of effaced texts linger, and even if those are wiped away, used wax is not as suited to clean inscription as new. The invocation of wax tablets thus testifies both to Hamlet's desire to actively remake the self and begins to suggest why his project of radical reinscription fails.

While Hamlet does not erase his mind and re-imprint it with only the ghost's command, his wax metaphor helps illuminate his inner conflict around the possibility of revenge. It also reveals his sense of his own malleability and his belief in the possibility of self-shaping. He returns to that possibility later in Act 3, when he praises Horatio for his Stoic traits. He claims,

> Since my dear soul was mistress of her choice
> And could of men distinguish, her election
> Hath sealed thee for herself...[42]

Again, in this speech to Horatio, Hamlet does not explicitly invoke a wax materiality. Yet his claim that his soul has "sealed" Horatio "for herself," implies as much. While there is some dislocution of the self here, with the soul both separate and a part of Hamlet, this figuration again suggests a kind of self-inscription. This time, Hamlet comes closer to describing the kind of practice described by Hugh of St. Victor. Horatio serves as a model man and Hamlet internalizes that model and with it the shape of Horatio's virtue.[43] As he goes on to say:

> ... Give me that man
> That is not passion's slave, and I will wear him
> In my heart's core, ay, in my heart of heart,
> As I do thee...[44]

Enshrined in Hamlet's heart, Horatio's print occupies space we have elsewhere seen reserved for a beloved, because his virtues are beloved by Hamlet's soul.[45] Yet again we must ask what kind of transformative possibilities are truly afforded to Hamlet here? Does wearing Horatio in his "heart's core" allow him to become like Horatio? Certainly, Hamlet does not seem to have freed himself from passion. Indeed, the positioning of this speech right before the staging of "The Mousetrap" and Hamlet's emotional confrontation with Gertrude underscores just how far Hamlet is from achieving that ideal. Hamlet's use of wax metaphorics to figure his mind, soul, and heart reveals something of the instability of the self and its vulnerability to writing pressures. At the same time, the failure of Hamlet's writing projects suggests a kind of resistance to inscription that can also be figured in wax.

Together these wax moments raise questions about authority, authorship, and agency, that largely remain unresolved within the play. The act of stamping seems to matter: It helps generate Hamlet's shape as son and would-be revenger and becomes the mechanism through which he is able to seal Rosencrantz and Guildenstern's doom. Yet, his project of radically rewriting himself fails. He is a text that is already written—at least in part—and he can neither erase his own selfhood nor replace it with a substitute text that would allow him to act as only his father's instrument. The play complicates the question of who is authoring what. When Hamlet imagines his mind as wax, is he imagining that he might rewrite it? Or that his father could? When he finds the opportunity to trade out the order for his own execution with one for Rosencrantz and Guildenstern, is he writing his fate by usurping the signet ring? Or is, "heaven ordinant," as he tells Horatio?[46] The competing possibilities for authorship and impression here show the impossibility of resolving how selfhood and agency are achieved in the play.

3.3   Imprinting Charlemont

Many of the same questions about what it means to be a wax self recur in Cyril Tourneur's *The Atheist's Tragedy*. This later Calvinist play repeats many elements present in *Hamlet*, including the suspicious death of a father and a son who must decide whether to take revenge. Yet despite the familiar contours of the play, *The Atheist's Tragedy* adopts a different view on the relation between father and son and the cultural imperative to revenge. Where the ghost of Hamlet senior advocates revenge, the ghost of Charlemont's father, Montferrers warns Charlemont away from that course of action, admonishing that revenge is God's prerogative. A conflicted Charlemont is prevented from taking action against his murderous uncle when he is himself accused of murder and arrested. The play then performs the promise of divine justice when that same uncle accidentally brains himself in the act of falsely executing Charlemont. As this brief summary suggests, *The Atheist's Tragedy* is deeply invested in a providential understanding of the universe and in affording tremendous agency to God. In such a play, the value of agency becomes less clear, as Charlemont reluctantly learns that the most virtuous action may be inaction.

Throughout the play, Charlemont's use of wax metaphorics shows a complicated sense of his own agency and what it means to be cast in relation to others. As in *Hamlet*, wax is caught up in questions of inscription and authority, but Charlemont plays on the propensity of wax to change and melt in order to show the vulnerability of that writing. Thus early in the play, Charlemont tells his father:

> My noble father,
> The weakest sigh you breathe hath power to turn
> My strongest purpose, and your softest tear
> To melt my resolution to as soft
> Obedience...[47]

Unlike Shakespeare's Hermia who refuses to be "as a form in wax" for her father to shape as he desires, Charlemont understands his filial duty to require just such obedience.[48] He figures himself not simply as obedient, but as completely malleable to his father's wishes. He will respond to the slightest application of force, "the weakest sigh," the "softest tear." His own "strongest purpose" is weaker than these signs of his father's disappointment. The rhetoric of softening, melting, and molding that permeates this speech suggests Charlemont see his mind and his desires as susceptible to authoring pressures.

Yet Charlemont's resolution does not actually melt away at the first hint of his father's displeasure. Instead, he attempts to manipulate his father into acceding to his own wishes, explaining:

> ... But my affection to the war
> Is as hereditary as my blood
> To ev'ry life of all my ancestry.
> Your predecessors were your precedents,
> And you are my example...[49]

By inscribing his duty to his father into a larger obligation to their shared ancestry, Charlemont suggests that his very "affection to the war" is a matter of filial imprint, "Your predecessors were your precedents, / And you are my example." A long history of precedent has stamped Charlemont into the would-be soldier and to turn away from that impressive history would require him to embrace the formlessness of melted wax. Thus while he claims that he would be willing to soften to his father's objections, he also suggests that those objections go against a deeply inscribed history of heroism. Ultimately Montferrers relents, and Charlemont is able to simultaneously occupy the roles of obedient son and soldier by manipulating the metaphorics of wax. While Charlemont is able to win his father over, that victory is hollow since it plays into the villain D'Amville's hands and sets up the tragedy that unfurls. Indeed, Charlemont's decision to go to war also reflects the danger of being malleable, insofar as D'Amville manipulates him into it.[50]

Charlemont uses wax metaphorics to figure himself as malleable, not only to his father, but also to his beloved. When he and Castabella kiss right before he leaves for war, he uses a vocabulary of impression and sealing that again figure him as malleable and void of agency:

> My noble mistress, this accompliment
> Is like an elegant and moving speech
> Composed of many sweet persuasive points
> Which second one another with a fluent
> Increase and confirmation of their force,
> Reserving still the best until the last,

> To crown with strong impulsion of the rest
> With a full conquest of the hearer's sense;
> Because th'impression of the last we speak
> Doth always longest and most constantly
> Possess the entertainment of remembrance.[51]

Here Charlemont suggests that Castabella's farewell kiss makes a greater impression than any of the other kisses that preceded it because it came last, just as the last speech in a series of speeches is most persuasive. By Charlemont's logic, both speeches and kisses make impressions and promise a "full conquest" of the passive recipient. Thus Castabella's kiss promises Charlemont a new and enduring shape for his memory, one that will comfort and entertain him when he is away. When Charlemont invokes wax impression at this moment, he again imagines himself in the passive position, upsetting the expected gender binaries of passive woman and active man. Their kiss, which could be understood as a mutual act, becomes Castabella's kiss, and she becomes the active shaper of his interior.

Castabella, however, rejects Charlemont's theorization of the kiss. She tells him:

> My worthy servant, you mistake th' intent
> Of kissing. 'Twas not meant to separate
> A pair of lovers, but to be the seal
> Of love, importing by the joining of
> Our mutual and incorporated breaths
> That we should breathe but one contracted life.
> Or stay at home, Or let me go with you.[52]

Where Charlemont reads the kiss as a farewell and understands it as a powerful unilateral action, akin to a persuasive speech, Castabella sees it as an act of union. Adopting her own version of wax metaphorics, Castabella suggests that a kiss is "the seal of love." Here, she plays on the role of wax seals on contracts, suggesting that the kiss as seal testifies to the "joining of / Our mutual and incorporated breaths" and signals that they should "breathe but one contracted life. She insists on the mutuality of the kiss and the bodily union that creates it, rejecting Charlemont's construction of himself as passive recipient, while transforming his wax metaphor into one that better suits her purpose—to convince Charlemont to either "stay at home, Or let me go with you."

Despite Charlemont and Castabella's disagreement about the meaning of the kiss, their shared reliance on a language of wax impression suggests a fundamental agreement about the transformative power of kissing and the virtue of being shaped by a beloved. Interestingly, although the kiss might move both of them, the emphasis is on Charlemont's malleability. Indeed, elsewhere in the play, Castabella is figured as hard, perhaps to escape the negative associations of women with wax. Languebeau tells D'Amville "She's like your diamond, a temptation in every man's eye, yet not yielding to any light impression herself."[53] By figuring Castabella as a diamond, Languebeau aligns her with one of the hardest substances possible and testifies to her chastity. She also defies Levidulcia's claim that "hot diet and soft ease make [ladies], like wax always kept warm, more easy to take impression,"[54] although Levidulcia embodies that description herself.[55] The contrast between Castabella's hardness and Charlemont's softness has the effect of reversing the gender roles implicit in their union.

If Charlemont's waxiness makes him an unusual man, it also seems to make him a good man within the universe of the play.[56] After D'Amville has imprisoned him for killing an assassin, Castabella pleads for him to show Charlemont mercy:

> O father, mercy is an attribute
> As high as justice, an essential part
> Of His unbounded goodness, whose divine
> Impression, form, and image man should bear.
> And, methinks, man should love to imitate
> His mercy, since the only countenance
> Of justice were destruction, if the sweet
> And loving favour of His mercy did
> Not meditate between it and our weakness.[57]

Castabella very clearly invokes a religious understanding of the trope of signet–seal. We should model ourselves after God and take on his "divine / Impression, form, and image," just as a piece of wax takes the print of a seal.[58] In Castabella's speech, the impression of God is what should allow D'Amville to take mercy on Charlemont and also seems to be the most direct way that God can "meditate between [justice] and our weakness." Yet D'Amville fails to live up to his responsibility as God's creature. As Castabella laments:

> ...neither the impression in your soul
> Of goodness, nor the duty of your place
> As goodness' substitute can move you...[59]

As one of God's creations, he should carry God's form and be moved by that shape. Moreover, since he has civil power, he is duty-bound to serve as "goodness' substitute" and apply the laws of mercy. Yet neither constitution nor position moves him to mercy. Indeed, Tiffany Jo Werth has argued that D'Amville is strongly associated in the play with stoniness, and thus materially opposed to the bearing of God's print.[60]

Of course, D'Amville rejects Castabella's logic and implies that by arguing for his release, she has revealed her own feminine weakness and softness for Charlemont, endangering her honor in the process. Yet given the play's commitment to Christian morality and D'Amville's role as villain and atheist, his dismissal of this claim of divine impression suggests that Castabella has articulated the code by which he should live.[61] We never see this code in action, however. Since our Christian hero, Charlemont, does not have the opportunity to exercise the virtue of mercy, as he occupies the role of prisoner rather than judge. Yet since Charlemont is frequently depicted as soft, we can imagine that given the chance, he would be more responsive to both the "impression ... of Goodness" and the "duty of [his] place / as goodness' substitute."[62] Certainly, his understanding of filial duty suggests that he has a much firmer grasp on the demands of "duty" than D'Amville does. Extrapolating from this scene therefore, we can begin to claim that Charlemont's softness may be the very quality that makes him a good Christian, and D'Amville's failure to be soft, or to live his life in relation to God, causes his eponymous damnation.

Charlemont's malleability and passivity predominate the play and in the first three acts might seem to connote weakness. He is susceptible to D'Amville's manipulation, Montferrers' tears, and changes his course of action easily when admonished by the ghost of Montferrers. Yet in the last two acts, Charlemont also displays his willingness to suffer punishment and death. Both Charlemont and Castabella leap onto the scaffold when faced with D'Amville's accusations. Charlemont declares:

> D'Amville to show thee with what light respect
> I value death and thy insulting pride,
> Thus, like a warlike navy on the sea,

> Bound for the conquest of some wealthy land,
> Passed through the stormy troubles of this life
> And now arrived upon the armèd coast,
> In expectation of the victory
> Whose honour lies beyond this exigent,
> Through mortal danger, with an active spirit,
> Thus I aspire to undergo my death.[63]

Charlemont's speech reveals that his seeming passivity is actually both active and virtuous. While throughout the play, he has seemed to change direction whenever anybody provides the slightest push, he has in fact always been setting a course toward heaven, and his movement sideways or backwards has been largely the result "the stormy troubles of this life," of the tempestuous winds and waves that push even the most "warlike navy" off course. Thus what has appeared to be passivity, has instead always been activity, even if it is only at this final moment that he can show his willingness to leap forward to "undergo [his] death." Similarly, his malleability has been a carefully cultivated state put on to facilitate virtuous forms. When faced with D'amville's assault, he stands his ground.

Charlemont's speech at this moment is also interesting because it aligns with his earliest speeches of the play when he articulated his desire to go to war. While his inclination to the war played into D'Amville's hands and proved to be one of his key mistakes in the tragedy, the honor and heroism that he attached to being a soldier are reclaimed in the end for any good Christian. Charlemont's passage through life has prepared him for the final battle with death and allows him to face death with an ease of conscience that inspires and confuses D'Amville, leading him to ask first for Charlemont's body after death so that he might discover "what thing there is in Nature more exact / Than in the constitution of myself" and then for mercy from the judges so that Charlemont can serve as his "physician" and teach him "th'efficient cause of a contented mind."[64] In this last Act of the play, Charlemont becomes the model man, because he is a man that God has modeled. What first seemed weakness and passivity becomes in the final equation both strength and activity, and is enough to make even the avowed atheist change his tune. As for Castabella, she also adopts the same rhetoric of martial heroics, declaring "And thus I second thy brave enterprise," as she leaps to join Charlemont on the scaffold.[65] In doing so, she suggests that she is his equal in Christian goodness and in strength. Yet while her speech begins as an echo of his, she continues in a different vein, taking on the more traditionally female role of providing emotional support and reassurance.

Ultimately, both survive when D'Amville brains himself with the executioner's axe. Charlemont makes clear the moral of the play, exclaiming:

> Only to Heav'n I attribute the work,
> Whose gracious motives made me still forebear
> To be mine own revenger. Now I see
> That *patience is the honest man's revenge*.[66]

The play resolves the seeming inconsistencies between the mission of revenge and the demands of faith by leaving revenge to God. Further, in marked contrast to most revenge tragedies, which end in the death of the revenging hero, *The Atheist's Tragedy* ends with the promise of a marriage which will not even be delayed long enough to bury the dead.

As we have seen, Hamlet and Charlemont both occupy similar subject positions as would-be revengers, and both try to understand the possibilities of selfhood through wax. While *The Atheist's Tragedy* was likely influenced by *Hamlet*, there might also be something about the genre of the revenge tragedy that foregrounds problems that are aptly figured with wax. Certainly, the conventions of the genre require a failure of the state to respond to a perceived injustice which creates a crisis for an individual. By jeopardizing the relationship between an individual and the state, the genre places pressure on an individual to find new ways of being, to adopt a new shape, even if that new shape is itself imitative. At the same time, the shape of the revenger is, as we have seen, always at odds with scripture which puts additional pressure on these projects of selfhood. Perhaps then it is not surprising to find wax in both Hamlet's and Charlemont's interior, since wax can speak simultaneously to the pressure of authority, the possibility of writing oneself, the lasting impressions others can make upon the self, and the instability of all these forms of selfhood while also raising questions about virtue and agency—which are often contested spaces in narratives of revenge.

Before bringing this chapter to a close, I want to pause for a moment over the problem of gender, which lurks on the edges of this chapter. The philosophical and pedagogical texts that rely on the model seem mostly to presume male subjects and many of the negative associations that we saw with female waxiness in Chapter 1 do not seem to pertain to articulation of the male wax mind. Yet in *The Atheist's Tragedy*, the wax qualities that are celebrated in Charlemont are not ascribed to Castabella, who must be hard like a diamond in order to be virtuous. Further, as we saw at the end of Chapter 1, men can be feminized through an association with wax. Yet while the possibilities of weakness and vulnerability are still present in these texts, the wax's association with Hamlet and Charlemont seems to speak more to questions of agency and self-realization then to questions of gender.

Reading *The Atheist's Tragedy* together with *Hamlet*, we can see how the wax model of the mind allows authors to express a wide variety of ideas about how the mind might be influenced by encounters with others. These plays raise the possibility that vulnerability might be an act of will—an openness to reshaping or reinscription that proves agential even as it might foreclose or reshape future possibilities of agency. It may be, as in *The Atheist Tragedy*, that maintaining a malleable wax mind is a virtuous possibility, one that allows a person to perform one's duty to father, country and God. Yet as we saw in *Hamlet*, it may also be that the mind resists effacement, and that the radical reinscription of the self is mere fantasy. The model of the wax mind is complex and allows for wide range of possibilities around questions of agency, authority, inscribability, and erasability. From the earliest articulations of the model, in Plato and Aristotle, it has been clear that not all wax minds are of the same quality and not all are equally inscribable, or likely to retain inscription. The power of the model is in this capacity to figure learning and forgetting, change, and endurance, agency, and passivity.

NOTES

1. William Shakespeare, "Hamlet," in *The Norton Shakespeare: Based on the Oxford Edition*, eds. Stephen Greenblatt et al. (New York: W. W. Norton, 1997), 1.5.100. References are to act, scene, and line.
2. Plato, "Theaetetus," in *The Dialogues of Plato*, ed. and trans. Benjamin Jowett, vol. 4, 3rd edition (London: Oxford University Press, 1892), 191c–191d. All references are to Stephanus number. In the Greek, "Θὲς δή μοι λόγου ἕνεκα ἐν ταῖς ψυχαῖς ἡμῶν ἐνὸν κήρινον ἐκμαγεῖον, τῷ μὲν μεῖξον, τῷ δ' ἔλαττον, καὶ τῷ μὲν καθαρωτέρου κηροῦ, τῷ δὲ κοπρωδεστέρου, καὶ σκληροτέρου, ἐνίοις δὲ ὑγροτέρου, ἔστι δ' οἷς μετρίως ἔχοντος." *Plato VII, Theaetetus. Sophist*, ed. and trans. Harold North Fowler, Loeb Classical Library (Cambridge, MA: Harvard

University Press, 1921). All Greek transcriptions of *The Theaetetus* that follow in the notes are from this edition.

3. Ibid., 191d–191e. In the Greek, "ὥσπερ δακτυλίων σημεῖα ἐνσημένους."
4. Ibid., 298, 194e. In the Greek, "οἱ δὲ δὴ λάσιον καὶ τραχὺ λιθῶδές τι ἢ γῆς ἢ κόπρου συμγείσης ἔμπλεων ἔχοντες ἀσαφῆ τὰ ἐκμαγεῖα ἴσχουσιν."
5. Plato, "Meno," in *The Dialogues of Plato*, ed. and trans. Benjamin Jowett, vol. 2, 3rd edition (London: Oxford University Press, 1892), 82a. In the Greek, "διδαχὴν εἶναι ἀλλ᾽ ἀνάμνησιν." Plato, *Plato: Laches, Protagoras, Meno, Euthydemus*, trans. W. R. M. Lamb (Cambridge, MA: Harvard University Press, 1977).
6. Ultimately, Plato discards the idea that virtue might be a kind of knowledge, but he does not discard the concept of knowledge as memory within the dialogue.
7. Mary Carruthers, *The Book of Memory: A Study of Memory in Medieval Culture* (Cambridge, 1990), 18.
8. Aristotle, "On the Soul," in *The Complete Works of Aristotle*, ed. Jonathan Barnes (Princeton, NJ: Princeton University Press, 1984), 424a12. Citations are to Bekker number. In the Greek: "Καθόλου δὲ περὶ πάσης αἰσθήσεως δεῖ λαβεῖν ὅτι ἡ μὲν αἴθησίς ἐστι τὸ δεκτικὸν τῶν αἰσητῶν εἰδῶν ἄνευ τῆς ὕλης, οἷον ὁ κηρὸς τοῦ δακτυλίου ἄνευ τοῦ σιδήρου καὶ τοῦ χρυσοῦ δέχεται τὸ σημεῖον." Aristotle, "On the Soul," in *Aristotle: On the Soul. Parva Naturalia. On Breath*, trans. Walter Stanley Hett, rev. edition, Loeb Classical Library (Cambridge, MA: Harvard University Press, 1957).
9. Aristotle, "On Memory," in *The Complete Works of Aristotle*, ed. Jonathan Barnes (Princeton, NJ: Princeton University Press, 1984), 450a11–450a12. Citations are to Bekker number. In the Greek: ὥστε φανερὸν ὅτι τῷ πρώτῳ αἰσθητικῷ τούτων ἡ γνῶσίς ἐστιν· ἡ δὲ μνήμη, καὶ ἡ τῶν νοητῶν, οὐκ ἄνευ φαντάσματός ἐστιν, καὶ τὸ φάντασμα τῆς κοινῆς αἰσθήσεως πάθος ἐστίν." All Greek transcriptions are from Aristotle, "On Memory," in Aristotle: On the Soul. Parva Naturalia. On Breath., trans. Walter Stanley Hett, Revised edition, Loeb Classical Library (Cambridge, MA: Harvard University Press, 1957).
10. Ibid., 450a27–450a32. In the Greek: "δῆλον γὰρ ὅτι δεῖ νοῆσαι τοιοῦτον τὸ γιγνόμενον διὰ τῆς αἰσθήσεως ἐν τῇ ψυχῇ καὶ τῷ μορίῳ τοῦ σώματος τῷ ἔχοντι αὐτήνοῖον ζωγράφημά τι [τὸ πάθος] οὗ φαμεν τὴν ἕξιν μνήμην εἶναι· ἡ γὰρ γιγνομένη κίνησις ἐνσημαίνεται οἷον τύπον τινὰ τοῦ αἰσθήματος, καθάπερ οἱ σφραγιζόμενοι τοῖς δακτυλίοις."
11. Ibid., 450b1–450b5. In the Greek: "διὸ καὶ τοῖς μὲν ἐν κινήσει πολλῇ διὰ πάθος ἢ δι᾽ ἡλικίαν οὖσιν οὐ γίγνεται μνήμη, καθάπερ ἂν εἰς ὕδωρ ῥέον ἐμπιπτούσης τῆς κινήσεως καὶ τῆς σφραγῖδος· τοῖς δὲ διὰ τὸ ψήχεσθαι, καθάπερ τὰ παλαιὰ τῶν οἰκοδομημάτων, καὶ διὰ σκληρότητα

τοῦ δεχομένου τὸ πάθος οὐκ ἐγγίγνεται ὁ τύπος. διόπερ οἵ τε σφόδρα νέοι καὶ οἱ γέροντες ἀμνήμονές εἰσιν· ῥέουσι γὰρ οἱ μὲν διὰ τὴν αὔξησιν, οἱ δὲ διὰ τὴν φθίσιν."

12. Gen. 1:27, 5:27. All biblical citations are to the 1616 King James Bible. References are given by chapter and verse.

13. Prov. 3:3.

14. Song 8:6.

15. Trans. in Caroline Walker Bynum, *Jesus as Mother: Studies in the Spirituality of the High Middle Ages* (Berkeley: University of California Press), 97–98. In the Latin: "Quare putatis, fratres, uitam et conuersationem bonorum imitari precipimur, nisi ut per eorum imitationem ad noue uite similitudinem reformemur? In ipsis siquidem similitudinis Dei forma expressa est et idcirco, cum eis per imitationem imprimimur, ad eiusdem similitudinis imaginem nos quoque figuramur. Sed sciedum est quia, sicut cera, nisi prius emollita fuerit, formam non recipit. sic et homo quidem per manum actionis aliene ad formam virtutis non flectitur: nisi prius per humilitatem ab omni elationis et contradictionis rigore molliatur." Hugh of St. Victor, *De institutione novitiorum*, ed. Jod. Chlichtoveus (Paris: Henricus Stephanus, 1506), 7–8.

16. Ibid., 97–98. In the Latin: "Quid ergo aliud in isto nobis innuitur, nisi quia nos qui per exemplum bonorum, quasi per quoddam sigillum optime exsculptum reformari cupimus: quedam in eis sublimia et quasi eminentia, quedam vero abiecta et quasi depressa operum vestigia inuenimus," Hugh, *De institution novitorum*, 8.

17. Pierre Hadot, *Philosophy as a Way of Life*, ed. Arnold I. Davidson (Malden, MA and Oxford: Blackwell, 1995), 81–126.

18. Hadot, *Philosophy as a Way of Life*, 82.

19. Interestingly, Plotinus uses a different metaphor of sculpture to describe the process of self-perfection, exhorting his followers to "never stop sculpting your own statue, until the divine splendor of virtue shines in you" (qtd. in Hadot, 100). Hadot suggests that this metaphor works precisely because classical sculpture was always an art of subtraction. Thus, the cultivation of a self-involved the removal of all extraneous matter (102).

20. Thomas Bentley, ed., *The Monument of Matrones Conteining Seuen Seuerall Lamps of Virginitie, or Distinct Treatises; Whereof the First Fiue Concerne Praier and Meditation: The Other Two Last, Precepts and Examples, as the Woorthie Works Partlie of Men, Partlie of Women; Compiled for the Necessarie vse of Both Sexes Out of the Sacred Scriptures, and Other Approoued Authors, by Thomas Bentley of Graies Inne Student* (London: Printed by H. Denham, 1582), 414–415.

21. Ibid., 415.

22. These examples are only a few of the many available in such texts, suggesting that the idea of a divine signature writ on the human soul or psyche was widely maintained in the early modern period. Even texts that reject the trope, such as Richard Bentley's "A Confutation of Atheism" (1692), affirm it as common belief through their engagement with it: "As to that natural and indelible signature of God, which human souls in their first origin are supposed to be stamped with … that it is a mistake, and that we have no need of it in our disputes against Atheism," Richard Bentley, "A Confutation of Atheism, Sermon 1," in *A Defence of Natural and Revealed Religion: Being a Collection of the Sermons Preached at the Lecture Founded by the Honourable Robert Boyle, Esq;… With the Additions and Amendments of the Several Authors, and General Indexes. In Three Volumes: I* (London: D. Midwinter et al., 1739), 2.

23. Roger Ascham, "The Scholemaster," in *English Works: Toxophilus, Report of the Affaires and State of Germany, The Scholemaster*, ed. William Aldis Wright (Cambridge, 1904), 200.

24. Ibid., 190–191.

25. Ibid., 191.

26. Ibid., 201.

27. Ibid., 202.

28. Ibid., 200.

29. Thomas Overbury, *Sir Thomas Overbury His Wife with Additions of New Characters, and Many Other Witty Conceits Never Before Printed* (London: Printed by Peter Lillicrap for Philip Chetwin, 1664), Sig. Q4r–Q4v. For further discussion, see Jonathan Goldberg, *Voice Terminal Echo* (New York, 1986), 86–98.

30. For an excellent discussion on the relation between memory and revenge in the play, see Stephen Greenblatt's *Hamlet in Purgatory*. See also, A. C. Bradley, *Shakespearean Tragedy* (London: Macmillan, 1905), 409–412 and Peter Mercer, *Hamlet and the Acting of Revenge* (Iowa City, IA: University of Iowa Press, 1987), 168–172.

31. Shakespeare, *Hamlet*, The Norton Shakespeare: Based on the Oxford Edition, eds. Stephen Greenblatt et al. (New York, 1997), 1.5.95–104.

32. In "Hamlet's Tables and the Technologies of Writing in Renaissance England," *Shakespeare Quarterly* 55, no. 4 (2004): 379–419, Peter Stallybrass, Roger Chartier, J. Franklin Mowrey and Heather Wolfe argue that on the early modern stage the actor may have carried wax tablets to supplement this speech, and that those tablets must have been small, rigid, and erasable. While other materials could have been used to provide an erasable surface, including a mixture of gesso and glue, wax is the material most strongly associated with such tablets, and because of its association with the mind in philosophy, would have been most strongly evoked by Hamlet's speech.

33. Jonathan Goldberg, *Shakespeare's Hand* (University of Minnesota Press, 2003), 111.
34. Ibid.
35. Garret Sullivan, *Memory and Forgetting in English Renaissance Drama: Shakespeare, Marlowe, Webster*, 13.
36. 3.1.58.
37. There has been considerable debate over the extent to which Hamlet's monologue should be read as consideration of suicide. See Vincent F. Petronella, "Hamlet's 'To Be or Not to Be' Soliloquy: Once More Unto the Breach," *Studies in Philology* 71, no. 1 (1974): 27–88, for a good discussion of the debate.
38. Rom. 12:19.
39. Margreta de Grazia, *'Hamlet' Without Hamlet* (Cambridge: Cambridge University Press, 2007), 2.
40. Shakespeare, *Hamlet*, 5.2.50–54.
41. De Grazia, *'Hamlet' Without Hamlet*, 203.
42. Ibid., 3.2.36–38.
43. Although as Angus Fletcher suggests, Hamlet also seems to critique Horatio's rigidity at various points in the play. See *Evolving Hamlet: Seventeenth-Century English Tragedy and the Ethics of Natural Selection* (New York, NY: Palgrave Macmillan, 2011), 53.
44. Shakespeare, *Hamlet*, 3.2.64–67.
45. In "'I Am More an Antique Roman Than a Dane': Suicide, Masculinity and Identity in *Hamlet*,' in *Identity, Otherness and Empire in Shakespeares Rome*, ed. Maria del Sapio Garbero (Farnham, UK, 2009), 75–90, Drew Daniel examines the relationship between Horatio and Hamlet and suggests that Horatio's willingness to die with Hamlet at the end of the play reveals a homosocial affect. Daniel does not want to name either Horatio or the relationship as queer, but the closeness of the friendship is revealed both in this moment and others through metaphors that resemble those of erotic love.
46. Shakespeare, *Hamlet*, 5.2.49.
47. Cyril Tourneur, "The Atheist's Tragedy," in *Four Revenge Tragedies*, ed. Katharine Eisaman Maus (Oxford, 2000), 1.2.10–14. Citations are to act, scene, and line.
48. William Shakespeare, *A Midsummer Night's Dream, The Norton Shakespeare: Based on the Oxford Edition*, eds. Stephen Greenblatt et al. (New York, 1997), 1.1.49. Citation is to act, scene, line.
49. Tourneur, "The Atheist's Tragedy," 1.2.14–18.
50. D'Amville urges Charlemont to go to war, celebrating it as the most honorable activity of man. Charlemont insists that he does not need such urging, as his soul already inclines to the activity.

51. Tourneur, "The Atheist's Tragedy," 1.2.68–78.
52. Ibid., 1.2.88–94.
53. Ibid., 1.2.167–168.
54. Ibid., 2.5.21–23.
55. For more on Levidulcia's character, see William E. Gruber, "Building a Scene: The Text and Its Representation in *The Atheist's Tragedy*," *Comparative Drama* 19, no. 3 (1985): 193–208.
56. Bruce R. Smith suggests that "nobility, honesty, gentleness, honour, [and] virtue" might be "the very qualities that define ideal manhood in early modern England," *Shakespeare and Masculinity* (Oxford, UK and New York, USA: Oxford University Press, 2000), 42. However, he suggests that those qualities mean different things for different social classes, see 42–60.
57. Tourneur, "The Atheist's Tragedy," 3.4–12.
58. The idea that the Christian heart must be like wax appears in other texts as well. For example, in a mother's prayer from the late sixteenth century, God is asked to soften the hearts of children, "make them fleshie, that being softened by the deaw of thy blessings, they may beare the seales of adoption in thy Sonne Christ." Thomas Bentley, *The Fift Lampe of Virginitie Conteining Sundrie Forms of Christian Praiers* (London, 1582), L1R.
59. Ibid., 3.4.19–21.
60. Mary Jo Werth, "A Heart of Stone: The Ungodly in Early Modern England," in *The Indistinct Human in Renaissance Literature* (New York, NY: Palgrave Macmillan, 2012), 181–204. See also Jennifer Waldron, "Of Stones and Stony Hearts: Desdemona, Hermione, and Post-Reformation Theater," in *The Indistinct Human in Renaissance Literature* (New York, NY: Palgrave Macmillan, 2012), 205–227 for a further discussion on the possibility of stony humans.
61. There are several competing readings of what is at stake in D'Amville's atheism. See for example Robert Ornstein, "'The Atheist's Tragedy' and Renaissance Naturalism," *Studies in Philology* 51, no. 2 (1954): 194–207; Matthew Kendrick, "Neostoicism and the Economics of Revenge in Cyril Tourneur's *The Atheist's Tragedy*," *College Literature* 41, no. 3 (Summer 2014): 7–26; and R. J. Kaufmann, "Theodicy, Tragedy, and the Psalmist: Tourneur's Atheist's Tragedy," in *Drama in the Renaissance: Comparative and Critical Essays*, eds. Clifford Davidson, C. J. Gianakaris, and John H. Stroupe, AMS Studies in Renaissance: 12 (New York: AMS, 1986), 192–215.
62. Tourneur, "The Atheist's Tragedy," 3.4.19–21.
63. Ibid., 5.2.120–129.
64. Ibid., 5.2.145–146, 164–165.

65. Ibid., 5.2.130.
66. Ibid., 5.2.273–276.

REFERENCES

Aristotle. "On Memory." In *Aristotle: On the Soul. Parva Naturalia. On Breath.* Translated by Walter Stanley Hett, Rev. edition. Loeb Classical Library. Cambridge, MA: Harvard University Press, 1957.

———."On Memory." In *The Complete Works of Aristotle: The Revised Oxford Translation*, edited by Jonathan Barnes, 1:714–20. Princeton, NJ: Princeton University Press, 1984.

———. "On the Soul." In *The Complete Works of Aristotle: The Revised Oxford Translation*, edited by Jonathan Barnes, 1:641–92. Princeton, NJ: Princeton University Press, 1984.

Ascham, Roger. "The Scholemaster." In *English Works: Toxophilus, Report of the Affaires and State of Germany, The Scholemaster*, edited by William Aldis Wright, 171–237. Cambridge: Cambridge University Press, 1904.

Bentley, Richard. "A Confutation of Atheism, Sermon 1." In *A Defence of Natural and Revealed Religion: Being a Collection of the Sermons Preached at the Lecture Founded by the Honourable Robert Boyle, Esq;... With the Additions and Amendments of the Several Authors, and General Indexes. In Three Volumes: I*, 1–11. London: D. Midwinter et al., 1739.

Bentley, Thomas, ed. *The Monument of Matrones Conteining Seuen Seuerall Lamps of Virginitie, or Distinct Treatises; Whereof the First Fiue Concerne Praier and Meditation: The Other Two Last, Precepts and Examples, as the Woorthie Works Partlie of Men, Partlie of Women; Compiled for the Necessarie vse of Both Sexes Out of the Sacred Scriptures, and Other Approoued Authors, by Thomas Bentley of Graies Inne Student.* London: Printed by H. Denham, 1582.

Bentley, Thomas. *The Fift Lampe of Virginitie Conteining Sundrie Forms of Christian Praiers and Meditations, to Bee Vsed Onlie of and for All Sorts and Degrees of Women, in Their Seuerall Ages and Callings ... A Treatise Verie Needful for This Time, and Profitable to the Church: Now Newlie Compiled to the Glorie of God, & Comfort of Al Godlie Women, by the Said T.B. Gentleman.* Early English Books, 1475–1640/377:02. Imprinted at London: By H. Denham, dwelling in Pater noster Rowe, at the signe of the Starre, being the assigne of William Seres, 1582.

Bradley, A. C. *Shakespearean Tragedy: Lectures on Hamlet, Othello, King Lear, and Macbeth.* Edited by John Bayley. Harmondsworth: Penguin Classics, 1991.

Bynum, Caroline Walker. *Jesus as Mother: Studies in the Spirituality of the Middle Ages.* Berkeley: University of California Press, 1984.

Carruthers, Mary. *The Book of Memory: A Study of Memory in Medieval Culture.* 2nd edition. Cambridge, UK and New York: Cambridge University Press, 2008.

Daniel, Drew. "'I Am More an Antique Roman Than a Dane': Suicide, Masculinity and National Identity in Hamlet." In *Identity, Otherness and Empire in Shakespeare's Rome*, edited by Maria Del Sapio Garbero, 75–87. Anglo-Italian Renaissance Studies. Farnham, UK: Ashgate, 2009.

De Grazia, Margreta. *"Hamlet" without Hamlet.* Cambridge, New York: Cambridge University Press, 2007.

Fletcher, Angus. *Evolving Hamlet: Seventeenth-Century English Tragedy and the Ethics of Natural Selection.* New York: Palgrave Macmillan, 2011.

Goldberg, Jonathan. *Voice Terminal Echo: Postmodernism and English Renaissance Texts.* 1st edition. New York: Routledge Kegan & Paul, 1986.

Goldberg, Jonathan. *Shakespeare's Hand.* Minneapolis: University of Minnesota Press, 2003.

Greenblatt, Stephen. *Hamlet in Purgatory.* Princeton, NJ: Princeton University Press, 2001.

Gruber, William E. "Building a Scene: The Text and Its Representation in The Atheist's Tragedy." *Comparative Drama* 19, no. 3 (1985): 193–208.

Hadot, Pierre. *Philosophy as a Way of Life: Spiritual Exercises from Socrates to Foucault*, edited by Arnold Davidson. 1st edition. Malden, MA: Wiley-Blackwell, 1995.

Hugo. *De institutione novitiorum ….* Edited by Jod. Chlichtoveus. Paris: Henricus Stephanus, 1506.

Kendrick, Matthew. "Neostoicism and the Economics of Revenge in Cyril Tourneur's The Atheist's Tragedy." *College Literature* 41, no. 3 (Summer 2014): 7–26.

Kaufmann, R. J. "Theodicy, Tragedy, and the Psalmist: Tourneur's Atheist's Tragedy." In *Drama in the Renaissance: Comparative and Critical Essays*, edited by Clifford (ed.) Davidson, C. J. (ed. & pref.) Gianakaris, and John H. (ed.) Stroupe, 12: 192–215. AMS Studies in Renaissance. New York: AMS, 1986.

Mercer, Peter. *Hamlet and the Acting of Revenge.* 1st edition. Iowa City: University of Iowa Press, 1987.

Ornstein, Robert. "'The Atheist's Tragedy' and Renaissance Naturalism." *Studies in Philology* 51, no. 2 (April 1, 1954): 194–207.

Overbury, Thomas, Sir. *Sir Thomas Overbury His Wife with Additions of New Characters, and Many Other Witty Conceits Never Before Printed.* Early English Books, 1641–1700/1023:14. London: Printed by Peter Lillicrap for Philip Chetwin, 1664.

Petronella, Vincent F. "Hamlet's 'To Be or Not to Be' Soliloquy: Once More unto the Breach." *Studies in Philology* 71 (1974): 72–88.

Plato. "Meno." In *The Dialogues of Plato Translated into English*, edited and translated by Benjamin Jowett, 3rd edition, 2:1–64. Abingdon, OX: Oxford University Press, 1892.

———. *Plato: Laches, Protagoras, Meno, Euthydemus*. Translated by W. R. M. Lamb. Cambridge, MA: Harvard University Press, 1977.

———. *Plato, VII, Theaetetus. Sophist*. Translated by Harold North Fowler. Loeb Classical Library edition. Cambridge, MA: Harvard University Press, 1921.

———. "Theaetetus." In *The Dialogues of Plato Translated into English*, edited and translated by Benjamin Jowett, 3rd edition, 4:109–281. Abingdon, OX: Oxford University Press, 1892.

Shakespeare, William. "A Midsummer's Night's Dream." In *The Norton Shakespeare*, edited by Stephen Greenblatt, Walter Cohen, Jean E. Howard, and Katharine Eisaman Maus, 805–64. New York: W. W. Norton, 1997.

———. "Hamlet." In *The Norton Shakespeare*, edited by Stephen Greenblatt, Walter Cohen, Jean E. Howard, and Katharine Eisaman Maus, 1659–1760. New York: W. W. Norton, 1997.

Smith, Bruce R. *Shakespeare and Masculinity*. 1st edition. Oxford, UK and New York, USA: Oxford University Press, 2000.

Stallybrass, Peter, Roger Chartier Mowery, J. Franklin, and Heather Wolfe. "Hamlet's Tables and the Technologies of Writing in Renaissance England." *Shakespeare Quarterly* 55, no. 4 (Winter 2004): 379–419.

Sullivan, Garrett A. *Memory and Forgetting in English Renaissance Drama: Shakespeare, Marlowe, Webster*. Cambridge, UK and New York: Cambridge University Press, 2005.

Tourneur. "The Atheist's Tragedy." In *Four Revenge Tragedies*, edited by Katharine Eisaman Maus, reissue edition, 249–330. Oxford and New York: Oxford University Press, 2008.

Waldron, Jennifer. "Of Stones and Stony Hearts: Desdemona, Hermione, and Post-Reformation Theater." In *The Indistinct Human in Renaissance Literature*, edited by J. Feerick and V. Nardizzi, 2012 edition, 205–30. New York, NY: Palgrave Macmillan, 2012.

Werth, Mary Jo. "A Heart of Stone: The Ungodly in Early Modern England." In *The Indistinct Human in Renaissance Literature*, edited by J. Feerick and V. Nardizzi, 2012 edition, 181–204. New York, NY: Palgrave Macmillan, 2012.

CHAPTER 4

Wax Patterning: Cavendish and the Physics of Wax

We have already begun to see that wax's malleability allows it to speak to a wide variety of concerns, and that the signet–seal trope was deployed in the period to talk about gender, reproduction, sense perception, memory, cognition, and subjectivity. Still, despite the range of possibilities that attach to the trope in the texts, we have considered, by and large, the trope has been constrained by a shared sense that impression depends on the hard, unrelenting pressure of metal on the soft, yielding, and surface of wax. While physics was contested in the period, as we will see in this chapter, both Aristotelian and mechanistic natural philosophies would have located the onus of impression primarily in the signet ring and the hand that moved it. Thus, wax is seen largely as a passive material, a material of vulnerability, of susceptibility to change and impression, and often of weakness. Given the material qualities of wax such associations may seem inevitable. Yet in her *Philosophical Letters* (1664), Margaret Cavendish re-conceptualizes the physics of the encounter of signet and seal and calls into question the extent to which wax should be read as a passive, inscribable material. She writes:

> [I]f a seal be printed upon wax, 'tis true, it is the figure of the seal, which is printed on the wax, but yet the seal doth not give the wax the print of its own figure, but it is the wax that takes the print or pattern from the seal, and patterns or copies it out in its own substance, just as the sensitive motions in the eye do pattern out the figure of an object, as I have declared heretofore.[1]

© The Author(s) 2019
L. M. Maxwell, *Wax Impressions, Figures, and Forms in Early Modern Literature*, Early Modern Cultural Studies 1500–1700, https://doi.org/10.1007/978-3-030-16932-9_4

In this brief passage, Cavendish rewrites the physics of signet and seal and, whether she fully intends it or not, offers up new possibilities for wax, women, and all positions traditionally construed as passive. She replaces forceful impression with patterning and locates agency not in the signet, nor even in the hand that moves the ring, but rather in "the wax that takes the print or pattern from the seal." That she performs this rewriting in an epistolary treatise filled with her responses to an imagined female correspondent about some of the most preeminent male philosophers of her day, raises questions about what Cavendish might be saying about epistemology, gender relations, and gender politics with her natural philosophy and invites us to reconsider what it might be possible to think via wax.[2]

Cavendish's *Philosophical Letters* is a small part of her prolific and sometimes contradictory output regarding natural philosophy. Reading it in isolation risks distorting its place within her thought, thus before discussing it further, I would like to situate it within the larger landscape of Cavendish's natural philosophy. Over a fifteen-year period, Cavendish wrote several treatises on natural philosophy and her ideas about nature and physics changed dramatically over time. Her early poetry collection, *Poems and Fancies*, contains reveries on atoms, borrowing both topic and genre from Lucretius's *De Rerum Natura*.[3] Where Lucretius held that the material world was created when atoms falling in a void swerved ever so slightly and collided with each other giving rise to new forms and possibilities, Cavendish's atoms are more joyful:

> Small Atoms of themselves a *World* may make,
> As being subtle, and of every shape:
> And as they dance about, fit places finde,
> Such *Formes* as best agree, make every kinde.[4]

Here Lucretius's swerve is reimagined as a dance and his accidental collisions are replaced by something more collaborative consisting of "fit places" and agreement. Without direct access to Lucretius's texts, and with considerable imagination, these poems offer a creative rewriting of Epicurean atomism, one that through the relentless personification of atoms prefigures the thoroughly vitalist philosophy that Cavendish later develops.[5]

Cavendish ultimately rejects atomism, and even within *Poems and Fancies*, she seems to anticipate that her poems do not contain her finished thoughts. She explains in the preface that the poems might contain errors and are recreational in nature: "the Reason why I write it in *Verse*, is, because I thought *Errours* might better pass there, then in *Prose*; since *Poets* write most *Fiction*, and *Fiction* is not given for *Truth*, but *Pastime*; and I feare my *Atomes* will be as small *Pastime*, as themselves: for nothing can be lesse then an *Atome*."[6] While this apology might be less than genuine—Cavendish does not seem to limit her serious thinking to prose or actually find truth and pastime irreconcilable, as we can see in her playful invocation of the atom's size—it reflects her unwillingness to commit herself to the truth value of her poems.

Indeed, she quickly moves away from atomism. *Philosophical Fancies*, published later in 1653, scarcely mentions atoms, focusing instead on developing her materialist ideas, while her 1655 *Philosophical and Physical Opinions* abandons atomism entirely in favor of infinitely divisible and self-moving matter. There she claims, "the old opinions of atoms seems not so clear to my reason as my own and absolutely new opinions."[7] Cavendish's rejection of atomism is twofold, as Susan James has shown.[8] First, she refuses the possibility of indivisible matter. Second, she finds the idea that nature, in all its beauty, variety, and order could be created from "the concussions of minute particles of inert matter" to be absurd.[9] Instead, she embraces a vitalist philosophy that holds that everything is material, self-moving, and mixture. As Jonathan Goldberg put its, for Cavendish "the bottom line is mixture and motion."[10] Her later philosophical writings build on those "new opinions" and offer further elaborations of her theories and responses to many of her male contemporaries. In addition to *Philosophical Letters* (1664), which I will be discussing at length, Cavendish published *Observations Upon Experimental Philosophy* (1666) and *Grounds of Natural Philosophy* (1668), which further elaborate her philosophical views vis-à-vis the emerging scientific community and its methods. Together with her fictional narrative *The Blazing World* (1666) and her mixed-genre *Worlds Olio* (1655), which also explore aspects of her theories, Cavendish's philosophical writings represent a tremendous effort to intervene in natural philosophy, one that while not influential still merits consideration.[11]

Philosophical Letters, then, is only one articulation of Cavendish's natural philosophy, written significantly after Cavendish had moved away from atomism. It represents neither Cavendish's first nor her final articulation of her materialist, vitalist, and non-atomist philosophy. Yet it is important because it embeds her theory of how objects relate in a text that is itself relational. As suggested above, the theory of patterning that she lays out in its pages posits that objects affect each other not through impacts or collisions, but instead through meetings that serve as occasions for one object to copy out the form of another. For Cavendish, patterning explains a wide range of phenomena, from sense perception in which "the sensitive motions of the eye pattern out the figure of an object in the eye,"[12] to the generation of an image in a mirror, the print of signet on wax, or the seeming transference of motion from one object to the next.[13] By offering that theory within an epistolary volume that considers the works of several significant male natural philosophers, Cavendish may be trying to extend the physics of patterning to the world of intellectual discourse. Suggesting that the reader is actively involved in choosing how a work might move them and imagining that her work might be able to inspire voluntary self-movements in her own readers.

Reading *Philosophical Letters* not only allows us to see new possibilities in wax, but also in all kinds of relations, as we shall see in the last part of this chapter when we turn to Cavendish's *Blazing World*. There, the flexibility of patterning seems to infuse Cavendish's depictions of the various same-sex and cross-sex relationships entered into by the Lady-turned-empress, suggesting that social relations, like physical relations, might be better understood through the possibilities of self-moving wax.

4.1   THINKING PATTERNS AND IMPRESSIONS IN *PHILOSOPHICAL LETTERS*

In *Philosophical Letters*, Cavendish offers her theory of patterning to explain how sensation works and how objects interact. When she first invokes patterning, it is in response to Thomas Hobbes' *Leviathan* and his mechanistic description of sense perception, which holds that external objects press on the sense organs and cause perception. Specifically, Hobbes writes:

> The cause of sense is the external body, or object, which presseth the organ proper to each sense, either immediately, as in the taste and touch, or mediately, as in seeing, hearing, and smelling; which pressure, by the mediation of nerves and other strings and membranes of the body continued inwards to the brain and heart, causeth there a resistance,

or counter-pressure, or endeavour of the heart, to deliver it self; which endeavour, because *outward*, seemeth to be some matter without.[14]

This formulation depends on both an external pressure and an internal counter-pressure to generate sensation. While Hobbes does not invoke a signet–seal analogy, the metaphorics of impression seems implicit in the pressing on organs, and even perhaps in the "resistance, or counter-pressure, or endeavor of the heart" that responds to that pressure. After all, for all its flexibility, wax is not simply soft; its ability to take and hold a print depends on some measure of resistance to pressure. As Hobbes continues, he argues that not only sensation, but also imagination, is a product of impression, "For after the object is removed, or the eye shut, we still retain an image of the thing seen, though more obscure than when we see it. And this is it, the Latins call *imagination*, from the image made in seeing."[15] Further, for Hobbes, "*imagination* and *memory*, are but one thing" and both are simply decayed versions of sense perception.[16]

Cavendish disagrees with Hobbes about the nature of sense perception and its relation to impression. She insists:

> [A]lthough Matter by the power of self-motion is as much composeable as divideable, and parts do joyn to parts, yet that doth not make perception; nay, the several parts, betwixt which the Perception is made, may be at such a distance, as not capable to press: As for example, Two men may see or hear each other at a distance, and yet there may be other bodies between them, that do not move to those perceptions, so that no pressure can be made, for all pressures are by some constraint and force; wherefore, according to my Opinion, the Sensitive and Rational free Motions, do pattern out each others object, as Figure and Voice in each others Eye and Ear.[17]

Impression fails to explain sense perception for Cavendish because it does not adequately take into account the problem of objects acting over a distance, and because it relies on "constraint and force."[18] When she discusses hearing later, she makes more explicit her objection to the idea that sensation might occur via concussions, explaining "I fear, if the Ear was bound to hear any loud Musick, or another sound a good while, it would soundly be beaten, and grow sore and bruised with so many strokes; but since a pleasant sound would be rendred very unpleasant in this manner, my opinion is, that like as in the Eye, so in the Ear the corporeal sensitive motions do pattern out as many several figures, as sounds are presented to them."[19] If every sensation is an impact, surely such impacts would cause damage. Much more plausible for Cavendish is the possibility that sensitive organs are responsive to external stimuli but self-moving.

Similarly, Cavendish rejects Hobbes's claim that imagination and memory are decayed sense perceptions. For Cavendish sensation is double because all nature is composed of rational and sensitive matter and "these self-moving parts ... caus[e] a double perception in all Creatures, whereof one is made by the Rational corporeal motions, and the other by the Sensitive."[20] Where sense perception is a double perception, memory occurs when rational matter alone repeats those figures that were once copied out in both sensitive and rational matter, thus "the figure patterned out in the sensitive organs, being altered, and remaining onely in the Rational part of matter, is not so perspicuous and clear, as when it was both in the Sense and in the Mind."[21] Thus, while perception, memory, and imagination all depend on self-moving matter taking up new figures, they differ in their composition of rational and sensitive matter and the extent to which their figure has an external reference. For "a Man may Imagine that which never came into his Senses," while memory depends on sensation for its initial shape.[22] In this early discussion of patterning, Cavendish does not tackle the physics of impression or invoke the materials commonly associated with it, such as wax, except in passing, when she takes up the possibility that air might make impressions on sensitive organs "as a seal do[es] print another body," before discarding it as unlikely.[23]

However, when Cavendish takes up Descartes and his theories of motion she revisits classic examples of impression, including the signet–seal trope to argue that impression itself should be understood as patterning. She begins by asking, "when a bodies figure is printed on the snow, or any other fluid or soft matter, as air, water, and the like; whether it be the body, that prints its own figure upon the snow, or whether it be the snow, that patterns the figure of the body?"[24] She then answers that it is "the snow that patterns out the figure of the body."[25] The snow is not a passive recipient in this account since, for Cavendish, all matter is capable of self-motion and perception. As a result, all matter has a certain kind of agency. Thus, the exchange between the body and the snow is not an interaction between one active and one passive object, but between two active objects. Immediately after the snow example,

Cavendish takes up wax, as quoted earlier. Just as she does with the snow Cavendish argues that the wax is active. It *"takes* the print or pattern" and *"patterns* or *copies* it out in its own substance" (emphasis added).[26] This self-figuration is possible because the wax is able to perceive the signet and move itself in imitation of the pattern it perceives.

While it might appear that the signet is moved by the hand, and the wax is moved by the signet, for Cavendish these movers only offer an occasion for movement. The concept of occasioning provides Cavendish a framework to consider motion that does not seem to be self-generated. As Cavendish explains in her *Observations on Experimental Philosophy*:

> [W]hen a man moves a string, or tosses a ball, the string or ball is no more sensible of the motion of the hand, than the hand is of the motion of the string or ball; but the hand is only an occasion that the string or ball moves thus or thus. I will not say, but that it may have some perception of the hand, according to the nature of its own figure; but it does not move by the hand's motion, but by its own: for, there can be no motion imparted, without matter or substance.[27]

Thus to occasion movement is in some sense to cause it. Yet as Cavendish takes great pains to establish, there is still a mutuality; "the string or ball is no more sensible of the motion of the hand, than the hand is of the motion of the string or ball," which is to say that they perceive each other equally. Moreover, the movement of the ball or string is fundamentally its own motion "for, there can be no motion imparted." Thus, while the signet and the wax in the above example might not move if not for the hand, their movement is still fundamentally their own.

Cavendish's understanding of motion is crucially different from Descartes' and both are different from the Aristotelian or scholastic theory of motion. In *Principles of Philosophy*, Descartes offers a theory of motion that in many ways prefigures Newtonian physics. He argues that "each and every thing, in so far as it can, always continues in the same state," thus bodies in motion remain in motion, and bodies at rest remain at rest.[28] Under this schema, the wax would have no propensity to move in and of itself. Instead, it would change only because of the application of force and because its ability to resist change is less than the force applied to it: "when a moving body collides with another… if its power of continuing is greater than the resistance of the other body, it carries that body along with it, and loses a quantity of motion equal to that which it imparts to the other body."[29] Descartes embraces transference of motion from one object to the next that Cavendish finds nonsensical. Aristotle, on the other hand, would describe impression as a violent or unnatural motion that occurs as the result of a movent that has a capacity to move itself. As he explains in Book VIII of his *Physics*, "it is impossible for that with which a thing is moved to move it without being moved by that which imparts motion by its own agency."[30] Some entity with intrinsic motion must be responsible for all violent or unnatural motion. At the same time, objects are moveable because they possess a potentiality for motion. Thus, wax changes both because it has the capacity for change and because the signet pushes against it, while the signet moves because the hand which grasps it has the capacity for self-motion. Fundamentally, Aristotle's account of motion depends on force and thus is fundamentally different from Cavendishian physics, in which no object causes the movement of another object.

Cavendish's choice of examples to explain her theory of patterning and her understanding of movement is strategic. Since both Aristotle and Descartes explain sense perception by analogy to the process of imprinting wax with a signet ring, Cavendish's uses the trope of signet–seal as one of her examples works to signal her awareness of those previous philosophies as well as her departure from them. Yet it is not simply Cavendish's choice of wax that is calculated, but also her decision to make wax one example of many. In the passage just quoted, the initial question does not invoke wax, but instead considers footprints in the snow. This image, of course, shares many similarities with that of a printed seal. The footprint, too, is a figure of impression and one frequently invoked in the literature of the period to figure theft. For example, in John Donne's "Sappho to Philaenis," which I take up in the next chapter, Sappho laments, "Men leave behind them that which their sin shows, / And are as thieves traced, which rob when it snows."[31] Here impressing women's wombs is like leaving footprints in the snow and both kinds of prints testify to men's sins. When Cavendish invests footprints with the physics of patterning, she frees the snow from connotations of passivity and recasts the footprint as evidence not of violence, but of the snow's self-motion and voluntary figuring. As Cavendish continues to develop her philosophy, she returns to vision and the "sensitive motions of the eye" to solidify her claims. This move not only connects her theory of motion to her theory of sense perception, as we saw above, but also emphasizes that for Cavendish all matter works the same way, whether it is part of human bodies or not.[32]

By positioning wax as one of many objects, locating it between the example of the footprint and the eye, Cavendish makes the point that patterning does not apply only to malleable objects, or only to encounters between hard and soft objects. Instead, patterning is the system that governs all natural movement because all things are composed of the rational, sensitive, and grosser parts of matter.[33] Consequently, all things are perceptive and self-moving. One consequence of Cavendish's theory of patterning is that it starts to suggest that it is not that exceptional to be human as everything has the power of self-motion and perception. Cavendish's de-emphasis of wax, given its philosophical connection to the human mind, participates in this leveling process by placing the human mind on the same continuum with every other object including other parts of the body which might have different sympathies and antipathies than the mind itself.

Yet at the same time that Cavendish's contextualization of the wax model suggests that there is nothing exceptional about being human, her invocation of wax invites the reader to connect Cavendish's philosophy to the human mind and to human interactions. After all, for Cavendish everything is material: "not anything in Nature, what belongs to her, is immaterial," which means that not only physical objects but also, "Motions, Forms, Thoughts, Ideas, Conceptions, Sympathies, Antipathies, Accidents, Qualities, as also Natural Life and Soul, are all Material."[34] Cavendish articulates a physics that applies to thoughts, psyches, and subjectivities, as well as the more traditional objects of snow, wax, and eyes. Thus, Cavendish makes it possible to conceive of a physics of subjects in which their interactions proceed just as relations do between all things in the natural world. Precisely because humans are not so different from anything else, her physics can be applied to human interaction of all kinds. Since wax has a long philosophical history of figuring biological and epistemological reproduction, Cavendish's turn to wax helps her readers recognize the ways that her physics apply to people. In fact, if we return to the passage we first quoted, we see that the examples of patterning Cavendish supplies take us closer and closer to considerations of human relationships. The footprints in the snow evoke human impact on nature. From this starting point, Cavendish transitions to the figure of the signet and seal, a figure connected to human interaction both through the philosophical resonances and through its connection to writing. Finally, Cavendish addresses human perception and human agency when she moves from discussing the wax to detailing the "sensitive motions of the eye."[35] Rather than moving away from human concerns, Cavendish seems to be zeroing in on them.

4.2   Waxing Social and Political

As the discussion above has suggested, *Philosophical Letters* is a deeply social and relational text, not simply because it takes up the questions of how exterior objects might affect a subject and how two objects might affect each other, but also because the text itself is written in conversation, inviting the question of how human relationships might be understood differently if we take seriously the possibility of patterning.

In her prefatory materials, Cavendish addresses briefly her choice to write in response to other natural philosophers. She suggests that she has chosen to present her ideas in relation to those of other natural philosophers because the contrast will help "to make [her philosophy] more perspicuous and intelligible by the opposition of other Opinions, since two opposite things placed near each other, are the better discerned."[36] She also insists that her opinions are entirely her own, "being new, and never thought of, at least not divulged by any."[37] Since she places her philosophy in opposition to other natural philosophies, these claims might be read as combative. Yet, her emphasis is not on conflict but on understanding. She hopes her ideas will be "better discerned" by her readers and that they will internalize the forms of her thought more ably because they can better trace its contours through the contrast of her thought and those of her contemporaries.

Of course, because reading relies on sensory perception, the first way a reader would experience a text would be via patterning. Viewing a text would lead to the double perception of sensitive and rational matter, but this experience would not make impressions for Cavendish, as it would for Hobbes. Reading would, instead, provide figures that could be copied or compared to other figures by the rational motions of the mind. She explains, "Thoughts are not like *Water upon a plain Table, which is drawn and guided by the finger this or that way,* for every Part of self-moving matter is not always forced, perswaded or directed."[38] Instead, thoughts experience considerable freedom: "[T]hey are several figures, made by the mind, which is the Rational Part of matter, in its own substance, either voluntarily, or by imitation"[39] and the mind then makes examination and arrives at conclusion by "a comparing of Figures to Figures… and when the mind makes voluntary Figures with those repeated Figures, and compares them together, this comparing is Examination; and when several Figures agree and join, it is Conclusion or Judgment: likewise doth Experience proceed from repeating and comparing of several Figure in the Mind."[40] Thought, analysis, judgment, and experience then are all material for Cavendish and are formed out of an intricate dance of patterning, figuring, and comparing of figures. The result is that reading becomes a tremendously active experience, regardless of whether the reader ultimately agrees with material being read. Thus just as Cavendish's reworking of the signet–seal trope locates agency in the seemingly passive position, so too does Cavendish's version of epistemology. As a writer too, she must have hoped for her thoughts to resonate with readers and inspire voluntary figurations, but it seems important to her that such relations not proceed through force.

At the same time, Cavendish imagines that her act of writing has been impelled. In addition to the famous male philosophers that Cavendish invokes, and the readers she anticipates, there is also the specific figure of her female interlocutor, whom critics generally agree is imagined. This friend purportedly provides Cavendish with the impetus for writing: sending her the books of the male philosophers and asking her to "give [her] judgment of them."[41] Cavendish suggests that she sees this request as an opportunity to clarify her opinions, but claims that her chief reason for writing is "the Authority of [her friend's command], which did work so powerfully with me, that I could not resist, although it were to the disgrace of my own judgment and wit."[42] This friend, with whom Cavendish claims to regularly correspond, possesses so much influence over her, that her request becomes an irresistible command, a force that moves Cavendish to write even against her better judgement. By framing her exposition in these terms, Cavendish asks us to consider social forces and how obligations and commands might work in relation to voluntary motions. In a world of figures that can be copied, or not, following a command is a choice, even when it seems to work so powerfully that one "could not resist."

The difference between forced and voluntary motions is an important component of Cavendish's natural philosophy as we saw through her rewriting of the signet–seal trope which allows for freedom in movement that might seem forced. Yet Cavendish's philosophy does not erase the possibilities of violence. For Cavendish, all matter has "the freedom" to work against reason, move irregularly, and be combative.[43] Motion can be forced, but that is the exception, rather than rule. Cavendish explains:

> 'Tis true, 'tis the freedom in Nature for one man to give another a box on the Ear, or to trip up his heels, or for one or more men to fight with each other; yet these actions are not like the actions of loving Imbraces and Kissing each other... and so is likewise the action of impression, and the action of self-figuring not one and the same, but different; for the action of impression is forced, and the action of self-figuring is free.[44]

Here, Cavendish allows that the action of impression exists, but she likens it to the violence of men fighting. If we fail to recognize the difference between patterning and impression, it is equivalent to not recognizing the difference between fighting and "loving Imbraces," and thus not understanding the nature of relations—in the natural world or the social.

When Cavendish claims that she cannot resist her friend's request, she is not attributing to her the kind of force that she would equate with impression or with men fighting. Instead, she is investing affective bonds, voluntary self-figuring, and "the actions of loving Imbraces and Kissing" with a kind of persuasive force that allows influence and freedom to coexist. Pushed to its logical conclusions, Cavendish's natural philosophy would directly challenge Hobbes's political philosophy because she believes in a more harmonious state of nature than he does and because she allows for power and influence to derive from friendship, love, and other positive bonds.[45]

Yet in *Philosophical Letters*, Cavendish refuses to engage directly with political considerations. While she responds to the first part of Hobbes's *Leviathan*, in which he outlines his natural philosophy in order to lay the grounds for his views on the state of nature, she refuses to comment on his political ideas, explaining:

> but seeing he treats in his following Parts of the Politicks, I was forced to stay my Pen, because of these following reasons. First, that a Woman is not imployed in State Affairs, unless an absolute Queen. Next, That to study the Politicks, is but loss of Time, unless a man were sure to be a Favourite to an absolute Prince. Thirdly, That it is but a deceiving Profession, and requires more Craft then Wisdom.[46]

Even as Cavendish's natural philosophy could provide the grounds for a politics that would challenge Hobbes's absolutism, patriarchy and even human-centrism, she refuses to engage in a political debate, claiming that such engagement would be a waste of time on multiple levels, not the least that she is a woman. Instead, Cavendish insists that she does not "discourse or write of either Church or State" and seems to explicitly shut down such possibilities.[47]

Still, while Cavendish claims that she stays her pen and avoids politics. Her text invites political considerations through her frequent invocation of social relations and her choice to situate her text within a community. When we apply Cavendish's physics and particularly her conception of patterning to human interactions, we find that traditionally vulnerable positions are rendered less so or are at least afforded agency within that vulnerability. These possibilities might afford more power to women and challenge patriarchal norms. As Misty Anderson argues, "Cavendish's animism carries both a philosophical challenge to Cartesian objectivity and a political challenge to the characterization of women as mere body or legal chattel exchanged by Lockean subjects by claiming the intelligence of the body."[48] John Rogers similarly suggests that the purpose "behind the lessons in spiritualized matter that fill so many volumes of her natural philosophy is to supply the metaphysical foundations for a social agenda for which she had almost no contemporary support—the liberation of women from the constraints of patriarchy."[49] Both Anderson and Rogers locate egalitarian possibilities in Cavendish's philosophy.

Yet if we return to wax and the trope of the signet–seal, we see that even as Cavendish's philosophy seems progressive, it might not be. What, we can ask again, is the value of imagining that the movement of the wax is voluntary? If, as I suggested earlier, such a reading can be translated into social relations by imagining more agency in passive positions, what becomes of rape? It could still be read as violence and force since Cavendish's philosophy allows for such. After all, "'tis the freedom in Nature for one man to give another a box one the Ear."[50] However, conception from rape might also be read as a kind of consent. Cavendish's insistence on the mixture of sensitive and rational matter in all things and all parts of things makes consent tricky, just as it also makes selfhood slippery. Since the womb contains both rational and sensitive matter imbued with self-motion, consent could be local and the self-divided. Cavendish does not devote considerable attention to the question of reproduction, but she does differentiate generation from patterning, which again further complicates these questions. She explains, "Generation must needs be performed by the way of translation, which translation is not required in the act of patterning."[51] The two are different in that translation requires the imparting of matter and motion, "for to pattern out, is nothing else but to imitate, and to make a figure in its own substance or parts of matter like another figure. But in generation every producer doth transfer both Matter and Motion, that is, Corporeal Motion."[52] This distinction suggests that Cavendish's concept of reproduction might require an entirely different trope—if women are like wax, then reproducing might be like pulling a piece of wax off the block and allowing it to shape itself. The problem of how to understand the effects of violence on agency is not easily solved by Cavendish's philosophy, or her fiction, where she also displays deep ambivalence about female culpability with regard to rape.[53]

Similarly, Cavendish's explicit engagement with gender politics is not as progressive as a modern reader might desire. Cavendish does not always seem to think highly of her sex. She writes in a preface to *Worlds Olio*, "although Nature hath not made women so strong of Body, and so clear of understanding, as the ablest of Men, yet she hath made them fairer, softer, slenderer, and more delicate than they, separating as it were the finer parts from the grosser."[54] Since elsewhere she describes the highest type of matter—rational matter—in similar terms, John Rogers argues that this moment shows her high opinion of women and their capacity to lead. Yet as Deborah Boyle has pointed out, such a reading ignores Cavendish's clear assertion that women are less in both body and mind. We find similar assertions in a preface to *Philosophical Letters*, when she preemptively apologizes: "And if I should express more Vanity then Wit, more Ignorance then Knowledg, more Folly then Discretion, it being according to the Nature of our Sex, I hoped that my Masculine Readers would civilly excuse me, and my Female Readers could not justly condemn me."[55] The implication of this apology is that anything deficient in her work could be attributed to the "Nature of our sex." While these apologies may not be sincere, Cavendish often seems to see herself as an exceptional woman, one who has singularly overcome the deficiencies of her sex. While it is clear that she wishes for her work to be taken seriously, it is less clear that she means to uplift her gender in general. So too in the realm of politics, Cavendish is undeniably conservative and would not advocate for the more egalitarian positions that her philosophy suggests.

What then can we say about what it means to be human and engage in social and political relationships by way of Cavendish's philosophy. First, as the discussion about consent implies, Cavendish's natural philosophy challenges the possibility of a stable, integrated self. Instead, as Eve Keller suggests, "Cavendish's acceptance of organic materialism ... holds implications for her vision of the self: like the object of its study the self for Cavendish is irregular, prone to contradiction, and non-discrete."[56] Because every part of every thing and person includes rational self-moving matter, rationality is not confined to the mind and decisions can be local, which makes for a flexible vision of selfhood.

At the same time, Cavendish's philosophy erases differences between man and the rest of nature. While she suggests that man might be different from the rest of nature because he has "a supernatural Soul, whose actions also are supernatural,"[57] she mostly denies meaningful difference between men and animals or other things. She asks:

> [F]or what man knows, whether Fish do not Know more of the nature of Water, and ebbing and flowing, and the saltness of the Sea? or whether Birds do not know more of the nature and degrees of Air, or the cause of Tempests? or whether Worms do not know more of the nature of Earth, and how Plants are produced? or Bees of the several sorts of juices of Flowers, then Men? And whether they do not make there Aphorismes and Theoremes by their manner of Intelligence? For, though they have not the speech of Man, yet thence doth not follow, that they have no Intelligence at all. But the Ignorance of Men concerning other Creatures is the cause of despising other Creatures, imagining themselves as petty Gods in Nature, when as *Nature* is not capable to make one God, much less so many as Mankind[58];

By extending perception, rationality, and knowledge to animals, Cavendish de-privileges the human, insisting that we are not so different from other parts of nature. Later in her treatise, she extends these claims even further, writing "that Sense and Reason are in other Creatures as well as in Man and Animals; for example, Drugs, as Vegetables and Minerals, although they cannot slice, pound or infuse, as man can, yet they can work upon man more subtilly, wisely, and as sensibly either by purging, vomiting, spitting, or any other way, as man by mincing, pounding and infusing them, and Vegetables will as wisely nourish Men, as Men can nourish Vegetables."[59] By infusing every part of nature with motion, and perception, she affords every part of nature with vitality and power.

With the erasure of these boundaries comes not only a more flexible idea of selfhood, but also more flexible, wax-like possibilities for relationships between selves, parts of selves, and other parts of nature. Goldberg, writing about Cavendish's move away from atomism, writes "Cavendish … denies the atom for the sake of an analysis that can never come to an end; in place of the aporia at the heart of Lucretian atomism, she finally offers an endless decipherment that maintains the problematic of sameness and difference as irresolvable."[60] Without these boundaries, gender difference, species difference, even the differences between imagination and reality begin to fall away. Self-moving matter can respond to other self-moving matter and pattern itself after it—regardless of initial form or function. Or it can move creatively or transformationally, figuring out new shapes at every turn. Like wax, each part of nature is flexible, moldable, and receptive to new prints. When relationships proceed neither according to difference, nor sameness, but simply perception, reason, and perhaps desire, the queer possibilities abound within and without same-sex relations.

4.3   PATTERNING WORLDS AND RELATIONS IN *THE BLAZING WORLD*

While Cavendish's philosophy implies social and political possibilities made visible by patterning, her fiction, particularly her *Blazing World*, more actively explores such possibilities, although without reference to wax and with only a few invocations of patterning. Still, I would suggest, that both patterning and wax provide us with a way of understanding how the relationships in *The Blazing World* function and how the relationship of the empress and the Duchess of Newcastle becomes the most intimate and profound relationship in the book.

Cavendish explicitly connects her natural philosophy and her fiction, inviting us to read them together as intimately related projects. Indeed, she published *Observations Upon Experimental Philosophy* and *The Blazing World* together, as part of the one volume. In a preface, she places the two in conversation, explaining that where philosophy "enquires after the true causes of natural effects," fiction is freer and "creates of its own accord whatsoever it pleases, and delights in its own work."[61] Still, she sees both of these enterprises as rewarding and as complementary endeavors. In particular, the pursuit of natural philosophy, because it is "laborious and difficult … requires sometimes the help of fancy, to recreate the mind, and withdraw it from its more serious contemplations."[62] Here, the work of natural philosophy takes priority, with fiction serving as a recreational aid. However, as Cavendish continues, it becomes clear that the relationship is more complex than that. She explains that she "added this piece of fancy to my philosophical observations, and joined them as two worlds at the ends of their poles; both for my own sake, to divert my studious thoughts, which I employed in the contemplation thereof, and to delight the reader with variety, which is always pleasing."[63] The figure of two worlds being joined at their poles proves to also be the relation between Earth and the blazing world that Cavendish's heroine explores within the pages of the *Blazing World*. The trope and the text insist on richness and completeness of both realms; each world is a world unto itself even as it is held in intimate relation with the other. Thus, her fiction is not auxiliary to her philosophy, but equally vital.

Further, the two are integrated. The fictional text, responds to, repeats and augments the philosophical one. Cavendish explains that the text of the *Blazing World* can be understood as composed of multiple parts: "the first part whereof is *romancical*, the second philosophical, and the third is merely *fancy*, or (as I many call it) *fantastical*, which if it add any satisfaction to you, I shall account my self a happy *creatoress*."[64] The *Blazing World*, then, is not simply a fictional text, but itself a philosophical work. Indeed, within its pages, we find that the empress debates the merits of experimental philosophy with her new subjects, allowing them to carry out experiments and make observations, before deciding that such endeavors are more trouble than they are worth. After the Bearmen disagree about what they see through telescopes, the empress tells them, "that if their Glasses were true informers, they would rectify their irregular sense and reason; but … nature has made your sense and reason more regular then art has your glasses, for they are mere deluders, and will never lead you to the knowledge of truth."[65] Thus, the empress comes to the same conclusion about the merits of experimental philosophy as Cavendish does in *Observations Upon Experimental Philosophy*.

While patterning is not of primary interest in either *Observations Upon Experimental Philosophy* or *The Blazing World*, it obviously still underlies Cavendish's thought on sense perception, object relations, and epistemology. When another set of the empress's scientists, the Bird-men, is discussing why the sun and moon "often appear in different postures and shapes, as sometimes magnified, sometimes diminished," some of them decide that those differences are the result of air choosing to pattern itself in various ways, "for like as painters do not copy out one and the same original just alike at all times, so said they, do several parts of the air make different patterns of the luminous bodies of the sun and moon: which patterns, as several copies, the sensitive motions do figure out in the substance of our eyes."[66] Here, the air has the same freedom as an artist to creatively figure the celestial bodies, and those figures are then copied—and perhaps transformed—through the act of vision, which is also an act patterning. This explanation is only one of several offered by the Bird-men, but "the Empress liked [that response] much better than the former."[67] Since the empress is one of Cavendish's doubles in the book it is not surprising that her views on natural philosophy align with Cavendish's own.

Similarly, toward the end of the book, when the duchess is trying to create her own world within herself, she first tries to use classical models as patterns for that world. However, they lead her to chaos and nothingness, so "she fully resolved, not to take any more patterns from the ancient philosophers," turning instead to Descartes, and Hobbes, before finding that "no patterns would do her any good in the framing of her World."[68] Ultimately, she makes "a world of her own invention," one composed of "sensitive and rational self-moving matter," that is, a world very much in line with Cavendish's understanding of our world.[69] She drops the grosser, inanimate matter, which is "dull, stupid, and immoveable in its own nature," to create a world that is more animate and perceptive than she believes ours to be.[70] Such a world might surpass our own. The duchess certainly seems to think so, declaring that it "so curious and full of variety, so well order'd and wisely govern'd, that it cannot possibly be expressed by words." Just as Cavendish found the natural philosophy of other thinkers to be nonsensical in *The Philosophical Letters*, so the duchess finds them absurd, incoherent, or terrifying, when she tries to create imaginary worlds according to the patterns of their thoughts. Cavendish's own thoughts about nature are, however, reflected in the duchess's idealized imaginary world, and the most crucial component of that world is its absolute reliance on rational and sensitive self-moving matter, i.e., the type of matter that makes patterning work. While she does not expound upon the physics of her new creation, her insistence on animate and perceptive matter strongly implies that the duchess's imaginary world works through patterning.

A world composed of such matter is "curious and full of variety," as is *The Blazing World* itself—what with its "men of several different sorts, shapes, figures, dispositions, and humors" including, "bear-men, some worm-men, some fish- or mear-men, otherwise called syrens; some bird-men, some fly-men, some ant-men, some geese-men, some spider-men, some lice-men, some fox-men, some ape-men, some jack-daw-men, some magpie-men, some parrot-men, some satyrs, some giants, and many more."[71] It also is "well order'd and wisely govern'd" raising the question of how the order, government, and various social and political relationships within *The Blazing World* might connect to the wax possibilities of figuring and patterning.[72] As we will see, Cavendish investigates female rule—upturning traditional gender roles in the process—and explode the possibilities for relationships and selfhood by imagining intimate, albeit spiritual, relations between women that transcend physical boundaries and push against narrow understandings of selfhood. These more flexible structures, relationships, and selves seem animated by Cavendish's vitalism and particularly the infusion of motion and perception into traditionally passive locations, like wax, especially since so many of these possibilities are also traditionally figured through wax metaphors such as the signet–seal.

Cavendish explores female rule through the heroine of her fiction, the Lady, who accidentally crosses into the Blazing World. When the Lady arrives in that world, she is taken to the emperor, who immediately falls in love with her and hands over power to her:

> No sooner was the Lady brought before the Emperor, but he conceived her to be some goddess, and offered to worship her; which she refused, telling him, (for by that time she had pretty well learned their language) that although she came out of another world, yet was she but a mortal; at which the Emperor rejoicing, made her his wife, and gave her an absolute power to rule and govern all that world as she pleased. But her subjects, who could hardly be persuaded to believe her mortal, tendered her all the veneration and worship due to a deity.[73]

Marriage here does not follow the traditional gender roles that we have seen narrated by the signet–seal trope. Instead, the emperor moves into the passive position, granting his empress "absolute power to rule and govern all the world as she pleased." In the pages that follow, she uses her absolute power to experiment with the systems of science, and religion, and while she ultimately discards some of her own innovations, she proves to be a good ruler by returning things to the status quo when necessary.

As the narrative continues, the relationship between the empress and the emperor continues to defy gender norms. The emperor is scarcely mentioned in the pages that follow until the second part of the narrative, when the empress hears that there is a great war in her native world. At this point, he encourages her to intervene and to use "all the assistance that the Blazing World was able to afford."[74] At his suggestion, she does so, leaving him behind. On her return, he is pleased to show off the stables that he had built in her absence, and the narrative ends with some description of the pastimes enjoyed by the emperor and empress. Our narrator relays, "you may sooner imagine than expect that I should express the joy which the emperor had at her safer return; for he loved her beyond his soul; and there was no love lost, for the empress equaled his affection with no less love to him."[75] Again the emperor occupies the more passive position, simply awaiting his beloved's return, while she travels to a different world and intervenes in a war. At the same time, the narrative insists on their mutual love for each other and that mutuality seems informed by Cavendish's insistence that all parts of matter are rational and self-moving—an insistence that destabilizes gender difference and patriarchal norms.

Cavendish not only explores female rule and possibilities of greater female power and agency in cross-sex relationships, she also takes up female relationships in ways that push the limits of relationality and selfhood. Arguably the most important relationship in the book is that between the empress and the Duchess of Newcastle, Cavendish's double, whose spirit moves between the two worlds and becomes the empress's platonic lover. This same-sex relationship is far more substantially developed in the text than that of the empress and emperor. The empress and the duchess meet when the duchess decides to write a Cabbala and requires a scribe for the undertaking. After requesting first an "ancient famous writer," and next "one of the most famous modern writers," the immaterial spirits, with whom she is consulting suggest instead "a lady, the Duchess of Newcastle, which although she is not one of the most learned, eloquent, witty and ingenious, yet is she a plain and rational writer, for the principle of her writings, is sense and reason, and she will without question, be ready to do you all the service she can."[76] The empress acquiesces to this suggestion in part because the emperor will have no "reason to be jealous, she being one of my own sex."[77]

Despite this foreclosing of anything erotic between the two, they become quite intimate. Indeed, the narrator relays:

> The Empress thanked the Duchess, and embracing her soul, told her she would take her counsel: she made her also her favorite, and kept her some-time in that world ... and after some time the Empress gave her leave to return to her husband and kindred into her native world, but upon condition, that her soul should visit her now and then; which she did, and truly their meeting did produce such an intimate friendship between them, that they became platonic lovers, although they were both females.[78]

While the two share the same sex, and the duchess is not embodied when she visits the empress, they achieve "such an intimate friendship" that the aptest description for it is that of "platonic lovers." Earlier, in the text, the empress learns from the immaterial spirits that, "Platonics believed, the souls of lovers lived in the bodies of their beloved"[79] and that, "in truth... husbands have reason to be jealous of platonic lovers, for they are very dangerous, as being not only very intimate and close, but subtle and insinuating."[80] Cavendish clearly positions the possibility of the platonic lover as something that infringes on the prerogatives of marriage and as a relationship that may be erotically charged. Indeed, in *Philosophical Letters*, Cavendish opines:

> I am no Platonick; for this opinion is dangerous, especially for married Women, by reason the conversation of the Souls may be a great temp-tation, and a means to bring Platonick Lovers to a neerer acquaintance, not allowable by the Laws of Marriage, although by the sympathy of the Souls.[81]

Here, even as Cavendish eschews the Platonic philosophy for being against the laws of marriage, she seems to suggest that there is some-thing more natural about such arrangements since they depend on "the sympathy of the Souls," and for Cavendish sympathy is an important

governing force in nature. In adopting the position of scribe, the duchess agrees to help physically manifest the empress's thoughts and make
material the figurations of her fancy—as they ultimately agree not to
write a spiritual or philosophical cabbala, but rather to produce "a poetical or romancical Cabbala, wherein you can use metaphors, allegories,
similitudes, etc. and interpret them as you please."[82] She is essentially
promising to move her own thought in the same patterns as the duchess
and help reproduce the duchess's fancy. This relation blurs the boundaries of selfhood and authorship, while intimately connecting the two
women.

At the same time, their behavior raises questions about the lines
between erotic and non-erotic relations as they frequently engage in
spiritual kisses and embraces.[83] The intimacy of the relationship is further
heightened when the two women decide to visit the duchess's husband.
Their souls leave the Blazing World and travel in an aerial vehicle, until
they reach the home of the duke. At which point, the duchess's soul
enters her husband, and "the Empress's soul perceiving this, did the like:
and then the duke had three souls in one body; and had there been but
some such souls more, the duke would have been like the Grand Signior
in his seraglio, only it would have been a platonic seraglio."[84] Again, the
insistence on the Platonic nature of the meeting does not remove an
erotic charge, as the narrative makes clear:

> But the Duke's soul being wise, honest, witty, complaisant and noble,
> afforded such delight and pleasure to the Empress's soul by her conver-
> sation, that these two souls became enamored of each other; which the
> Duchess's soul perceiving, grew jealous at first, but then considering
> that no adultery could be committed amongst Platonic lovers, and that
> Platonism was divine, as being derived from divine Plato, cast forth of her
> mind that Idea of jealousy. Then the conversation of these three souls was
> so pleasant that it cannot be expressed; for the Duke's soul entertained the
> Empress's soul with scenes, songs, music, witty discourses, pleasant recre-
> ations, and all kinds of harmless sports; so that the time passed away faster
> than they expected.[85]

Being Platonic lovers is posited as being close to and possibly in competition with the intimacy of a marital relationship; the duke's and empress's
souls "be[come] enamored with each other" and the duchess's soul
"gr[ows] jealous" at that closeness. The duchess's jealousy reveals that she

perceives this closeness as a threat, and while she ultimately decides that "no adultery can be committed amongst Platonic lovers" and joins with the others in conversation and recreation, the possibility that such relations might encroach on the intimacies of marriage is left open in the text. Certainly, as the description continues we see that this platonic seraglio is intensely pleasant. The narrator insists that the conversation was so "so pleasant that it cannot be expressed," and that "time passed away faster than they expected." The combination of pleasure and intimacy certainly suggests that we might be skeptical of the narrative's insistence that this union consist solely of "harmless sports."

Since multiple souls occupy the same body, at times, the limits of identity are also blurred. The very intimacy and closeness that make the relationships close also make it challenging to tell where one soul ends and the other begins. This danger is the "subtle and insinuating" influence that the immaterial spirits warned the empress about before she and the duchess became Platonic lovers.[86] At the same time, selfhood is also challenged in the narrative, by the fact that it is possible to read both the empress and the duchess of Newcastle as proxies for Cavendish herself, as both separate and the same, further problematizing the stability of selfhood.[87] Again, we can relate these ideas on selfhood to Cavendish's infusion of motion and perception into virtually all matter. In such a system, all parts of the self are vital and identity becomes flexible. Further, if patterning is the dominant means of interaction, then difference becomes less important than similarity, and the boundaries between one object and another or one self and another begin to blur.

Cavendish shows us is that in the realm of philosophy, reimagining the relationship between wax and signet can create new models of subjectivity, epistemology, and physics. Since the model of wax seal and signet occupies a crucial position in the inherited scholastic legacy, disrupting it is an important tactic to offering new versions of natural philosophy. Yet as we began to see with regard to Shakespeare, in Chapter 1, the signet–seal model also has considerable power to figure the relationships between men and women. Thus, Cavendish's intervention in natural philosophy also has implications for understanding desire and destabilizes figures of impression by offering new possibilities for agency. Cavendish's philosophy allows us to locate agency in both the object that provides a pattern, and the object that adopts that pattern as its own. When mapped on to new relations, such re-conceptualization provides women with considerably more power in determining their own futures by affording them some measure of control over their own desires.

NOTES

1. Margaret Cavendish, *Philosophical Letters: Or, Modest Reflections Upon Some Opinions in Natural Philosophy, Maintained by Several Famous and Learned Authors of This Age, Expressed by Way of Letters: By the Thrice Noble, Illustrious, and Excellent Princess, the Lady Marchioness of Newcastle* (London, 1664), 105.

2. See Susan M. Fitzmaurice "'But Madam': The Interlocutor in Margaret Cavendish's Writing," *In-Between: Essays and Studies in Literary Criticism* 9.1, no. 2 (2000), 17–27 for a discussion of the interlocutor in *The Philosophical Letters.*

3. See Emma Rees, *Margaret Cavendish* (Manchester, Manchester University Press, 2004), 54–79 for a discussion of Cavendish's use of Lucretius.

4. Margaret Cavendish, *Poems, and Fancies Written by the Right Honourable, the Lady Margaret Newcastle* (London: Printed for T. R. for J. Martin, and J. Allestrye, 1653), 5. Hereafter, *Poems, and Fancies.*

5. See Susan James, "The Philosophical Innovations of Margaret Cavendish," *British Journal for the History of Philosophy* 7, no. 2 (1999): 219–244 for a discussion of the relationship between Cavendish's atomism and her later philosophy.

6. Cavendish, *Poems, and Fancies*, sig. a6v.

7. Margaret Cavendish, *The Philosophical and Physical Opinions Written by Her Excellency the Lady Marchionesse of Newcastle* (London: Printed for J. Martin and J. Allestrye, 1655), unnumbered.

8. See James, "The Philosophical Innovations of Margaret Cavendish," 222–225.

9. James, "The Philosophical Innovations of Margaret Cavendish," 222.

10. Jonathan Goldberg, *The Seeds of Things: Theorizing Sexuality and Materiality in Renaissance Representations* (New York: Fordham University Press, 2009), 126.

11. Recent criticism has explored Cavendish's relationship with her contemporaries and placed her natural philosophy in conversation with more widely known views. For a start, see Anna Batigelli, *Margaret Cavendish and the Exiles of the Mind* (Lexington: University of Kentucky Press, 1998). See also, James, 219–244; Goldberg, 122–151; Eileen O'Neill's 'Introduction' to Margaret Cavendish, *Observations Upon Experimental Philosophy*, ed. Eileen O'Neill (Cambridge: Cambridge University Press, 2001), x–xxxvi; and Karen Detlefsen, "Atomism, Monism, and Causation in the Natural Philosophy of Margaret Cavendish," *Oxford Studies in*

Early Modern Philosophy, vol. 3, ed. Daniel Garber and Stephen Nadler (Oxford: Oxford University Press, 2005), 199–240.

12. Cavendish, *Philosophical Letters*, 64.
13. Ibid., 84 and 105.
14. Thomas Hobbes, *Leviathan* (Indianapolis, IN and Cambridge, UK: Hackett, 1994), 6.
15. Ibid., 8.
16. Ibid., 9.
17. Cavendish, *Philosophical Letters*, 18.
18. Cavendish discards the possibility that objects might transfer prints to the next adjacent substance, such as the air, and so on until the eye unless each of those parts has self-motion because "rare parts of matter… are not able to retain a print without self-motion," Cavendish, *Philosophical Letters*, 62.
19. Ibid., 72.
20. Ibid., 19.
21. Ibid., 26.
22. Ibid., 27.
23. Ibid., 81.
24. Ibid., 104.
25. Ibid., 105.
26. Ibid.
27. Cavendish, *Observations Upon Experimental Philosophy*, ed. Eileen O'Neill (Oxford and New York: Cambridge University Press, 2001), 140.
28. René Descartes, "Principles of Philosophy," in *The Philosophical Writings of Descartes*, trans. John Cottingham, Robert Stoothaff, and Dugald Murdoch (Cambridge: Cambridge University Press, 1985), 240. In the Latin: "quód unaquaeque res, quantum in se est, semper in eodem statu perseveret" *Principia philosophiae*, vol. 8 of *Oeuvres de Descartes*, eds. Charles Adam and Paul Tannery (L. Cerf, Paris, 1897), 62. In the French "Que tout corps qui se meut, tend á continuer son mouuement in ligne droit" *Méditations et Principes*, vol. 9 of *Oeuvres de Descartes*, eds. Charles Adam and Paul Tannery (L. Cerf, Paris, 1897), 85.
29. Descartes, "Principles of Philosophy," 242. In the Latin: "ubi corpus quod movetur alteri occurrit…si uero habeit maiorem, tunc alterum corpus secum mouet, ac quatum ei dat de suo motu, tantundem perdit" *Principia philosophiae*, 65. In the French: "si un corps qui se meut & qui en rencontre un autre… s'il a plus de force, il meut auec Iby cet autre corps, & perd autant de son mouvement qu'il luy en donne" *Méditations et Principes*, 86–87.
30. Aristotle, "Physics," *The Complete Works of Aristotle*, ed. Jonathan Barnes, 2 vols. (Princeton, NJ: Princeton University Press, 1984), vol. 1, 428,

256a25–256a28. References to Aristotle are to page and Bekker number unless otherwise noted. In Greek: "Ἀδύνατον δὲ κινεῖν ἄνευ τοῦ αὐτὸ αὑτῷ κινοῦντος τὸ ᾧ κινεῖ· ἀλλ᾽ εἰ μὲν αὐτὸ αὑτῷ κινεῖ, οὐκ ἀνάγκη ἄλλο εἶναι ᾧ κινεῖ, ἂν δὲ ᾖ ἕτερον τὸ ᾧ κινεῖ, ἔστιν τι ὃ κινήσει οὐ τινὶ ἀλλ᾽ αὑτῷ, ἢ εἰς ἄπειρον εἶσιν." Aristotle, *Aristotle: The Physics: Books V–VIII*, trans. P. H. Wicksteed and F. M. Cornford (Cambridge, MA: Harvard University Press, 1934).

31. John Donne, "Sappho to Philaenis," in *The Major Works*, ed. John Carey (Oxford, 1990), 39–40. Citation is to line.

32. We looked briefly at the Aristotelian model of sense perception in the Introduction. Aristotle treated all perception as impression, and his conception of vision was highly influential. Both Hobbes' and Descartes' theories of vision also depend upon impression. Cavendish first offers her theory of sense perception in response to Hobbes. However, in the passage that is quoted she is responding to Descartes.

33. Susan James, "The Philosophical Innovations of Margaret Cavendish," 225.

34. Cavendish, *Philosophical Letters*, 12.

35. Ibid., 64.

36. Ibid., 2.

37. Ibid.

38. Ibid., 31.

39. Ibid., 33.

40. Ibid.

41. Ibid., 1.

42. Ibid., 3.

43. Ibid., 23.

44. Ibid., 23–24.

45. Cavendish directly challenges Hobbes's state of nature in *Philosophical Letters*. She writes "I Cannot well conceive what your *Author* means by the *Common Laws of Nature*... I say Nature hath but One Law, which is a wise Law, viz. to keep Infinite matter in order, and to keep so much Peace, as not to disturb the Foundation of her Government," 146. See Deborah Boyle, "Fame, Virtue, and Government: Margaret Cavendish on Ethics and Politics," *Journal of the History of Ideas* 67, no. 2: 281–289 for a discussion of Cavendish's political philosophy.

46. Cavendish, *Philosophical Letters*, 47.

47. Ibid. Sig. b1v.

48. Misty G. Anderson, "Tactile Places: Materializing Desire in Margaret Cavendish and Jane Barker," *Textual Practice* 13, no. 2 (1999): 335.

49. John Rogers, *The Matter of Revolution: Science, Poetry and Politics in the Age of Milton* (Ithaca, NY, 1996), 181.

50. Cavendish, *Philosophical Letters*, 23.
51. Ibid., 428.
52. Ibid., 420.
53. When the possibility of rape arises in "Assaulted and Pursued Chastity," in *Natures Picture Drawn by Fancies Pencil to the Life Being Several Feigned Stories, Comical, Tragical, Tragi-Comical, Poetical, Romancical, Philosophical, Historical, and Moral: Some in Verse, Some in Prose, Some Mixt, and Some by Dialogues* (London: Printed by A. Maxwell, 1671), for example, Cavendish sidesteps the issue by having nature intervene. She explains, "Heaven doth not always protect the Persons of Virtuous Souls from rude Violences: neither doth it always leave Virtue destitute, but sometimes lends a Human Help, yet so, as never but where Necessity was the Cause of their Dangers, and not Ignorance, Indiscretion, or Curiosity: for, Heaven never helps, but those that could not avoid the Danger" (395).
54. Margaret Cavendish, *The Worlds Olio Written by the Right Honorable, the Lady Margaret Newcastle* (London: Printed for J. Martin and J. Allestrye, 1655), unnumbered.
55. Cavendish, *Philosophical Letters*, 2.
56. Eve Keller, "Producing Petty Gods," in *Margaret Cavendish*, ed. Sara Heller Mendelson (Farnham: Ashgate, 2009), 458.
57. Cavendish, *Philosophical Letters*, 35.
58. Ibid., 40.
59. Ibid., 43.
60. Goldberg, *The Seeds of Things*, 125–126.
61. Margaret Cavendish, "The Blazing World," in *The Blazing World and Other Writings*, ed. Kate Lilley (London; New York: Penguin, 1994), 123.
62. Ibid., 124.
63. Ibid.
64. Ibid.
65. Ibid., 141–142.
66. Ibid., 137.
67. Ibid., 138.
68. Ibid., 187, 188.
69. Ibid.
70. Cavendish, *Philosophical Letters*, 512.
71. Cavendish, *Blazing World*, 133–134.
72. Ibid., 188.
73. Ibid., 132.
74. Ibid., 203.
75. Ibid., 219.

76. Ibid., 181.
77. Ibid.
78. Ibid., 183.
79. Ibid., 175.
80. Ibid., 181.
81. Cavendish, *Philosophical Letters*, 219.
82. Ibid., 183.
83. Cavendish, "The Blazing World," 181.
84. Ibid., 194.
85. Ibid., 195.
86. Ibid., 181.
87. See Goldberg, *The Seeds of Things*, 127–128 for a discussion of the duchess as a figure for Cavendish.

REFERENCES

Anderson, Misty G. "Tactile Places: Materializing Desire in Margaret Cavendish and Jane Barker." *Textual Practice* 13, no. 2 (1999): 329–52.

Aristotle, "Physics." In *The Complete Works of Aristotle*, edited by Jonathan Barnes, 2 vols, vol. 1. Princeton, NJ: Princeton University Press, 1984.

———. *Aristotle: The Physics Books V–VIII*. Translated by P. H. Wicksteed and F. M. Cornford. Cambridge, MA: Harvard University Press, 1934.

Batigelli, Anna. *Margaret Cavendish and the Exiles of the Mind*. Lexington: University of Kentucky Press, 1998.

Boyle, Deborah. "Fame, Virtue, and Government: Margaret Cavendish on Ethics and Politics." *Journal of the History of Ideas* 67, no. 2 (2006): 281–89.

Cavendish, Margaret. "The Blazing World." In *The Blazing World and Other Writings*, ed. Kate Lilley. London and New York: Penguin, 1994.

———. *Natures Picture Drawn by Fancies Pencil to the Life Being Several Feigned Stories, Comical, Tragical, Tragi-Comical, Poetical, Romancical, Philosophical, Historical, and Moral: Some in Verse, Some in Prose, Some Mixt, and Some by Dialogues*. London: Printed by A. Maxwell, 1671.

———. *Observations Upon Experimental Philosophy*. Edited by Eileen O'Neill. Oxford and New York: Cambridge University Press, 2001.

———. *Poems, and Fancies Written by the Right Honourable, the Lady Margaret Newcastle*. London: Printed for T. R. for J. Martin, and J. Allestrye, 1653.

———. *The Philosophical and Physical Opinions Written by Her Excellency the Lady Marchionesse of Newcastle*. London: Printed for J. Martin and J. Allestrye, 1655.

———. *Philosophical Letters: Or, Modest Reflections Upon Some Opinions in Natural Philosophy, Maintained by Several Famous and Learned Authors of This Age, Expressed by Way of Letters: By the Thrice Noble, Illustrious, and Excellent Princess, the Lady Marchioness of Newcastle*. London, 1664.

————. *The Worlds Olio Written by the Right Honorable, the Lady Margaret Newcastle*. London: Printed for J. Martin and J. Allestrye, 1655.

Detlefsen, Karen. "Atomism, Monism, and Causation in the Natural Philosophy of Margaret Cavendish." In *Oxford Studies in Early Modern Philosophy*, vol. 3, edited by Daniel Garber and Stephen Nadler. Oxford: Oxford University Press, 2005, 199–240.

Descartes, René. "Principles of Philosophy." In *The Philosophical Writings of Descartes*, translated by John Cottingham, Robert Stoothaff, and Dugald Murdoch. Cambridge: Cambridge University Press, 1985.

————. "Principia philosophiae." In *Oeuvres de Descartes*, edited by Charles Adam and Paul, vol. 8. Tannery. L. Cerf, Paris, 1897.

————. "Méditations et Principes." In *Oeuvres de Descartes*, edited by Charles Adam and Paul, vol. 9. Paris: L. Cerf, 1897.

Donne, John. "Sappho to Philaenis." In *The Major Works*, edited by John Carey. Oxford, 1990, 39–40.

Fitzmaurice, Susan M. "'But, Madam': The Interlocutor in Margaret Cavendish's Writing." *In-Between: Essays and Studies in Literary Criticism* 9, no. 1–2 (March 2000): 17–27.

Goldberg Jonathan. *The Seeds of Things: Theorizing Sexuality and Materiality in Renaissance Representations*. New York: Fordham University Press, 2009.

Hobbes, Thomas. *Leviathan with Selected Variants from the Latin Edition of 1688*. Edited by Edwin Curley. Indianapolis, IN and Cambridge, UK: Hackett, 1994.

James, Susan. "The Philosophical Innovations of Margaret Cavendish," *British Journal for the History of Philosophy* 7, no. 2 (1999): 219–44.

Keller, Eve. *Generating Bodies and Gendered Selves: The Rhetoric of Reproduction in Early Modern England*. Seattle: University of Washington Press, 2007.

————. "Producing Petty Gods." In *Margaret Cavendish*, edited by Sara Heller Mendelson. Farnham: Ashgate, 2009.

O'Neill, Eileen. Introduction to *Observations Upon Experimental Philosophy*, by Margaret Cavendish, edited by Eileen O'Neill, x–xxxvi. Cambridge: Cambridge University Press, 2001.

Rees, Emma L. E. *Margaret Cavendish: Gender, Genre, Exile*. Manchester, UK: Manchester University Press, 2004.

Rogers, John. *The Matter of Revolution: Science, Poetry and Politics in the Age of Milton*. Ithaca, NY: Cornell University Press, 1996.

CHAPTER 5

Wax Arts: Projects of Transformation in Webster's *The Duchess of Malfi* and Donne's *Sappho to Philaenis*

Thus far, we have seen that wax is a material used to figure both men and women in the early modern period via the trope of signet–seal, and that it plays an important conceptual role for early modern authors in thinking about gender, selfhood, and relationality, and the malleability of those constructions. We saw too that wax's usefulness for thinking through such questions has much to do with its perceived status as passive, vulnerable, and malleable to external forces. Thus, in Chapter 4, reading the signet–seal trope through a vitalist lens with Margaret Cavendish fundamentally changes the meanings of that trope, allowing more possibilities for agency in seemingly passive positions. In this chapter, we will leave behind, at least for the most part, the trope of signet–seal, shifting instead to possibilities of sympathy, or to wax-acting-on-wax. John Webster's *The Duchess of Malfi* and John Donne's *Sappho to Philaenis* both explore the possibility that wax might transform wax on the basis of likeness and shared affinities, a possibility that we can understand through both wax artistic practices and wax magic. Together these two possibilities help figure the power of art more broadly and its ability to mediate the relationship between subjects and objects.

Early modern artistic practices reveal that wax played an important role in transforming an artist's vision into form. As we saw in the introduction, wax was an important sculptural material in the early modern period, used both for finished, albeit ephemeral, sculptures and for working out forms to be transferred into other mediums such as marble and

© The Author(s) 2019   133
L. M. Maxwell, *Wax Impressions, Figures, and Forms in Early Modern Literature*, Early Modern Cultural Studies 1500–1700,
https://doi.org/10.1007/978-3-030-16932-9_5

paint. In numerous treatises, Italian art critics extolled the virtue of wax as a material for realizing the artist's vision. As Vasari explains: "sculptors, when they wish to work a figure in marble, are accustomed to make what is called a model for it in clay or wax or plaster...because they can exhibit in it the attitude and proportion of the figure that they wish to make."[1] Working "with judgement and manipulation," the sculptor can perfect his vision by rendering it material, refining the models until they "exhibit in it the attitude and the proportion of the figure" that will be carved in marble.[2] Further, wax models allowed artists to gain new understanding of their subjects by allowing artists to manipulate their forms. Such manipulation is advantageous not only to sculptors, but also to painters who can use wax to see the human form in positions that it does not easily occupy. Thus, as we saw earlier, Tintoretto's practice of placing models in perspective boxes or suspending them from the ceiling allowed him to see the human form differently and thus make "humans fly" in his finished paintings.[3]

If wax sculpture provides a medium for the working out of artistic vision, wax tablets offer a similar space for writing. While our discussion of the signet–seal trope has frequently touched on possibilities of wax writing, there is more to say about the kind of mediating space that a wax tablet can provide for a poet's vision. Just as wax models can be shaped and refined, wax tablets provide a provisional surface for writing, one that can be erased and re-inscribed, worked and re-worked until the inscription matches the poet's mind. As we saw in the introduction, wax tablets are particularly aligned with love poetry in classical culture. In the early modern period, such tablets were often used for accounting and other more mundane inscriptions. Still, the wax tablet conjures up all the possibilities of drafting and re-drafting, erasing and re-inscribing that govern the writing process. Thus, wax writing like wax sculpture provides a bridge between mind and art, subject and object, and represents the process through which ideas and dreams are made physical.

Since wax can model the transformation of thoughts into objects through art, it can also model the power of art to work on its viewer or reader. This possibility is perhaps best evoked through the possibility of magic in the period, as magic offers a model for how external forces might work upon interiors indirectly or from a distance. Recent work on the role of magic in the early modern period has shown that belief in magic ranging from the benign to the diabolical was widespread in the period.[4] Although there was some skepticism around magical practices, by and large, magic was regarded as a practice with real power to act in the world even as that power might require the assistance of devils or other supernatural forces.[5] Further, as Stuart Clark claims, the study of witchcraft, magic, and demonology was "a composite subject consisting of discussions about the workings of nature, the processes of history, the maintenance of religious purity, and the nature of political authority and order."[6] Thus, contemplating witchcraft or magic was part of larger attempts to understand the world and the relations between man, devils, angels, and God. Indeed, as Clark also holds, "the subject of witchcraft seems to have been used as a means for thinking through problems that originated elsewhere and that had little or nothing to do with the legal prosecution of witches."[7] Magic then, like wax, was useful to think with.

The possibilities of thinking with magic and thinking with wax converge in the possibility of wax magic, which is to say magic intended to impact a person through the manipulation of wax simulacra. Wax magic is not an early modern term. Instead, such acts would have been understood in the period to be a kind of sympathetic magic, or perhaps, more specifically, a kind of image magic. Sympathetic magic works—to the extent that any magic can be said to work—on the basis of shared qualities or characteristics and an underlying neo-Platonic belief in the oneness of the universe capable of transcending any particularity and thus of making such linkages between all subjects and all objects.[8] However, I offer the term wax magic here to emphasize the role of materiality, and particularly wax materiality in the performance of sympathetic magic.[9] While wax magic might be understood as a subset of sympathetic magic, I separate it out here to emphasize the multiple and complex ways that wax objects might connect to human subjects through all of the wax possibilities of body, womb, heart, and mind that I have been tracing in this project. Thus, when sympathetic magic is performed through wax, it relies on both visual affinities and material ones, troubling the distinction between subject and object by relying on the thingness of people and the people-ness of things.[10]

If the artistic uses of wax reveal how the artist's mind becomes material, wax magic reveals how art—magical and otherwise—might shape our interior spaces through possibilities of likeness and sympathy. Thus, the wax statues in *The Duchess of Malfi* embody Ferdinand's vision of torture and work on the duchess's psyche—and perhaps ours—as though by magic, making malleable the boundaries between inside and outside, self and other. Similarly, Sappho's poetic efforts both translate her interior spaces into legible inscriptions and imagine that Philaenis might be drawn by and in her poetry as though through enchantment, suggesting that there is little difference, at least for Sappho, between writing to one's beloved, and writing one's beloved.

5.1   Deforming Wax in *The Duchess of Malfi*

In *The Duchess of Malfi*, Ferdinand stages a tableau of wax figures to "bring [his sister] to despair."[11] Enraged at her secret marriage and her refusal to be ruled by his desires, Ferdinand first captures his sister and then proceeds to psychologically torture her. He arranges to have wax sculptures made of her husband and children as corpses and reveals them to her as the climax of a complicated scene of deception and revelation that begins with a promise of reconciliation. Primed to believe both that Ferdinand is fully capable of performing murder and that he is committed to the truth, the duchess takes the wax figures to be "true substantial bodies" and is devastated by what she believes to be the corpses of her family.[12]

The wax figures that Ferdinand stages can be read, at least in part as his artistic creation, even as they are actually crafted by an Italian artist.[13] While he does not sculpt the figures, the conception of the forms is Ferdinand's, as is their presentation, and he revels in their success, telling his henchman Bosola:

> Excellent; as I would wish; she's plagued in art.
> These presentations are but framed in wax,
> By the curious master in that quality,
> Vincentio Lauriola, and she takes them
> For true substantial bodies.[14]

This speech serves several purposes including alerting the audience to the exact nature of the display that they have just witnessed along with the duchess. More importantly, for our purposes, Ferdinand's speech reveals his interest in the artful nature of the figures. He delights in the deception and the fact that his sister is "plagued in art." By mentioning the artist's name, he elevates the wax figures from curiosity to art object and underscores the extravagance of his ruse.[15] In order to stage these figure, Ferdinand had to go to great length, securing a master craftsman, giving that craftsman time to create the artful corpses, and devising a strategy to present the forms to the duchess in such a way that she would take them to be true. Yet the result seems to be worth the effort, not simply because the duchess despairs, but because her misapprehension of the nature of the corpses is the cause of that despair.[16]

By reveling in the artful nature of the corpses, Ferdinand's speech begins to suggest that the wax figures might be better for his purposes than real corpses would have been. The deceptive nature of the display affirms his power over his sister, even more than the possession of the corpses would, since he need not actually catch her family and execute them to destroy her. This point may be especially important to Ferdinand whose entire problem with his sister relates to her decision to remarry and reproduce. By making corpses of wax, he obviates his only potential need for Antonio—as a body he can use to torture his sister. Instead, his artfulness, together with the skill of Vincentio Lauriola, is sufficient to remake his sister's world and drive her to despair. We can think again of Tintoretto, suspending wax figures from his ceiling in order to transform his perspective and create new worlds. Ferdinand, likewise, uses wax to subvert the constraints of reality. If Tintoretto can make "human figures fly" by way of wax, Ferdinand shows his mastery over reality by using artful wax forms to convince the duchess that her family is dead and that she should abandon all hope.[17]

Further, we can read the entire scene of torture as art, as wax-filled theatrics designed to demonstrate Ferdinand's power as a consummate artist, able to bend reality to his will and simultaneously reshape the duchess into a form of despair. The tableaux after all is only the final revelation in a performance that begins with Ferdinand visiting the duchess under the cover of darkness in order to offer her a hand of reconciliation without violating his vow to never see her again. Instead of offering his own hand, however, he gives her a dead man's hand to kiss, and when she recoils in horror, he calls for lights to illuminate his macabre display. By controlling the duchess's access to sensory information, Ferdinand manipulates her perception of her surroundings and begins the work of remolding her. Similarly, the dead hand participates in his wax art both because it might be "ta'en" from Antonio's wax corpse and because it becomes an instrument of impression, while her heart is figured as a material in which a "print" might be "bur[ied]" and thus a soft, retentive, wax locale.[18] By imagining his sister as wax, he imagines her as material he can mold and inscribe. Thus, Ferdinand's art extends beyond staging sculptures to transforming the duchess's interiority and modeling her as though she too was simply material for art.

To an extent, Ferdinand's efforts prove successful. Certainly, the wax figures impact the duchess profoundly and drive her to the "despair" that motivates his spectacle. Believing her family to be dead, the duchess loses, at least temporarily, her will to live. She suggests to Bosola, Ferdinand's henchman, that it would be a mercy "if they would bind me to that lifeless trunk, / And let me freeze to death."[19] Here, the "lifeless trunk" refers doubly to Antonio's corpse and also their dead legacy, their truncated family tree. She wants to be bound to those forms and also to die, as "the greatest torture souls feel in hell, / In hell: that they must live, and cannot die."[20] Over the course of several speeches, the duchess continues this line of thought, fantasizing first about emulating the famous Roman example of Portia and killing herself by consuming live coals and then, when Bosola admonishes her about the ethics of suicide, of starving herself to death since "the church enjoins fasting."[21] Bosola recognizes the suicidal fantasies for what they are, exclaiming "O fie! Despair?"[22] He exhorts her to "[l]eave this vain sorrow. / Things being at the worst begin to mend."[23] However, the duchess rejects the possibilities of recovery implicit in his speech. She exclaims:

> Good comfortable fellow,
> Persuade a wretch that's broke upon the wheel
> To have all his bones new set; entreat him live
> To be executed again. Who must dispatch me?
> I account this world a tedious theatre,
> For I do play a part in't 'gainst my will.[24]

Her metaphor makes clear both the extent to which Ferdinand's display has wrecked her and her rationale for preferring death to life. By comparing herself to "a wretch that's broke upon the wheel," she suggests that her internal pain is tantamount to the most extreme physical torture. Being broken on a wheel was a form of execution in which the prisoner was bound to a wheel and then bludgeoned such that every bone broke in multiple places and the body was severely mangled.[25] By referencing this form of torture, the duchess conveys both the extent of her pain and the impossibility of healing the damage that the torture has caused.[26] It would be impossible to set all of the bones of a body damaged to such an extent, and even if it were possible, the physical pain would continue to be unbearable. After sustaining that amount of damage, nobody would desire to continue to live, especially if one were to live just "to be executed again." The duchess is suggesting that the same promise of continuous torture is hers for as long as she remains alive. Stripped of her political power, deprived of her family, and held captive by her brother, the duchess knows that she is powerless and that things cannot mend. If she continues to live, it will be to "play a part... 'gainst [her] will," while being crippled by grief. Since Ferdinand's torturous spectacle has already taught her the pain of such playing, her preference for death is unsurprising.[27]

If Ferdinand's torture of the duchess can be understood via the possibilities of artistic creation and performance, and especially those that attach to wax, the duchess understands the result—her profound sense of despair—as a product of wax magic. When she first confronts the tableau, she exclaims:

> There is not between heaven and earth one wish
> I stay for after this. It wastes me more
> Than were't my picture, fashioned out of wax,
> Stuck with a magical needle, and then buried
> In some foul dunghill...[28]

Since she invokes wax magic to understand the impact of the wax figures, it may be that she knows the figures she looks upon are wax.[29] However, given the duchess's relief at Bosola's revelation that Antonio lives later in the act, it seems more likely that she turns to wax magic not because she understands that corpses are themselves wax figures, but rather that even without knowing the true nature of the figures, the duchess intuitively knows that this is a wax matter, something best conceptualized through the possibilities of wax materiality. Indeed, wax magic seems to serve as a conceptual upper bound for the duchess. For her, it represents the most extreme attack on a person's psyche and agency that does not result in death, or at least it did prior to Ferdinand's spectacle. The sight of the wax corpses, which she mistakes as real, drives her beyond that limit. His figures "waste [her] more" than any magical attack could, more than she can conceive without reference to wax magic or articulate through language other than analogy.

The duchess's comparison between the impact of these figures and that of wax magic raises the question of how Ferdinand's wax figures might be like those employed in witchcraft. As the duchess's speech suggests, when wax magic is performed a wax image of the intended target is abused and buried, and because the wax figure connects to a particular subject in various ways, whatever is done to it also impacts the target. Ferdinand, of course, does not show the duchess an image of her own wax corpse, nor for that matter do we have any reason to believe that he has a wax image of her pierced with needles and buried in a dunghill. Still, the wax corpses do have a similar relation to herself as the imagined "picture, fashion'd out of wax"—they represent her and connect to her through the bonds of flesh and family. Indeed, her family is, perhaps, more her "picture" than her own image is and for this reason more capable of affecting her. Certainly, the effect of seeing the figures is sudden, dramatic, and devastatingly destructive and her reaction to this presentation reveals the duchess as vulnerable to outside attack and manipulation through her affective bonds to other subjects, especially once those subjects are reduced to objects. Her turn to wax magic to understand the way the wax figures work on her also suggests that the figures could work on her through the power of likeness or sympathy. As Lynn Enterline argues, "It is as though she has an unconscious intuition of becoming like what she sees – and perishing for it."[30] Since her family is important to the duchess's self-identity, their forms of death might become her form, just as her portrait "stuck with a magical needle, and then buried / In some foul dunghill" might cause her to waste away.

Of course, Ferdinand's wax sculptures are not actually part of a magical attack. Indeed, Ferdinand explicitly rejects the possibility of magic earlier in the play. After reporting the rumor that the duchess has had three bastard children, Ferdinand's henchman, Bosola, suggests that sorcery might have caused the duchess to "dote on some desertless fellow, / She shames to acknowledge."[31] For Bosola, the duchess's love of a "desertless fellow" is proof that her agency has been compromised and sorcery seems to him the most likely culprit. When Ferdinand asks him:

> Can your faith give way
> To think there's power in potions, or in charms,
> To make us love, whether we will or no?[32]

Bosola replies, "most certainly." Yet while for Bosola such enchantment seems the most logical explanation for the duchess's illogical love choices, Ferdinand rejects the possibility outright:

Away, these are mere gulleries, horrid things
Invented by some cheating mountebanks
To abuse us. Do you think that herbs or charms
Can force the will? Some trials have been made
In this foolish practice; but the ingredients
Were lenitive poisons, such as are of force
To make the patient mad; and straight the witch
Swears, by equivocation, they are in love.[33]

Ferdinand's rejection of sorcery reveals both his skepticism and careful study of displays of magical prowess. For Ferdinand, magic is a deception, a "mere guller[y]," as he makes clear in his discussion of the "trials" that have been made "in this foolish practice." The witch or "cheating mountebank" deceives by a combination of artfulness and artifice, mixing poisons and lies to fool a susceptible audience. Ferdinand sees that sorcerers, mountebanks, and witches have a real power "to abuse us." Indeed, he seems to have given a great deal of thought as to how practitioners of magic prey on their audiences. He has paid attention to the "trials" that "have been made / In this foolish practice" and thought about what those trials confirmed or failed to confirm about magic. He has also realized that truth is less important than perception.[34]

While he does not actually employ magic, Ferdinand borrows from its methods and its cultural power. Like the witch or mountebank who sells love potions, Ferdinand "swears, by equivocation" and his torture of his sister proves that he is master of deception. Indeed, if we revisit the larger performance that leads to the display of corpses, we can see that deception, perversion, and the occult all figure in his scene of torture. First, Ferdinand deceives the duchess into accepting his offer of peace and allowing the lights to be removed. Then, he perverts the formal reconciliation that he offers by proffering a dead man's hand in place of his own, a perversion might itself suggest dark magic since magic is often associated with inversion. Further, the wax hand itself may, as Katherine Rowe has suggested, invoke folk tales of the Hand of Glory, another form of witchcraft that impinges on agency.[35] Taken together, these elements lead the duchess to ask Bosola, "what witchcraft doth he practice, that he hath left / A dead man's hand here?"[36] Thus even before the duchess witnesses the wax corpses, she sees Ferdinand as participating in a kind of diabolical magic.

Thus far I have been suggesting that wax's place in art might enable us to read Ferdinand's torture of his sister through the process of artistic creation and the damage she experiences through the possibilities of wax magic. These possibilities, however, are not fully distinct from each other, as we can see in the duchess's attempts to process her own ruin. While the duchess turns to wax magic as the closest analogue to how the corpses move her, later in the act, Cariola suggests that the best way to understand who the duchess has become may be by reference to art objects. After declaring that she is "not mad yet," and describing her immense suffering, the duchess asks Cariola "Who do I look like now?"[37] expecting that her interior suffering will have an external manifestation. Cariola replies:

> Like to your picture in the gallery,
> A deal of life in show, but none in practice;
> Or rather like some reverend monument
> Whose ruins are even pitied.[38]

The first of these comparisons simultaneously suggests that the duchess's appearance is static and that something has drastically changed. By looking like her picture, the duchess must look like herself. However, Cariola inverts the chain of resemblance so that the subject resembles the object rather than the reverse, and this reversal signals a lack of vitality. The duchess now possesses "a deal of life in show, but none in practice." While people can live and die, art can only represent such states. It is always "show" not "practice." Thus, Cariola is suggesting that what has changed is not the duchess's appearance, but the relationship of that appearance to her reality. The disjuncture between the appearance of life or death and their reality is intrinsic to art. If Cariola is right that the effect of Ferdinand's display has been to make the duchess more like her portrait, then the spectacle also has made the duchess more like the forms she viewed. After all, while the wax corpses of the duchess's family appear dead, they are exactly as close to death as her portrait is to life.

Yet Cariola does not end with this comparison. She immediately follows up the portrait analogy with the second analogy in which she compares the duchess to "some reverend monument / Whose ruins are even pitied."[39] This second analogy both extends and revises the first. Again, Cariola insists that the duchess has become like an art object. By shifting the comparison from a portrait to a sculpture, she brings the analogy even closer to Ferdinand's wax sculptures. Yet the move from portrait to ruined sculpture also reintroduces the possibility that Ferdinand's display has physically marked her. The duchess is not simply like art; she is like ruined art. A monument in ruins still reveals hints of what used to be, but it no longer seems to live or die so much as it threatens to become nothing and dissolve into incoherence. Since monuments typically depict important figures who have died, as a form of art, the ruined monument suggests both the possibility of memorialization after death and the impermanence of that memorialization. Art is not as static as it seemed in the first comparison. Instead, it is vulnerable to the same ravages of time that bodies are. Essentially, this second analogy both reinforces the duchess's connection to art and makes clear that nothing about that similarity protects her. If she has become like art, she has become an object to be "pitied," broken, manipulated, and interpreted as any subject sees fit. Together the two analogies further the duchess's suggestion that the impact of Ferdinand's figures is like wax magic. Seeing the wax figures of the corpses has made the duchess more like those forms by making her more like an art object, or perhaps more aptly, a ruined art object. Her sympathetic identification with those figures gives them the power to transform her from sovereign to subject and subject to object.

When Cariola tells the duchess that she looks like a "reverend monument, whose ruins are even pitied," she offers a vision of exactly how successful Ferdinand's attack has been. He has not only transformed the duchess from subject to object and driven her to despair. He also has forced her to adopt a position that she explicitly rejected earlier in the play, that of "the figure carved in alabaster kneels at [her] husband's tomb."[40] The alabaster funeral sculpture represents a certain idealized form of widowhood, a frozen posture of grief that constrains a woman's identity in reference to her husband, and the duchess must reject that posture in order to marry Antonio. If Cariola's analogy is apt, Ferdinand's torture has managed to transform her into the same kind of frozen form. On the one hand, this transformation reveals the success of Ferdinand's project, after all his torturous spectacle is motivated by his disapproval of her secret marriage and family, which are the forms she chooses over the idealized form of widowhood. Thus insofar as his display makes her more like the statue, his methods return her to a previous, more acceptable version of herself. At the same time, that transformation has given her a certain hardness and strength. While she can still be harmed, she is no longer as moldable as she once was. Ferdinand surrounds her with the denizens of the local madhouse, intending that their madness will infect her, yet it proves not to be catching. Similarly, the form of her death, which according to Bosola "should much afflict [her]," does not.[41] The duchess exclaims:

> What would it pleasure me to have my throat cut
> With diamonds? or to be smothered
> With cassia? or to be shot to death with pearls?[42]

The wax figures seem to have inured her to further attacks, especially those of a psychological nature. Indeed, after being surrounded by mad-men, the duchess tells Cariola:

> nothing but noise and folly
> Can keep [her] in [her] right wits; whereas reason
> And silence make [her] stark mad.[43]

Everything that transpires after seeing the figures, including her own execution, amounts to mere "noise and folly." If wax magic represented her previous conceptual limit for how one subject could waste another, having witnessed the wax corpses she is no longer a vulnerable subject. The devastation wrought by her despair is so totalizing that no further ruin is possible.

The wax subjects and objects of *The Duchess Malfi* work on each other and threaten to become each other in the interchange between artist and art, art object and viewer, and these relations seem to function as though by magic, as the result of shared qualities, affinities, and sympathies as much as the application of pressure. Yet that distinction too seems malleable. Neither the shaping pressure of impression nor perhaps the practice of wax magic seems able to convey the power and impact of art in the play. Further that power is not limited to the characters on the stage. As spectators, we are also worked on by both Ferdinand's spectacle and Webster's play. Like the duchess, we are impacted by Ferdinand's display of corpses and his torture of the duchess, and that seems true even as our knowledge of the nature of the figures changes.

We first witness the figures with the duchess and believe with her that Antonio and her children are dead.[44] In that moment, we might be moved to pity, impacted both by the sight of corpses and the duchess's displays of grief.[45] Our own wax interiority might allow us to connect to the duchess and to internalize her figure of pain. Eventually, however, as David Bergeron puts it "Webster... widens the ironic gap."[46] When Ferdinand brags to Bosola about the effect of his art, the audience is informed of the nature of the figures, while the duchess is left uninformed. This gap between our knowledge and hers invites the audience to contemplate the nature of the spectacle and its relationship to theater. As Huston Diehl argues, the effect is to shift our attention from spectacle to spectator and force us to consider our own vulnerability to the workings of the stage.[47] While the audience may not have known the exact nature of Ferdinand's artful figures, we should always have known, or at least assumed that all of the action on the stage was fictional because we were at a play. Yet have we? To the extent that we sympathize with the plights of characters and mourn their deaths, we collapse together the actors playing and the characters being played, repeatedly forgetting that we are watching fiction. Indeed, moments when playwrights draw attention to the artificiality of their spectacle are noteworthy precisely because they rupture the illusion created on stage. When, one scene later, Bosola demands that Ferdinand look on his own spectacle of bodies, consisting of the duchess and her strangled children, we mourn their deaths and feel the pity that Bosola calls for, even though on a metatheatrical level these corpses are the same as the wax figures of the previous scene.[48] Artful corpses and actual corpses require the same material to be staged: living bodies posed as dead.[49]

This repetition of corpses and spectacles suggests that art has the power to plague even when we should know the difference between fiction and reality, since as an audience we are again moved by the presentation of bodies, even though we have just been reminded of the artificiality of the stage. Just as wax magic relies on the power of sympathy to work profound change on the targeted subject, so too does the theater. Ferdinand thinks the power of his art is its ability to deceive—and to a certain extent he may be right—but there is power beyond simple deception that inheres in the display, regardless of whether anyone is deceived by it.[50] That power lies in its ability to connect with, move, and influence its intended target, which is also the power of both wax art more broadly.[51]

5.2   INSCRIBING WAX IN SAPPHO TO PHILAENIS

If wax sculpture and wax theater can be understood through the twin possibilities of wax art and wax magic, those same possibilities also provide the conceptual bases for understanding Sappho's poetic project in Donne's *Sappho to Philaenis*. The poem is a lyrical lament in which Sappho mourns the loss of Philaenis's love and attempts to re-seduce her. Yet she begins having, it seems, already failed. The poem opens asking:

> Where is that holy fire, which verse is said
> To have? Is that enchanting force decayed?
> Verse that draws Nature's works, from Nature's law
> Thee, her best work, to her work cannot draw.[52]

From a position of loss and failure, Sappho attempts to write Philaenis back into her life and rediscover the enchanting force of poetry. Her verse seeks to doubly draw Philaenis, to describe and attract her, and that possibility depends on the connections between both women's hearts and the text that Sappho is creating, connections that can be understood through wax.

Where Ferdinand and the duchess understand the tableaux of corpses differently—Ferdinand viewing them as a feat of wax art and the duchess as an attack of wax magic—Sappho seems to see her poetic project as being at once a work of wax poetics and an attempt at wax magic. The link between poetry and magic is made in the first stanza, when Sappho asks what has happened to "that enchanting force" commonly ascribed to verse. Here, she plays on the etymological roots of "enchant"—in Latin, literally "to sing upon."[53] At the same time, the connection between poetry and magic is furthered by the figure of Orpheus. As Heather Meakin has argued, Sappho alludes to Ovid's Orpheus when she claims that "verse... draws Nature's work, from Nature's law."[54] In *The Metamorphoses* 11, immediately before Orpheus's death, Ovid describes the power of the Orphic voice: "Orpheus sang his minstrel's songs and charmed / The rocks and woods and creatures of the wild / To follow...."[55] Orpheus's power here to draw "rocks and woods and creatures of the wild" is the power that Sappho searches for in her poetry.[56] Yet while the Orpheus allusion conveys the force of poetic enchantment, it does not shed any light on how it might work.[57] Instead, to find the linkages between poetry, seduction, and enchantment we must turn to wax.

Classical poets used wax tablets for their poetry, both because writing on wax suited the fleeting nature of erotic desire, and because writing on wax evoked the intimacy that the poet sought. Inscribing wax is a mode of writing that is almost bodily as wax inscription depends on a stylus penetrating the surface of the wax. Moreover, wax tablets were often diptychs or triptychs that folded together. Thus, the beloved's answer would fold onto the original poem, creating a union that mirrored the one desired by the poet. Poets used the connections between bodies and wax to great effect. In the *Amores*, for example, Ovid imagines that the work a writer does upon a wax tablet can echo the work he wishes to perform on his beloved's body. Thus, the speaker of 1.11 tells a servant:

> receive and take early to your mistress these tablets I have inscribed, and care
> that nothing hinder or delay! ... Should she ask how I fare, you will say my
> hope of her favour lets me live; as for the rest, it is charactered in the wax by
> my fond hand.[58]

Here, Raphael Lyne argues, the wax not only holds the words of Ovid's poems, it "show[s] the stroked words, softened by a passionate heat."[59] Thus, the recipient of the poem can read the speaker's intention not only in the text of the poem but also in the way "it is charactered in the wax by [his] fond hand." Ovid's description of wax writing practices pertains to *Sappho to Philaenis* not only because it reveals the seductive possibilities of wax writing, but also because Donne had Ovid in mind when he wrote his poem. As Elizabeth Harvey has shown, Donne alludes to Ovid's *Heroides* XV in *Sappho to Philaenis*, so it may well be that Donne imagined his heroine inscribing her verses on wax tablets, just as the lover in the *Amores* does.[60]

This possibility is heightened by the way wax explicitly enters into Sappho's poetics. Immediately following this opening lament, Sappho looks into her heart for inspiration, as so many Petrarchan poets. What she finds is Philaenis's image inscribed on her own wax heart, melting from the fires of passion, and taking with it her last access to her beloved:

> Only thine image, in my heart, doth sit,
> But that is wax, and fires environ it.

> My fires have driven, thine have drawn it hence;
> And I am robbed of picture, heart, and sense.[61]

The image of loss borrows from the cross-sexed trope of signet and seal that we explored with some depth in Chapter 2 and seems to represent Sappho's attempt to find a lasting significance in lesbian love. In a world where only cross-gendered relationships lead to productive impressions, the melting landscape of her own wax heart, impossibly or not so impossibly impressed by a female beloved, shows both the fragility of relationships between women and testifies to their importance. The imprint of Philaenis threatens to melt away, but if the image of Philaenis melts, it will annihilate Sappho's heart as well.

The wax of Sappho's heart, her poetic project of seduction, and the history of wax as a material of classical love poetry suggest that the act writing and the act of seducing may be one and the same, a possibility also raised in Shakespeare's Sonnet 122 through the close association of writing tablets and minds.[62] There, the speaker figures his brain as a wax tablet, "full charactered with lasting memory" and chides his beloved for giving him actual wax tablets, as "to keep an adjunct to remember thee / Were to import forgetfulness in me."[63] Both the mind and the wax tablet are spaces that the beloved can write here, and they threaten to collapse together from the opening line of the poem, when the speaker asserts "[t]hy gift, thy tables, are within my brain."[64] The beloved's text coexists inside and outside of the speaker and both part of and "adjunct" to that self.

By inscribing her words on a wax tablet, Sappho may be figuratively caressing and impressing her beloved. Her inscription of words on wax may double the impressions she hopes to make on both Philaenis's body and her affective locations.[65] For although the poem is silent on the issue, we can easily imagine that Philaenis too has a heart of wax, or at least that Sappho imagines Philaenis's heart as wax since the poem insists on the likeness and oneness of Sappho and Philaenis. We find the fullest articulation of that likeness toward the end of the poem when Sappho relays:

> My two lips, eyes, thighs, differ from thy two,
> But so, as thine from one another do;
> And, oh, no more; the likeness being such,
> Why should they not alike in all parts touch?[66]

Here, Sappho insists on the bodily sameness of herself and Philaenis that might extend to their interior spaces. If Philaenis's heart is wax, it is another location that Sappho would like to write, and through that act of writing reclaim as her own. Thus, I would argue, the female heart is both represented in the poem and doubles it: Both are texts, and given the classical practice of writing amorous poetry on wax tablets, both are wax locales.

Since Sappho seeks to restore multiple wax images through her act of poetic inscription, the "enchanting force" she seeks seems to be that of wax magic. Certainly, the doubleness of "draw," noted earlier, begins to suggest that the force of poetry might rest in its ability to delineate or describe nature and that it might be an attractive force based on likenesses that it helps create and reinforce. Thus, Sappho's poem itself can be understood as a vehicle designed to reshape Philaenis's affect. Sappho hopes that inscribing the wax tablet will allow her to re-inscribe Philaenis's heart, thus drawing her back to her former love for Sappho and erasing the differences between the two women that Philaenis's encounters with her male lover may have introduced. Whether such transformation amounts to magic depends on how it is effected. If Sappho's poetry can only succeed if Philaenis reads her text or hears her poem, then her verse is not exactly magic, since, just as Ferdinand's torture of the duchess requires her perception of the wax figures, Sappho's seduction of Philaenis would depend on Philaenis's exposure to her words. Even so in both cases wax magic is useful conceptually because it reveals the uncanny extent that these subjects might be manipulated and transformed by art and the complex relationship imagined between interiors and exteriors.

Further, it is not clear that Sappho's seduction requires an act of reading. Within the space of the poem, the distances between the two subjects and their interiors and exteriors seem always on the verge of collapse. For example, Sappho laments, "[t]houghts, my mind's creatures, often are with thee, / But I, their maker, want their liberty."[67] Here, Sappho's thoughts are externalized entities that can literally visit Philaenis, and the extent to which Sappho is speaking metaphorically seems an open question. While she can no longer physically be with Philaenis, her preoccupation with Philaenis offers a kind of nearness that has its own reality. The metaphysical divide between body and soul that Donne explores in "The Ecstasy" seems very much in play.[68] If we imagine a world where thoughts might literally be able to be with another person, or where souls could leave the body to negotiate with each other, it begins to seem possible that an act of writing, an inscribing of wax, could work on a beloved's wax heart from a distance and without her participation.

Regardless, conceptualizing Sappho's project through wax magic allows us to understand both how her melting wax heart endangers her project and why she insists on similarity throughout the poem. If we take seriously the possibility of wax magic, then Sappho's heart itself, imprinted with Philaenis's image, might attract her beloved. However, as we saw above, that image is first imperiled, "fires environ it" and then destroyed as Sappho is "robbed of picture, heart, and sense." When the image of Philaenis melts, so does one link between Sappho and her beloved. At the same time, and perhaps more importantly, without this image, Sappho cannot "look in [her] heart and write."[69] Which is to say, the melting/melted wax heart threatens Sappho's attempts to describe Philaenis in her poem by depriving her of a stable reference for Philaenis's image. Without Philaenis's image inscribed on the wax surface of her heart or poem, Sappho cannot hope to attract her.

Her verse then can be understood as an attempt either to rescue the wax image in her own heart, or to inscribe Philaenis's heart itself, as both are essentially the same project. At various points in the poem, Sappho seems to try both tactics. Immediately after considering her own melting interior, she attempts to describe Philaenis. Yet as several critics have noted, she gets caught up in negations, rather than positive descriptions:

> ...Thou art so fair,
>   As, gods, when gods to thee I do compare
> Are graced thereby; and to make blind men see,
>   What things gods are, I say they are like to thee.
> For, if we justly call each silly man
>   A little world, what shall we call thee then?
> Thou art not soft, and clear, and straight, and fair
>   As down, as stars, cedars and lilies are,
> But thy right hand, and cheek, and eye, only
>   Are like thy other hand, and cheek, and eye.[70]

Again and again in these lines, Sappho resists actual description in favor of emphasizing similarity and self-identity. When she claims that by comparison with Philaenis, blind men would "see, / What things gods are," her words are ironic. As Paula Blank notes, "those blind men will not 'see the gods any better for the comparison Sappho makes, because they cannot see Philaenis to begin with" and Sappho's poem does not fill in for the deficiencies of their vision.[71] What can we learn of Philaenis from Sappho's assertion that she is "not soft, and clear, and straight, and fair," but instead only like herself? James Holstun suggests, "Sappho begins with a stock Petrarchan rejection of stock Petrarchan similes. But she does not move beyond them to a positive description of Philaenis through some rejuvenated language."[72] Instead, the poem simply fails to represent. Certainly, we never learn the color of Philaenis's eyes or hair, only that her cheeks are "red" and "white."[73] If the enchantment of Philaenis is supposed to proceed by drawing her in poetic verse, by describing her in such a way that she will recognize herself in the poem and be attracted to that image, the non-descriptiveness of this description may doom Sappho's efforts to failure.

Still, Sappho's failure to represent Philaenis may be less a failure and more a choice. She might fail to enchant Philaenis because she cannot bring herself to imprint Philaenis. After all, she vilifies cross-sex erotics precisely because of their propensity to produce impressions. In what Janel Mueller has described as a "brief for lesbianism."[74] Sappho reminds Philaenis:

> Thy body is a natural paradise,
>   In whose self, unmanured, all pleasure lies,
> Nor needs perfection; why shouldst thou then
>   Admit the tillage of a harsh rough man?
> Men leave behind them that which their sin shows,
>   And are as thieves traced, which rob when it snows.
> But of our dalliance no more signs there are,
>   Than fishes leave in streams, or birds in air.[75]

Here, Sappho's depiction of heteroerotics is cast in terms of impression. "Tillage" is "the act, operation, or art of tilling or cultivating land so as to fit it for raising crops,"[76] or, more specifically "to till" is "to plow," which is "to make furrows in and turn up (the earth, the land) with a plough, esp. as a preparation for sowing or planting."[77] The process of making furrows in the earth resembles the process of impressing wax as a furrow is made by pressure of the plow on the soft earth. Moreover, this image of planting is also a classic trope for writing, appearing, for example, in Quintilian's *Institutes of Oratory.*[78] Just as a furrow is a type of impression, so too are the footprints that "thieves" leave who "rob when it snows." The tread of feet in snow leaves a print just like the stamp of a signet ring on wax. In fact, the image of a footprint in the snow is so like to the impression of wax that the two images frequently appear together in early modern literature. Yet unlike the wax heart, these images of impression are negatively valenced within this poem. Tillage might make the land more fertile, but it mars its surface. Similarly, the footprints are evidence of robbery, disrupting the otherwise pristine snowy landscape with their impressions. Thus, as Valerie Traub has argued Donne's Sappho conceives of "women's erotic innocence, purity, gentleness, and pleasure…in explicit opposition to the difference, friction, and reproductive after-effects of heteroeroticism," which produces impression.[79] Moreover, as Traub further notes, the "dalliance" of Sappho and Philaenis which produces no "signs" is directly contrasted to "the 'tillage' of a harsh, rough man, a sin which leaves indelible traces (semen, pregnancy)."[80]

Wax magic offers a possibility of force that depends on likeness. Yet if it also requires bodily or affective inscription, perhaps it is a force that Sappho is ultimately unwilling to harness. While Sappho mostly decries the visible signs that would transform the exterior of the beloved, how different can imprinting a heart be from imprinting a body? Certainly, the printing of a wax heart or a wax poem offers a kind of reproduction insofar as it re-produces the image of lover or beloved, and to the extent that such acts are transformative they might belong to the same sphere as "the tillage of a harsh rough man." If there is a difference, the difference rests in the difference between exteriors and interiors, surfaces and depths or perhaps in the kind of lines created by desire. In Sara Ahmed's *Queer Phenomenology: Orientations, Objects, Others,* she theorizes "a model of affect as contact" that places impression at the center of all encounters, straight or lesbian.[81] For Ahmed, desire that deviates from the rules of heteronormativity "leaves its own marks on the ground, which can help generate alternative lines, which cross the ground in unexpected ways" and ultimately help "generate a lesbian landscape."[82] Ahmed theorizes precisely the ground that Sappho seems to be seeking in the poem. Yet Sappho struggles to locate a lesbian possibility that does not simply reinstate heteroerotics.

Sappho's turn to her own image in the glass at the end of the poem suggests that she is still searching for a way to draw Philaenis, and that wax magic might be the best way to conceptualize her strategy, despite her unease about the erotics of impression. As I mentioned earlier, the melting wax heart does not simply imperil Sappho's image of Philaenis, or her ability to enshrine her in love poetry, it also threatens Sappho herself. After all, she is robbed, of "picture, heart, and sense." Noting the similarities in their two female bodies, Sappho turns to her mirror as though her own image could rescue her heart, and perhaps with it, Philaenis's love. Sappho pines:

> Me, in my glass, I call thee; but, alas,
> When I would kiss, tears dim mine eyes, and glass.
> O cure this loving madness, and restore
> Me to me; thee, my half, my all, my more.[83]

At first glance, Sappho's act of gazing in the mirror seems to have nothing to do with the tropes of impression that we have been discussing and little to do with the image of the wax heart. Yet if we take into account theories of perception in the period, we are reminded that an act of vision is an act of impression.[84] Thus when Sappho looks at an image in her glass and calls it "thee," she is attempting to reconstitute her image of Philaenis and, through that image, the image of herself. If she can re-inscribe her heart with an image of herself, that she names Philaenis she can fool herself into believing that she posses not only "me" but also "thee." This image might have the power to "draw" Philaenis. Or it may be that such an impression will restore to Sappho a wholeness that could never again be threatened. With her own image inscribed on her heart, she might not need an external love object. Yet before such an impression can be fully made, "tears dim [her] eyes, and glass," preventing the act of vision that could lead to such a reinscription.

Still, Sappho's failure to draw Philaenis is not simply a problem of vision. Sappho's cry: "O cure this loving madness, and restore / me to me; thee, my half, my all, my more," returns us to the problems of agency raised by the image of the melting wax heart. Yet here that loss of selfhood occurs not because Sappho and Philaenis are the same, or because the loss of Philaenis has melted away all coherence, but because Philaenis exceeds Sappho in a way that seems to overwhelm: She is not just "all," she is "more." In the lines that follow, Sappho imagines that Philaenis's more-ness might make her akin to a celestial body, affording her power and influence over all mankind. This power might still be derived from likeness if we consider the popular microcosm/macrocosm tropes of the period, but it is also no longer human as it works on "all women" and "all men" on a galactic scale:

> So may thy cheeks' red outwear scarlet dye,
>   And their white, whiteness of the galaxy,
> So may thy mighty, amazing beauty move
>   Envy in all women, and in all men, love,
> And so be change, and sickness, far from thee,
>   As thou by coming near, keep'st them from me.[85]

The Philaenis who Sappho describes here is no longer the mortal woman that Sappho loves. Instead, Philaenis is both universal and immortal force and poetic creation. Sappho's act of writing, which is also Donne's act of writing, does not bring the two lovers back together bodily, and yet it does bring them "near" and hold them in relation.

Sappho's poem ultimately offers a possibility for queer union outside of the usual limits of time and space both through the metaphor of Philaenis as galaxy and through the poem itself, which offers both women a kind of afterlife. I call this union queer, not because it unites two women, but because it does so while abandoning the limits of biological time and space. Queerness can be read, as Jack Halberstam suggests, as "an outcome of strange temporalities, imaginative life schedules, and eccentric economic practices," and the poem embraces just such alternatives in its final moments.[86] Yet what kind of a union does Sappho achieve? By writing Philaenis as a galactic force, Sappho imagines a relationship between them which does not involve consent, mutuality, or even awareness on the part of Philaenis. It is also a relationship that is erotic only in the same way that devotion to a god or force of nature might be. Certainly, this relationship is not the one that Sappho wanted to regain at the beginning of the poem, and it seems doubtful that it could offer Sappho lasting satisfaction given the bodily interest in Philaenis that she expresses elsewhere. Further, since the poem is not actually Sappho's poem, but Donne's, we must also question the extent to which the possibility of queer union might be undercut by Donne's own identity and erotic sensibilities. Yet while the ending is not entirely satisfactory, it does provide an afterlife for Sappho's love, one achieved perhaps only through Sappho's failed attempt at wax magic or seduction through likeness.

Sappho's poetic enchantment, her wax magic, seems destined for failure or perhaps already abandoned by the end of the poem. Yet the possibility of wax magic still does important work. It makes visible the violence of impression and the uneasy relationship between desire, power, and force and also raises questions about whether any project of seduction is compatible with ideals of mutuality and equality since Sappho simply trades one shaping pressure for another. Still further, Sappho's allusion to the holy fire of verse asks us to consider if love poetry might always be a site for wax magic, given the history of wax tablets as a medium for amorous inscription and the shaping goals of all such poetic efforts, and to take seriously the possibility of poetry as enchantment and all the transformative power that invokes.

Thinking of Sappho and Ferdinand's projects as wax art and wax magic allows us to see them as both translative and transformative, at least in their ambitions. They both attempt to bridge the gap between their own desires and the world they inhabit and turn to wax in order to remake their realities. Despite the difference in genres, wax sculpture, wax theatrics, and wax poetics all work in similar ways, moving between subject and object in order to give form to the artist's vision and then again to transform their viewers, audience, readers, and targets. Thus, wax minds make wax art to invoke transformations in wax others and through it all, a certain shared malleability allows these connections to work. Further, such connections might always inhere in the production and consumption of art. Which is to say, that all art, not simply wax art, might seek to move us and succeed in moving us on the basis of similarity and sympathy.

At the same time, the shared qualities that link subjects and objects here also reveal the thingness of humans and the life of objects. The duchess and Philaenis occupy the positions of both subject and art object, and Ferdinand and Sappho find themselves unable to maintain the boundaries of selfhood. They can all be read as human-thing hybrids, perhaps as something akin to Donna Haraway's cyborgs.[87] So too can Ferdinand's tableaux, and Sappho's poem which each take on a kind of quasi-life beyond the control of their creator. We will take up the possibility of wax hybrids more fully in Chapter 6, but it is important to note here that the practices of wax art lead to and make visible these entities that occupy a middle space and whose boundaries may prove malleable.

NOTES

1. Giorgio Vasari, *Vasari on Technique. Being the Introduction to the Three Arts of Design, Architecture, Sculpture and Painting, Prefixed to the Lives of the Most Excellent Painters, Sculptors and Architects*, ed. G. Baldwin Brown, trans. Louisa Maclehose (New York: Dover Publications, 1960), 148. In the Italian: "Sogliono gli scultori, quando vogliono lavorare una figura di marmo, fare per quella un modello - che così si chiama -, cioè uno esemplo che è una figura di grandezza di mez[z]o braccio o meno o più secondo che gli torna comodo, o di terra o di cera o di stucco, purché e' possin mostrar in quella l'attitudine e la proporzione che ha da essere nella figura che e' voglion fare, cercando accomodarsi alla larghezza et alla altezza del sasso che hanno fatto cavare per farvela dentro" *Le Vite de' Piu Eccellenti Pittori Scultori e Architettori*, edizione Giuntina, vol. 1 (1568), 87.

2. Ibid., 149. In the Italian, "col giudicio e le mani lavorando," *Le Vite de' Piu Eccellenti Pittori Scultori e Architettori*, edizione Giuntina, vol. 1 (1568), 88.

3. Marco Boschini, "Ricche Minere Della Pittura Veneziana," in *Italy and Spain, 1600–1750; Sources and Documents*, eds. Robert Enggass and Jonathan Brown (Englewood Cliffs, NJ, 1970), 52. In Italian: "fanno volare le figure Humane." See Marco Boschini, *Le Ricche Minere Dell Pittura Venezia* (Venice, 1674), sig. e4r. See Introduction for more discussion of Tintoretto.

4. For discussions of the role of magic in early modern culture, see Bengt Akarloo and Stuart Clark, ed., *Witchcraft and Magic in Europe: The Period of the Witch Trials* (Philadelphia: University of Pennsylvania Press, 2002); Kathryn A. Edwards, "Introduction: What Makes Magic Everyday Magic," in *Everyday Magic in Early Modern Europe*, ed. Kathryn A. Edwards (Abingdon, UK: Routledge, 2016), 1–10. See also, Brian P. Levack, ed., *The Oxford Handbook of Witchcraft in Early Modern Europe and Colonial America* (Oxford: Oxford University Press 2013); David J. Collins, ed., *The Cambridge History of Magic and Witchcraft in the West: From Antiquity to the Present* (Cambridge: Cambridge University Press, 2015) for overviews of early modern magic and witchcraft.

5. For more on skepticism, see Kathleen Kamerick, "Shaping Superstition in Late Medieval England," in *Magic, Ritual and Witchcraft* 3, no. 1 (2008): 29–53. See also, Michael D. Bailey, "The Disenchantment of Magic: Spells, Charms, and Superstition in Early European Witchcraft Literature," *The American Historical Review* 111, no. 2 (2006): 383–404.

6. Stuart Clark, *Thinking with Demons: The Idea of Witchcraft in Early Modern Europe* (Oxford: Oxford University Press), viii.

7. Ibid.

8. For a discussion of the relationship between philosophy and magic in the period, see Ernst Cassirer, *The Individual and the Cosmos in Renaissance Philosophy*, trans. Mario Domandi (New York, 1964).

9. For further discussion of these possibilities, see Lynn Maxwell, "Wax Magic and *The Duchess of Malfi*," *The Journal for Early Modern Cultural Studies* 14, no. 3 (2014): 31–36.

10. At the same time, wax magic may also have been a useful material for witchcraft because of its importance in devotional practices, particularly within the Roman Catholic Church. From the vast numbers of candles that adorned Catholic churches and were lit to offer prayers, to the small wax figures or ex-votos left at shrines by parishioners when they prayed for heavenly intercession, and larger wax figures used by the church for ceremonial purposes, wax was a material that had strong associations with religious activity. See Brett Hirsch, "Three Wax Images, *Two Italian Gentlemen*, and One English Queen," in *Magical Transformations on the Early Modern English Stage*, eds. Lisa Hopkins and Helen Ostovitch (Routledge, 2014), 150. These associations matter since magic was often conceptualized as acts of "pure inversion." See Clark, *Thinking with Demons*, 13. In a Protestant country, such as England, this might have been even more true since Catholic practices themselves were outlawed, and thus the twisted versions of Catholic practices might seem doubly perverse. Wax magic then, while working through possibilities of likeness, might also be read as working in opposition to other, more orthodox uses of wax.

11. John Webster, *The Duchess of Malfi*, ed. Rene Weiss (Oxford, 1996), 4.1.116. All citations to the play are to act, scene, and line.

12. Ibid., 4.1.115.

13. Several critics have noted that these wax figures can be connected to the use of wax as a material for portraiture and funereal effigies and thus participate in a larger consideration of the role of art and memorialization in the play. See Michael Neill, *Issues of Death: Mortality and Identity in English Renaissance Tragedy* (Oxford, 1997), 340–41; David Bergeron, "The Wax Figures in *The Duchess of Malfi*," *SEL* 18 (1978): 331–39; Margaret Owens, "John Webster, Tussaud Laureate: The Waxworks in *The Duchess of Malfi*," *ELH* 79, no. 4 (2012): 851–77.

14. Webster, *Duchess of Malfi*, 4.1.111–115.

15. As Owens notes, critics have been unable to positively identify Vincentio Lauriola. See Owens, 862. See also R. G. Howarth, "Webster's Vincentio Lauriola," *Notes and Queries* 2 (1955): 99–100.

16. In this discussion of despair, I have in mind despair as a kind of spiritual death. Richard Burton's *The Anatomy of Melancholy* (Oxford: 1638), 693, discusses despair in this context.

17. Boschini, "Ricche Minere Della Pittura Veneziana," 52.

18. Webster, *Duchess of Malfi*, 4.1.56, 46.

19. Ibid., 4.1.68–69.

20. Ibid., 4.1.70–71.

21. Ibid., 4.1.72, 75–76.

22. Ibid., 4.1.74.

23. Ibid., 4.1.76–77.

24. Ibid., 4.1.80–85.

25. See Jean Kellaway, *The History of Torture and Execution: From Early Civilization Through Medieval Times to the Present* (Guilford, CT: Lyons Press, 2002), 56.

26. Elaine Scarry's *The Body in Pain: The Making and Unmaking of the World* (Oxford, 1987) theorizes the relationship between language and physical pain. Scarry suggests that "whatever pain achieves, it achieves in part through its unsharability, and it ensures that unsharability through its resistance to language" (4). The duchess's response suggests that mental pain could be theorized in similar terms. To describe her mental anguish, the duchess must resort to a series of metaphors, none of which prove sufficient alone.

27. A significant aspect of Ferdinand's torture is that he tricks the duchess into actively participating in it. She accepts the offered hand and kisses it. For further discussion on the duchess's active participation, see Hillary Nunn, *Staging Anatomies: Dissection and Spectacle in Early Stuart Tragedy*, 94.

28. Webster, *Duchess of Malfi*, 4.1.62–65.

29. Lynn Enterline and Brian Chalk both suggest the duchess's response to the wax figures as evidence that she might understand their true nature. See Lynn Enterline, *The Tears of Narcissus: Melancholia and Masculinity in Early Modern Writing* (Stanford, 1995), 271. See also Brian Chalk, "Webster's 'Worthyest Monument': The Problem of Posterity in *The Duchess of Malfi*," *Studies in Philology* 108, no. 3 (2011): 393–94.

30. Enterline, *Tears of Narcissus*, 271. In her reading of this scene, Enterline also suggests that Webster may be "attempt[ing] to invoke a blind transference of sympathetic, magical power in her 'direct' reaction to the theatrical tableau," 271.

31. Webster, *Duchess of Malfi*, 3.1.65–66.

32. Ibid., 3.1.66–68.

33. Ibid., 3.1.70–77.

34. Despite Ferdinand's rejection of magic, the play as a whole is more ambivalent, leaving open the possibility of the supernatural. Tricomi suggests the play demonstrates "the consequences of living in a world where the possibilities of spiritual intervention and demonic possession are continually in play," Albert Tricomi, "Historicizing the Imagery of the Demonic in *The Duchess of Malfi*," *Journal of Medieval and Early Modern Studies* 34, no. 2 (2004): 346. See also 345–72.

35. Katherine Rowe, *Dead Hands: Fictions of Agency, Renaissance to Modern* (Stanford, CA, 2000), 97–104.

36. Webster, *Duchess of Malfi*, 4.1.54–55.

37. Ibid., 4.2.24, 30.

38. Ibid., 4.2.31–34.

39. Ibid., 4.2.33–34.

40. For a further discussion of the alabaster funereal sculpture, see Neill, "Issues of Death," 338–41.

41. Webster, *Duchess of Malfi*, 4.2.206.

42. Ibid., 3.1.208–210.

43. Ibid., 3.1.5–7.

44. At first, the impact of the figures on the audience would be heightened by our ignorance of their true status as art within the world of the play. Critics have raised various theories about how the wax figures might have been staged in the seventeenth century. Some have suggested, for example, that the figures might have actually been made of wax by the same sculptor who made the funereal sculptures for Prince Henry. Yet the more plausible theory seems to be that the wax sculptures would have been played by actors in exactly the same way that corpses would have been. See Neill, *Issues of Death*, 339; David Bergeron, "The Restoration of Hermione in *The Winter's Tale*," *Shakespeare's Romances Reconsidered*, eds. Carol McGinnis Kay and Henry E. Jacobs (Lincoln, NE: University of Nebraska Press, 1978), 132.

45. A modern production could play with the obviousness of the materiality of the corpses through makeup, use of props, or actors, changing the audience's relationship to Ferdinand's spectacle.

46. Bergeron, "Wax Figures in *The Duchess of Malfi*," 335.

47. See Huston Diehl, *Staging Reform, Reforming the Stage: Protestantism and Popular Theater in Early Modern England* (Ithaca: Cornell University Press, 1997), especially 185.

48. Webster, *The Duchess of Malfi*, 4.2.248.

49. Even if the wax corpses are actually pieces of sculpture on the stage, it is still an analogous moment. The substitutions of actors for characters and live bodies for dead participate in the same network as the substitution of wax icon for corpse.

50. Presumably if the duchess knew that the corpses of her family were fake, she would still be moved. She would see the corpses as prefigurations of what would be and read them as wax magic, as witchcraft with the power to waste her family and through them herself. Her knowledge or lack of knowledge about the figures would change very little about how they impact her.

51. Ferdinand's desire to "plague[] in art" seems to anticipate Antonin Artaud in *The Theater and Its Double*, trans. Mary Caroline Richards, reprint edition (New York: Grove Press, 1994), where he posits "if the theater is like the plague, it is not only because it affects important collectivities and upsets them in and identical way. In the theater as in the plague there is something both victorious and vengeful," 27. Artaud's theater of cruelty, like Ferdinand's works on its audience in ways that are beyond rational comprehension.

52. John Donne, "Sappho to Philaenis," in *The Major Works*, ed. John Carey (Oxford, UK, 1990), 1–4. All citations to "Sappho to Philaenis" are to line number.

53. *Oxford English Dictionary*, s.v. 'enchant.'

54. Heather Meakin, *John Donne's Articulations of the Feminine* (Oxford: Oxford University Press, 1998), 113.

55. Ovid, *Metamorphoses*, trans. A. D. Melville, and E. J. Kenney (Oxford, 1986), 11.1–2. Citations are to book and line. In the Latin: "Carmine dum tali silvas animosque ferarum / Threicius vates et saxa sequentia ducit," Ovid, *Ovid IV: Metamorphoses, Books IX-XV*, ed. G. P. Goold, trans. Frank Justus Miller, Subsequent edition, Loeb Classical Library (Cambridge, MA: Harvard University Press, 1916).

56. Meakin, 113–14. Meakin also connects Sappho to Orpheus through their "unacceptably (homo)sexual bod[ies]" and by noting the connection both have to the island of Lesbos. For Meakin, Sappho's desire to "draw[] Nature's work, from Nature's law" references the discourse of unnaturalness that surrounded homosexuality in the early modern period.

57. We might read this line as drawing away from Nature's law or according to Nature's law. See the discussion around the ending of *Twelfth Night* in Chapter 2, and in Laurie Shannon, "Nature's Bias: Renaissance Homonormativity and Elizabethan Comic Likeness," *Modern Philology: A Journal Devoted to Research in Medieval and Modern Literature* 98, no. 2 (November 11, 2000): 207–8 for a discussion on how nature's law might be one of sameness.

58. Ovid, *Amores*, trans. in Raphael Lyne, "Lyrical Wax in Ovid, Marlowe, and Donne," in *Ovid and the Renaissance Body*, ed. Goran V. Stanivukovic (Toronto, 2001), 1.11.7–8, 13–14. Citation is to book, poem, and line. In the Latin: "accipe et ad dominam peraratas mane

tabellas /perfer et obstantes sedula pelle moras! / ... / .... / .... / ....
/ si quaeret quid agam, spe noctis vivere dices; /cetera fert blanda cera
notata manu."

59. Lyne, "Lyrical Wax," 193. Jenny C. Mann also takes up the question
of Ovid's wax and its connection to sixteenth century translations. See
Jenny C. Mann, "Marlowe's 'Slack Muse': *All Ovids Elegies* and an
English Poetics of Softness," *Modern Philology* 113, no. 1 (2015): 49–65.

60. For a further discussion of the relationship between Donne's poem and
Ovid's, see Elizabeth Harvey's *Ventriloquized Voices: Feminist Theory and
English Renaissance Texts* (London, 1995).

61. Donne, "Sappho to Philaenis," 9–12.

62. For a further discussion of sonnet 122, see the Introduction.

63. Shakespeare, Sonnet 122, 2, 13–14. Citation is to line.

64. Ibid., 1.

65. This comparison is complicated by the fact that Sappho and Philaenis are
both women and that elsewhere in the poem Sappho celebrates lesbian
erotics for not creating impressions, "of our dalliance no more signs there
are, / Than fishes leave in streams, or birds in air," 41–42. Still, Sappho's
description of her own wax heart as a location that has been stamped with
Philaenis's image suggests that some of the bodily connections between
writing on wax and seducing the body still figure.

66. Donne, "Sappho to Philaenis," 44–47.

67. Ibid., 7–8.

68. See Donne, "The Ecstasy," in *The Major Works*, ed. John Carey, reprint
(Oxford: Oxford University Press, 2000), 121.

69. Philip Sidney, Sonnet 1 of *Astrophil and Stella* in *The Major Works*, ed.
Katherine Duncan-Jones, 153, line 14.

70. Donne, "Sappho to Philaenis," 15–24.

71. Paula Blank, "Comparing Sappho to Philaenis: John Donne's
'Homopoetics,'" *PMLA: Publications of the Modern Language Association
of America* 110, no. 3 (1995): 361.

72. James Holstun, "'Will You Rent Our Ancient Love Asunder?' Lesbian
Elegy in Donne, Marvell, and Milton,' *English Literary History: ELH* 54:
840.

73. Donne, "Sappho to Philaenis," 59, 60.

74. Janel Mueller, "Troping Utopia: Donne's Brief for Lesbianism," in
Sexuality and Gender in Early Modern Europe: Institutions, Texts, Images,
ed. James Grantham Turner (Cambridge, UK, 1993), 182.

75. Donne, "Sappho to Philaenis," 35–42.

76. *Oxford English Dictionary*, s.v. "tillage."

77. Ibid.

78. Quintilian, *Institutes of Oratory or Education of an Orator*, trans. John Selby Watson (London, 1875), 284, 10.3.2.
79. Valerie Traub, *The Renaissance of Lesbianism in Early Modern England* (Cambridge, MA: 2002), 339.
80. Ibid.
81. Sarah Ahmed, *Queer Phenomenology: Orientations, Objects, Others* (Durham and London: Duke University Press, 2006), 2
82. Ahmed, *Queer Phenomenology*, 20.
83. Donne, "Sappho to Philaenis," 55–58.
84. Aristotle held that sense perception was a matter of impression, as we saw in the introduction, see Aristotle, "On the Soul," in *The Complete Works of Aristotle*, ed. Jonathan Barnes, 2 vols (Princeton, NJ, 1984), vol. 1, 424a18–424a23. Seventeenth-century philosophers articulated similar theories. Descartes, for example, claims in his "Rules for the Direction of the Mind," that "sense-perception occurs in the same way in which wax takes on an impression from a seal... thus in the eye, the first opaque membrane receives the shape impressed upon it by multi-coloured light," *The Philosophical Writings of Descartes*, trans. John Cottingham, Robert Stoothoff and Dugald Murdoch, 2 vols (Cambridge, UK, 1984), vol. 1, 40. In the Latin: "propriè tamen sentire per passionem tantùm, eâdem ratione quâ cera recipit figuram à sigillo... nempe primum opacum quod est in oculo, ita recipere figuram impressam ab illuminatione variis coloribus indutá," *Regulae ad directionem ingenii*, vol. 10, *Oevres de Descartes*, 412.
85. Donne, "Sappho to Philaenis," 58–64.
86. Jack (Judith) Halberstam, *In a Queer Time and Place: Transgender Bodies, Subcultural Lives* (New York and London: New York University Press, 2005), 1.
87. Donna Haraway, "A Cyborg Manifesto: Science, Technology, and Socialist-Feminism in the Late Twentieth Century," in *Simians, Cyborgs and Women: The Reinvention of Nature* (New York: Routledge, 1991), 147–81.

References

Ahmed, Sara. *Queer Phenomenology: Orientations, Objects, Others*. Durham and London: Duke University Press, 2006.
Akarloo, Bengt, and Stuart Clark, ed. *Witchcraft and Magic in Europe: The Period of the Witch Trials*. Philadelphia: University of Pennsylvania Press, 2002.
Aristotle. "On the Soul." In *The Complete Works of Aristotle: The Revised Oxford Translation*, edited by Jonathan Barnes, Vol. 1, 641–92. Princeton, NJ: Princeton University Press, 1984.

Artaud, Antonin. *The Theater and Its Double*. Translated by Mary Caroline Richards. New York: Grove Press, 1994.

Bailey, Michael D. "The Disenchantment of Magic: Spells, Charms, and Superstition in Early European Witchcraft Literature." *The American Historical Review* 111, no. 2 (2006): 383–404.

Bergeron, David. "The Restoration of Hermione in *The Winter's Tale*." In *Shakespeare's Romances Reconsidered*, edited by Carol Mcginnis Kay and Henry E. Jacobs. Lincoln: University of Nebraska Press, 1978.

Bergeron, David M. "The Wax Figures in The Duchess of Malfi." *Studies in English Literature, 1500–1900* 18, no. 2 (1978): 331–39.

Blank, Paula. "Comparing Sappho to Philaenis: John Donne's 'Homopoetics.'" *PMLA: Publications of the Modern Language Association of America* 110, no. 3 (May 1995): 358–68.

Boschini, Marco. "Ricche Minere Della Pittura Veneziana." In *Italy and Spain, 1600–1750: Sources and Documents; Compiled and Translated from the Italian and Spanish by Robert Enggass, Jonathan Brown*, edited by Robert Enggass and Jonathan Brown, 51–54. Englewood Cliffs, NJ: Prentice-Hall, 1970.

———. *Le ricche minere della pittura veneziana*. Venice: Appresso Francesco Nicolini, 1674.

Burton, Richard. *The Anatomy of Melancholy*. Oxford, 1638.

Cassirer, Ernst. *The Individual and the Cosmos in Renaissance Philosophy*. Translated by Mario Damandi. Philadelphia: University of Pennsylvania Press, 1963.

Chalk, Brian. "Webster's 'Worthyest Monument': The Problem of Posterity in *The Duchess of Malfi*." *Studies in Philology* 108, no. 3 (Summer 2011): 379–402.

Clark, Stuart. *Thinking with Demons: The Idea of Witchcraft in Early Modern Europe*. Oxford: Oxford University Press, 1999.

Collins, David J., ed., *The Cambridge History of Magic and Witchcraft in the West: From Antiquity to the Present*. Cambridge: Cambridge University Press, 2015.

Descartes, René. "Regulae ad directionem ingenii." In *Oeuvres de Descartes*, edited by Charles Adam and Paul Tannery, Vol. 10. Paris: L. Cerf, 1897.

———. "Rules for the Direction of the Mind." In *The Philosophical Writings of Descartes*, edited by John Cottingham, Dugald Murdoch, and Robert Stoothoff, Vol. 1, 7–78. Cambridge, UK: Cambridge University Press, 1985.

Diehl, Huston. *Staging Reform, Reforming the Stage: Protestantism and Popular Theater in Early Modern England*. Ithaca: Cornell University Press, 1997.

Donne, John. "The Ecstasy." In *The Major Works*, edited by John Cary, 121–22. Oxford and New York: Oxford World Classics, 1990.

———. "Sappho to Philaenis." In *The Major Works*, edited by John Cary, 65–67. Oxford and New York: Oxford World Classics, 1990.

Edwards, Kathryn A. "Introduction: What Makes Magic Everyday Magic." In *Everyday Magic in Early Modern Europe*, edited by Kathryn A. Edwards, 1–10. Abingdon, UK: Routledge, 2016.

Enterline, Lynn. *The Tears of Narcissus: Melancholia and Masculinity in Early Modern Writing*. 1 edition. Stanford, CA: Stanford University Press, 1995.

Halberstam, J. Jack. *In a Queer Time and Place: Transgender Bodies, Subcultural Lives*. 1st US Edition 1st Printing edition. New York: New York University Press, 2005.

Haraway, Donna. "A Cyborg Manifesto: Science, Technology, and Socialist-Feminism in the Late Twentieth Century." In *Simians, Cyborgs, and Women: The Reinvention of Nature*, 149–82. New York: Routledge, 1991.

Harvey, Elizabeth D. *Ventriloquized Voices: Feminist Theory and English Renaissance Texts*. London: Routledge, 1992.

Hirsch, Brett. "Three Wax Images, Two Italian Gentlemen, and One English Queen." In *Magical Transformations on the Early Modern English Stage*, edited by Lisa Hopkins and Helen Ostovich, 155–68. London: Routledge, 2014.

Holstun, James. "'Will You Rent Our Ancient Love Asunder?' Lesbian Elegy in Donne, Marvell, and Milton." *ELH* 54, no. 4 (Winter 1987): 835–67.

Howarth, R. G. "Webster's Vincentio Lauriola." *Notes and Queries* 2 (1955): 99–100.

Kamerick, Kathleen. "Shaping Superstition in Late Medieval England." *Magic, Ritual, and Witchcraft* 3, no. 1 (2008): 29–53.

Kellaway, Jean. *The History of Torture and Execution: From Early Civilization Through Medieval Times to the Present*. 1st edition. Guilford, CT: Lyons Press, 2002.

Levack, Brian P., ed., *The Oxford Handbook of Witchcraft in Early Modern Europe and Colonial America*. Oxford: Oxford University Press, 2013.

Lyne, Raphael. "Lyrical Wax in Ovid, Marlowe, and Donne." In *Ovid and the Renaissance Body*, edited by Goran V. Stanivukovic, 191–206. Toronto, ON: University of Toronto Press, 2001.

Mann, Jenny C. "Marlowe's 'Slack Muse': All Ovids Elegies and an English Poetics of Softness." *Modern Philology: Critical and Historical Studies in Literature, Medieval Through Contemporary* 113, no. 1 (August 2015): 49–65.

Maxwell, Lynn. "Wax Magic and *The Duchess of Malfi*." *The Journal for Early Modern Cultural Studies* 14, no. 3 (2014): 31–36.

Meakin, Heather L. *John Donne's Articulations of the Feminine*. 1st edition. Oxford and New York: Clarendon Press, 1999.

Mueller, Janel. "Troping Utopia: Donne's Brief for Lesbianism." In *Sexuality and Gender in Early Modern Europe: Institutions, Texts, Images*, edited by

James Grantham Turner, 182–207. Cambridge: Cambridge University Press, 1993.

Neill, Michael. *Issues of Death: Mortality and Identity in English Renaissance Tragedy*. Oxford: Clarendon Press, 1997.

Nunn, Hillary M. *Staging Anatomies: Dissection and Spectacle in Early Stuart Tragedy*. Aldershot, UK: Ashgate, 2005.

Ovid. *Metamorphoses*. Edited by E. J. Kenney. Translated by A. D. Melville. Oxford: Oxford University Press, 1998.

———. *Ovid III: Metamorphoses, Books I–VIII*. Edited by G. P. Goold. Translated by Frank Justus Miller. 3rd edition. Loeb Classical Library. Cambridge, MA: Harvard University Press, 1984.

———. *Ovid IV: Metamorphoses, Books IX–XV*. Edited by G. P. Goold. Translated by Frank Justus Miller. Subsequent edition. Loeb Classical Library. Cambridge, MA: Harvard University Press, 1916.

Owens, Margaret E. "John Webster, Tussaud Laureate: The Waxworks in *The Duchess of Malfi*." *ELH* 79, no. 4 (n.d.): 851–77.

Quintilian. *Quintilian's Institutes of Oratory; or, Education of an Orator*. Translated by John Selby Watson. London: G. Bell and Sons, 1875.

———. *The Institutio Oratoria of Quintilian*. Translated by Harold Edgeworth Butler. Vol. 4. Loeb Classical Library. Cambridge, MA: Harvard University Press, 1920.

Rowe, Katherine. *Dead Hands: Fictions of Agency, Renaissance to Modern*. Stanford, CA: Stanford University Press, 1999.

Scarry, Elaine. *The Body in Pain: The Making and Unmaking of the World*. 1 edition. Oxford: Oxford Paperbacks, 1987.

Shakespeare, William. "The Sonnets and 'A Lover's Complaint.'" In *The Norton Shakespeare*, edited by Stephen Greenblatt, Walter Cohen, Jean E. Howard, and Katherine Eisaman Maus, 1915–90. New York: W. W. Norton, 1997.

Shannon, Laurie. "Nature's Bias: Renaissance Homonormativity and Elizabethan Comic Likeness." *Modern Philology: A Journal Devoted to Research in Medieval and Modern Literature* 98, no. 2 (November 2000): 183–210.

Sidney, Philip. "Astrophil and Stella." In *Sir Philip Sidney: The Major Works*, edited by Katherine Duncan-Jones, Reissue edition, 153–211. Oxford: Oxford University Press, 2009.

Traub, Valerie. *The Renaissance of Lesbianism in Early Modern England*. Cambridge, UK: Cambridge University Press, 2002.

Tricomi, Albert. "Historicizing the Imagery of the Demonic in *The Duchess of Malfi*." *Journal of Medieval and Early Modern Studies* 34, no. 2 (2004): 345–72.

Vasari, Giorgio. *Vasari on Technique. Being the Introduction to the Three Arts of Design, Architecture, Sculpture and Painting, Prefixed to the Lives of the Most*

Excellent Painters, Sculptors and Architects. Edited by G. Baldwin Brown. Translated by Louisa Maclehose. New York: Dover Publications, 1960.

———. *Le Vite de' Piu Eccellenti Pittori Scultori e Architettori*. Vol. 1. 6 vols. Florence, 1568.

Webster, John. "The Duchess of Malfi." In *The Duchess of Malfi and Other Plays*, edited by Rene Weiss. Oxford: Oxford University Press, 2009.

CHAPTER 6

Wax Hybrids: Re-thinking Subjects and Objects in Ovid, Paré, Descartes, and Spenser

As we saw in Chapter 5, wax is caught up in projects of artistic creation. From Tintoretto's models to Ferdinand's sculptures and Sappho's poetic efforts, wax has proven an apt material for modeling forms and particularly human forms. Yet at the same time, as we have seen throughout this book, wax also models subjects. In doing so, it collapses the boundaries between male and female, exterior and interior, body and mind, suggesting that these distinctions might not be material. To be a wax human means to be inscribable, relational, changeable, vulnerable, and enmeshed in a material world which has transformative power. The self constituted in wax is open to revision and yet, as we saw in *Hamlet*, simultaneously resistant to erasure. Wax as a material has a certain stickiness, an intransigence, which allows it to function as more than a metaphor or a model of malleability, a thingness, which prevents it from disappearing into the human even as it models it. This is even more true, if we infuse wax with Cavendish's vitalism, as we saw in Chapter 4, and take seriously the possibility that wax might shape itself. Reading the metaphorical, philosophical, and cultural deployments of wax in the early modern period in relation to early modern selfhood, we discover a medium, material, and location where the distinction between thing and human gives way. Thus, paying attention to wax in the period reveals an early modern posthumanism, a vision of the self as, in Jane Bennett's words, "an impure, human-nonhuman assemblage."[1]

© The Author(s) 2019   167
L. M. Maxwell, *Wax Impressions, Figures, and Forms in Early Modern Literature*, Early Modern Cultural Studies 1500–1700, https://doi.org/10.1007/978-3-030-16932-9_6

While posthumanism has been used to describe a wide range of scholarly commitments, the kind of posthumanism I have in mind here is not that of "object-oriented" scholarship.[2] Nor does it lead toward "thinking a concept of life that is foundationally, and not incidentally, a nonhuman or unhuman concept of life."[3] While it would be interesting to ask how a block of wax might conceive life that does not seem of particular concern to the early modern authors and artists under consideration. Instead, they use wax in ways that prefigure a posthumanist criticism that sees the collapse of a distinction between thing and human as a vehicle for re-examining the subject together with its thingness. Bennett's subject as impure assemblage, Katherine N. Hayles's subject as "amalgam, a collection of heterogeneous components, a material-informational entity whose boundaries undergo continuous construction and reconstruction,"[4] and Rosa Braidotti's subject as "a relational subject constituted in and by multiplicity, that is to say a subject that works across differences and is also internally differentiated, but still grounded and accountable," share the most affinity with the waxy human we have been exploring.[5]

In this chapter, I will take up early modern engagements with prosthetics and automata. These categories play with the same possibilities of human-thing hybrids that I have just suggested lie at the heart of many early modern engagements with wax. Yet what might be implicit in the metaphor of self as writing tablet becomes explicit when early modern authors imagine building prosthetics or inhabiting a world peopled by non-peoples. Early modern discourse about such possibilities reveals both considerable excitement and anxiety around the possibilities of supplementing or supplanting the human and what it might mean to treat the self as a thing—as fixable, augmentable, and re-creatable—rather than divine. While wax is not a material of either prosthetics or automata, we find that it again serves to model their possibilities and limitations. Thus, in Ovid's *Metamorphoses* and its early modern retellings, Descartes' *Meditations*, and Spenser's *The Faerie Queene*, wax is embedded in the possibilities of human supplements and supplanters, prosthetics and automata, and the possibility of the wax human again troubles the stability and integrity of the human as such.

6.1   Dreaming Prosthetics

In Ovid's *Metamorphoses*, as the title reminds us, transformation and change are to be expected. Yet two myths in particular foreground the intersection of art and the human: the myth of Daedalus and Icarus, and that of Pygmalion. We can read the first as a fantasy about the power and limits of human supplementation, and the second as an exploration of human supplantation. Both myths and their early modern deployments rely on wax as a material that bridges the gap between human and thing. Yet as a bridge, wax proves vulnerable, revealing a cultural anxiety around such projects and troubling, once again, the dividing line between the two.

In the myth of Daedalus and Icarus, wax literally bridges human and thing, creating a hybrid capable of superhuman feats. Daedalus, desperate to escape Crete, undertakes a project in the "unimagined arts" that will "alter[] nature's laws,"[6] and allow him and his son to fly away from their island prison. The "unimagined arts" prove to be prosthetic wings, carefully crafted in his workshop:

> Row upon row of feathers he arranged,
> The smallest first, then larger ones, to form
> A growing graded shape, as rustic pipes
> Rise in a gradual slope of lengthening reeds;
> Then bound in the middle and the base with wax
> And flaxen threads, and bent them, so arranged,
> Into a gentle curve to imitate
> Wings of a real bird.[7]

Wax proves crucial to this project, serving as the glue that holds the wings together and allows humans to use feathers and pipes as instruments of flight. At the same time, as a material of sculpture and imitation, wax also represents the project, emphasizing the artfulness of Daedalus's creation and the extent to which it relies on copying the "wings of a real bird," and rendering nature in art. Thus, both literally and conceptually wax provides the link between art and nature, thing and human.

With the wings attached, Icarus and Daedalus seem to become new creatures. Once they are in flight, Ovid muses:

> An angler fishing with his quivering rod
> A lonely shepherd propped upon his crook,
> A ploughman leaning on his plough, looked up
> And gazed in awe, and thought they must be gods
> That they could fly...[8]

The angler, shepherd, and ploughman, each engaged in their daily activities, give perspective to the flight of Icarus and Daedalus through their awe.[9] From their perspective on the ground, the two figures seem to "be gods" because their abilities transcend those of man. Viewed from below, the wings would appear as organic extensions of Icarus and Daedalus, rather than as separate apparatuses. While to a certain extent this transformation is optical illusion, the two travelers are more than human as they fly across the sky insofar as they have access to abilities beyond those normally afforded to man and have successfully extended their bodies to include the artful wings. They are human-thing hybrids and their successful flight both optically and substantively erases the boundary between body and prosthesis so long as survival can only be ensured by the continued commingling of nature and art, body and prosthesis.

Of course, the myth does not end there. Instead, once in flight:

> ...[T]he boy
> Began to enjoy his thrilling flight and left
> His guide to roam the ranges of the heavens,
> And soared too high. The scorching sun so close
> Softened the fragrant wax that bound his wings;
> The wax melted; his waving arms were bare;
> Unfledged, they had no purchase in the air![10]

When the wax adhesive melts, the wings fail Icarus, leaving his "waving arms bare" as he falls to his death. All of the other materials used in the construction of the wings cease to matter as Ovid relays the wings' failure. It is the wax that changes, melts away, and causes the wings to fail. Without wax to bridge the gap between humanity and art, what is left is waving arms with "no purchase in the air," a body's last grasp for life. If the wax wings create human-thing hybrids, their melting leaves nothing but death. By propelling the human out of the realm of humanity and into the skies, the prosthetic wings change Icarus forever.

Yet what is the relationship of this wax hybrid, this winged boy, to the child that played in his father's studio? There, Icarus, ignorant of the danger that awaits him:

> … plays with his peril, tries to catch
> Feathers that float upon the wandering breeze,
> Or softens with his thumb the yellow wax.[11]

The pressure of Icarus's thumb on the wax suggests again man's power to give form, invent, and perform "wondrous work."[12] As much as the wax wings are an artificial addition, they also seem already a part of the boy and a part of what it means to be human in that they represent both Daedalus' faculties of creation and Icarus's propensity to play. The boy with wax wings who soars too close to the sun "thrilling" in his flight is the same boy that "plays with his peril" in the studio, and perhaps even in the studio he is already a hybrid, a composite of fleshy materials and wax dreams. Of course this passage serves to warn the reader of the impending tragedy, reminding us of the softness of wax and the vulnerabilities of thing, human, and hybrid alike, but in doing so it casts doubt on boundaries between these categories.

Undoubtedly, Icarus's tragic plunge into the sea attaches to a cultural anxiety about transgressively overstepping the bounds of the human body. On a simple level, Icarus falls because he literally flies too high and the wax melts. Yet the mythic importance of his flight and fall cannot be simply reduced to the fact that the sun melts wax. The myth has endured not as a lesson that engineers should be more careful in choosing their materials, but as a subtler warning about the need to limit human invention, and circumscribe human activities. Ovid clearly suggests that something about the flight of Icarus or Daedalus's project of creating prosthetic wings is transgressive, yet exactly how they overstep human bounds is more ambiguous. Perhaps the transgression is Daedalus's initial project of setting aside the "nature's laws" and enabling flight, perhaps the transgression is Icarus's propensity to play and be led by desire into abandoning the middle way prescribed by his father, or perhaps both father and son transgress when they actually take to the air. Yet Ovid leaves ambiguous the exact action that leads to Icarus' downfall, and as a result, the myth itself is not (simply) didactic. Instead, it raises questions about the boundaries between art, desire, and transgression and between human, supplement, and hybrid.[13]

If we look at early modern retellings of Ovid's myth, we find that sixteenth- and seventeenth-century translations and adaptations offer a range of possible lessons for the myth and do not necessarily attach it to worries about the limits of the human body or the possibility of prostheses. For example, in the prefatory poem to Arthur Golding's 1567 translation, he holds Daedalus up as an example of ingenuity in the face of hardship, or of how "streight distresse / Dooth make men wyse."[14] Far from being faulted for his willingness to overstep the natural of things, Daedalus is applauded for his "desyre[] too bee at libertie" and his ability to act on that desire.[15] Icarus, on the other hand, is admonished for "disobedience" and his lack of foresight.[16] He is an example of "how good it is to bee / In meane estate and not too clymb too hygh."[17] Here, "meane" suggests "occupying a middle or intermediate place."[18] Thus, for Golding, Icarus's flight is transgressive because he abandons the middle way, disregarding his father's warning, not because flight itself is forbidden to man. By applauding Daedalus and faulting Icarus, Golding suggests that art is not the problem at all.

However, Golding's text is, in many ways, an exception. More commonly, early modern texts attach the myth to warnings about the dangers of intellectual curiosity, as can be seen in early modern emblem books.[19] As Carlo Ginzburg has shown, in "High and Low: The Theme of Forbidden Knowledge in the Sixteenth and Seventeenth Centuries," illustrations of the myth in such books were often accompanied by the Pauline motto "noli altum sapere," and its vulgate translations, which ranged from the "be not high minded" of the *King James Bible* to the "non volere sapere le chose alte" or "do not seek to know high things" of Nicolò Malermi's Italian translation of the Bible.[20] Ginzburg traces the motto itself through the centuries, suggesting that in its original context the words "noli altum sapere" were intended to condemn moral pride. However, as a result of loose translation techniques and increasing decontextualization, the phrase came to serve primarily as warning against the pursuit of dangerous knowledge by the sixteenth and seventeenth centuries.[21] It may be that in the association of Icarus with these Pauline mottos, the myth experiences the same slippage in meaning as Ginzburg posits for the Pauline motto itself, coming to stand as a warning against the pursuit of knowledge, where it first stood as a warning against pride. Regardless of whether such slippage occurs, these emblem books suggest again that Daedalus's art is transgressive for reaching beyond the limits of what is properly human. What seemed in Ovid to be a warning against transgressing bodily limits instead becomes about the limits of human knowledge and power, and the fear that man's creative power might take something from the gods.

The boundaries between transgressive art, transgressive knowing, and transgressive bodies begin to lose distinction in these interpretations of the myth as does the value of Daedalus's creative capacity. Wax participates in that blending, representing the overreaching intellect, the artful creations of that intellect, and the redemptive possibilities of both. We can see this multiplicity in Emblem 104 of Andrea Alciato's *Emblematum Libellus*,[22] which translates:

> Wax melting made you, Icarus, while you were flying aloft, fall headlong into the sea. Now the same wax and the burning fire revive you, to teach with your example a well-defined truth. Let the astrologer beware of making predictions, for the impostor, while flying over the stars, will fall headlong to the earth.[23]

For Alciato, wax occupies the nominative case; it becomes the central performer of the action, making Icarus fall and reviving him. Wax is responsible for the fall because it melts, but perhaps also because it represents the project of constructing wings, and of dreaming up such a project in the first place. Wax allows Icarus to become an "imposter" and perhaps also, insofar as it represents the human mind, allows the astrologer to make "predictions" and trespass on the realm of the divine. Transgressive art, transgressive bodies, and transgressive minds become one in the figure of the imposter modeled in wax.

At the same time, Alciato insists on wax's redemptive possibilities, claiming "now the same wax and burning fire revive you." If we trace the poem back to its source in *The Greek Anthology*, an epigram by Julianus known as "On a Bronze Statue of Icarus which stood in a Bath," this rebirth begins to make sense.[24] In Julianus's poem, he tells the statue, "now by wax the worker in bronze has restored thee to thy shape," referring to the artistic process of lost wax casting.[25] A second epigram by Julianus, immediately following the first, treats Icarus's new bronze materiality ironically, exhorting the statue, "remember thou art of bronze, and let neither art nor the pair of wings on thy shoulders delude thee; for if, when alive, thou didst fall into the depths of the sea, how canst thou wish to fly when formed of bronze?"[26] For Julianus, the new life provided to Icarus is the life of a statue, a life governed by the material limits of bronze.

Yet by erasing any references to bronze and statues from his own text, Alciato offers Icarus a life that is not so materially bound, even while he connects that life to wax. Detached from the specific connotations of statue making, the combination of wax and fire might suggest a whole network of possibilities around writing itself. Since wax is both a material of writing and one that facilitates reading through illumination, we might read Alciato as suggesting that wax offers Icarus a new life within his book. Such a possibility is further strengthened by the connection of fire with the creative process that we discussed in Chapter 5. The connections between wax and writing help allow the wax in Alciato's poem to become a material of creativity beyond the specific process of casting bronze statues or fashioning of Icarus's wings.

If Alciato's poem ascribes a doubleness to wax that troubles an easy reading of the myth, I would argue that doubleness was always there. The same wax destroys Icarus and offers him new life as a mythic figure who circulates broadly through time and space. What starts as a warning about the limits of human art becomes a vehicle for new creations—in wax, in bronze, in ink, in paint, and in the mind of the artist who has not yet given his thought material form. The wax transforms Icarus and reveals that nothing about the boy has changed, other than the stakes of his play. Indeed, the wax prostheses that aid his flight are not so different from the wax tablets that aid our thought, and those tablets are not so different from the wax minds upon which we write our experience or our experience writes us. We can understand the body, with N. Katherine Hayles, "as the original prosthesis we all learn to manipulate, so that extending or replacing the body with other prostheses becomes a continuation of a process that began before we were born."[27] If we do so, the myth becomes not about the danger of the prosthesis, or of the human augmented by art, but simply about the danger of being human, with all its wax possibilities.

If Icarus's wings are only myth, their wax possibilities animate the actual early modern use of prosthetics, albeit in a more tempered form, as we can see in the early modern English and Latin translations of Ambroise Paré's *Works*.[28] In talking of Icarus's wings, we have been talking about the prosthetic as supplement, as an addition that promises new form and new capacity to the human body. Daedalus does not devise the wings to replace damaged limbs, but to give himself and his son the power of flight. According to The *Works*, however, a surgeon's goal should be to fix what is broken and "repair[] those things which are defective, either from infancy, or afterwards by accident, as much as Art and Nature will suffer."[29] Here, the text limits the scope of the surgeon's intervention and in so doing reveals a certain conception of the appropriate limits of human art. Yet at the same time in order for a surgeon to do his work of restoration, he has to see the body as an object that can be molded, as a place for art and ingenuity to act, and as material that can be imitated. We can see this attitude when the *Works* explains, for example, that after the loss of an eye, "you may put another eye artificially made of gold or silver, counterfeited and enameled, so that it may seem to have the brightnesse, or gemmie decency of the naturall eye, into the place of the eye that is so lost."[30] The best artificial eye is one that imitates a real one down to its "brightnesse, or gemmie decency." While wax might not be the material of artificial eyes, I would suggest that it symbolizes the blending of art and nature, and the artful possibilities that come with re-making the human form. Thus, when a surgeon tries to craft an artificial eye that will have the same "gemmie decency" as a natural eye, he is pushing the limits of surgery and art in ways made possible by wax.

6.2   ANIMATING ALLEGORIES

While Ovid's Icarus myth can provide us with insight into attitudes about early modern prosthetics, his "Pygmalion" invites us to consider animate things and how they might matter within the early modern cultural imagination, and again, to do so through wax. In the myth, a sculptor falls in love with his own creation, and Venus, pitying him, grants his prayer and gives the statue life. The statue transitions from immobile ivory to breathing flesh in a moment figured through wax. As the sculptor kisses her and touches her breast, her ivory hardness:

> ... Yield[s] to his hands, as in the sun
> Wax of Hymettus softens and is shaped
> By practised fingers into many forms.[31]

In many ways, this is a fantasy of male creation and domination—Pygmalion's statue is shaped in the image of his desires and gains life while fulfilling them. She yields to his hands even as she gains flesh, raising the question of whether she gains any capacity for agency in the transformation. What are we supposed to make of statue turned wife? The only sign of selfhood offered up is a blush, before the poet tells us of their marriage and that,

> when nine times the crescen moon had filled
> Her silver orb, and infant girl was born,
> Paphos, from whom the island takes its name[32]

The wax woman waxed with the moon and, in perhaps the most waxen act of reproduction imaginable, bore a child.

Pygmalion's wife bears a relation to the cyborg theorized by Donna Haraway.[33] Where Haraway positions the cyborg in relation to animals and machines, and claims them as a particularly modern phenomenon, with "no origin story in the Western sense,"[34] Pygmalion's wife's marble/wax/flesh hybridity provides her with a similar hybridity and ability to trouble the limits of the human.[35] Her created nature and threshold existence invite comparison to other real and imagined early modern automata and related constructions, and raise the question of whether the line between science fiction (or its early modern equivalents of myth and allegory) and social reality might have been as much an illusion in the sixteenth and seventeenth centuries as Haraway claims they are today.[36] Which is to say Pygmalion's wife, together with the other denizens of this chapter, continues to suggest that the boundaries between human and thing are unstable, that they are particularly unstable around women, and that the blurring of boundaries might be best understood through wax. Again, wax does not enter the story because it is the obvious material for creating either magical figures or automata. And yet, wax, as we will see, becomes a material associated with these possibilities, not only in Ovid, but also in the writings of both René Descartes and Edmund Spenser, perhaps because of its capacity to model mind, body, and reproduction, begins to model humanity itself. Indeed, if Joseph Campana is right that "the human lacks definition, experiences a radical plasticity, and as a consequence tends toward imitation," then wax might be the best material for modeling the human in all its malleability.[37]

Pygmalion's wife is visible in the *Metamorphoses* only for the brief moments of her creation and entry into the world of reproduction, and then she and her past as statuary are left behind as the poem churns on. We can only imagine the extent of her transformation and whether she would have passed in society. Yet her entrance into wife and mother-hood suggests that she would have—for what more is asked of women? The possibility of statues walking the streets, of fake people passing as real, is not a worry of *The Metamorphoses*, but it is of both Descartes' *Meditations* and Spenser's *Faerie Queene* and in both that possibility is raised around wax and automata.

Descartes' "Second Meditation" famously takes up wax in order to explain the limits of human knowledge and affirm his declaration, "I think therefore I am."[38] As I discussed in the introduction, wax proves an apt material for his investigation because it seems to change on every sensory register and yet is still "the same wax."[39] For Descartes, this sameness despite apparent change leads him to conclude that we can-not know wax through our senses, but only through our mind, which in turn leads him to the claim that the mind is the only knowable object, "every consideration whatsoever which contributes to my perception of wax, or of any other body, cannot but establish even more effectively the nature of my own mind."[40] This meditation on the nature of wax returns Descartes to the priority of the thinking mind as the object of knowledge. Yet importantly for this chapter, the meditation does not end there, nor does Descartes abandon wax. Instead, he uses wax to raise the question of how one might know that men are men and not automata. He writes:

> We say that we see the wax itself, if it is there before us, not that we judge
> it to be there from its colour or shape; and this might lead me to conclude
> without more ado that knowledge of the wax comes from what the eye
> sees, and not from the scrutiny of the mind alone. But then if I look out
> of the window and see men crossing the square, as I just happen to have
> done, I normally say that I see the men themselves, just as I say that I see
> the wax. Yet do I see any more than hats and coats which could conceal
> automatons? I *judge* that they are men. And so something which I thought
> I was seeing with my eyes is in fact grasped solely by the faculty of judge-
> ment which is in my mind.[41]

Descartes moves from his discussion of wax to a discussion of automata because he is "almost tricked by ordinary ways of talking" into saying that he "see[s] the wax itself" when, in reality, he is only judging that what is before him is wax.[42] The difference between seeing and judg-ing here triggers his turn to automata, a turn that is both striking and disturbing because the shift from wax to people underscores the divide between subject and object: The thinking subject only knows his own reality and can only judge the nature of objects, even when those objects might be other people.

Descartes' supposition that what he sees from the window might simply be "hats and cloaks which could conceal automatons" is certainly more rhetorically motivated than real. Yet to his readers, such machines would not have seemed utterly implausible. After all, while sixteenth- and seventeenth-century craftsmen could not create machines sophisticated enough to pass as people under careful scrutiny, they were making automata sufficiently complex to engender wonder and delight. Leonardo da Vinci is credited with crafting a flying bird automaton and a lion that walked, stood, and roared. He also designed a robot using a pulley system.[43] Gianello Torriano built a knight automaton and is also believed to have crafted a small clockwork monk for the Holy Roman Emperor Charles V. When wound up, the monk not only walked in a square, but also raised and lowered a cross in his left hand, moved his head back and forth, and mouthed a prayer. Other mechanical curiosities of the time include a miniature coach and horses designed for Louis the XIV.[44] All of these automata display complicated movements and intricate designs and suggest the creative power of humankind. Primarily curiosities for royal courts and the very rich, these automata suggested that art could mimic the motion of nature, and that the current limitations of machines could be overcome.[45] Artificial machines that could be mistaken for human when viewed from above, especially when covered by hats and cloaks, were not beyond the technological possibilities of the day. While early modern automata could not pass as human in the same way that Pygmalion's wife could pass as human, responding to his touch and offering the promise of reproduction, the gap between these machines and Venus's animation of the Pygmalion statue is not so great as it might seem. For the early modern thinker, both types of nonhuman lay just at the edge of possibility; since most viewers of these mechanical beings did not understand the mechanics of their movement, they were regarded as almost magical themselves.[46]

For Descartes, however, the possibility of automata on the street leads him not to magic, but to the mechanism of organic life. In a letter to Henry More, he writes:

> [S]ince art copies nature, and people can make various automatons which move without thought, it seems reasonable that nature should produce its own automatons, which are more splendid than artificial ones — namely the animals.[47]

Here, human art and ingenuity, our capacity to "make various automatons," invite us to imagine the existence of the same in nature.[48] Indeed, it makes the existence of natural automata "reasonable," by which Descartes means highly plausible. When Descartes suggests that animals might be automata, he means that they might move without possessing a mind, that "bones, nerves, muscles, animal spirits and other organs" might "give rise to all the movements we observe in animals."[49] He extends that mechanism even to the human body, which he explains, in his "Discourse on the Method," should be understood as "a machine which, having been made by the hands of God, is incomparably better ordered than any machine that can be devised by man, and contains in itself movements more wonderful than those in any such machine."[50] For Descartes, only our minds (and perhaps our souls) make us different from the animals.

Yet the existence of any mind, other than one's own, is for Descartes almost impossible to prove. Still, in "Discourse on the Method," he offers his own early modern Turing test. Taking up the possibility of human automata, he imagines how one might differentiate between humans and "machines [which] bore a resemblance to our bodies and imitated our actions as closely as possible for all practical purposes."[51] Such machines would reveal their natures through failures of language and performance. Descartes explains:

> we can certainly conceive of a machine so constructed that it utters words and even utters words which correspond to bodily actions causing a change in its organs (e.g. if you touch it in one spot it asks what you want of it, if you touch it in another it cries out that you are hurting it, and so on). But it is not conceivable that such a machine should produce different arrangements of words so as to give an appropriately meaningful answer to whatever is said in its presence, as the dullest of men can do. Secondly, even though such machines might do some things as well as we do them, or perhaps even better, they would inevitably fail in others, which would reveal that they were acting not through understanding but only from the disposition of their organs.[52]

Descartes takes seriously the possibility of very sophisticated machines that could mimic mankind almost perfectly. Yet these machines would be recognizable as imitations to any careful interlocutor because their capacity to respond to human speech would be limited, as would their ability to fully perform the full range of actions of which the human body is capable. While neither of these tests resolve the problem of the passerby, who can neither be carefully questioned nor observed, they begin to suggest the line that might be drawn between human and machine.

While wax might not be central to Descartes' consideration of automata, it haunts it. Wax's associations, as a material of replication and art, a material associated with both mind and body, and the material that models Descartes' attempts to divide subject from object, make logical the transition from wax to automata in *The Meditations*. Further, wax's flexibility—its ability to change shape and form—seems also to model the distinctions between machine and man that Descartes attempts to draw out in his "Discourse." Producing language and moving like a person are not sufficient proofs of humanity, but doing so flexibly and fluidly, might be.

In Spenser's *Faerie Queene*, wax actually does become the material of an automaton, or at least the material of a magical replica that function in many ways like an automaton, imitating human forms and actions to pass as a person. The question of personhood in *The Faerie Queene* is of course fraught from the beginning. The poem is as Spenser himself terms it "a continued Allegory, or darke conceit."[53] As such, none of the characters within the poem are intended to be exactly human. They stand not for complete people, but for particular virtues and vices, or for some combination of attributes that can be infused with allegorical meaning. Yet as Jonathan Goldberg suggests, these characters "are not themselves exactly singular, fetched as they are from so many anticipatory models, modeled as they are on real persons and fictional ones, divided and reassembled out of parts that are not always themselves self-identical."[54] Spenser's characters resist being quickly and irreducibly flattened into allegorical figures, yet they also never cease being allegorical. Amidst these allegorical humans (among whom I would include those of mixed fairy-human and god-human birth) are two entities that are created by artificial means, the false Florimell, made of wax, snow, and feathers, and Talus, comprised of iron. Spenser uses these two figures to question the nature of personhood.

We are first introduced to the false Florimell (and the true one), in Book III of *The Faerie Queene*, the book that deals with "Chastity, / That fayrest vertue, fare aboue the rest."[55] Since the false Florimell is a figure who is associated with art from the moment of her creation to that of her destruction, I want to pause over the opening of Book III, where Spenser raises the question of art and the truth of art together with the virtue of chastity. Spenser proclaims that the best example of chastity is Queen Elizabeth herself:

> Sith it is shrined in my Soueraines brest,
> And formd so liuely in each perfect part,
> That to all Ladies, which haue it profest,
> Neede but behold the pourtraict of her hart,
> If pourtrayd it might be by any liuing art.[56]

Like so many other female hearts, the heart of Queen Elizabeth holds an image or figure. Yet unlike the heart of Sappho, Hermia, or Olivia, the figure inscribed on the heart is not that of the beloved, but rather the perfect figuration of chastity, "formd so liuely in each perfect part." While Spenser does not mention the materiality of this image, the multiple figurations of female hearts as wax, and the "so liuely" figuration of chastity in Elizabeth's breast, raise the question: Is the Queen's heart wax? If Elizabeth's heart is wax, and thus the figure of chastity is a perfect figure formed in wax, would that suggest that chastity is a figure of change and malleability? Or that chastity is a virtue that only gains meaning to the degree that it faces change and malleability?

In Elizabeth's final speech to Parliament, she explicitly associates herself with wax. Reflecting on her reign, she reminds her audience that she has always put the country's interests first: "I have diminished my own revenue that I might add to your security, and been content to be a taper of true virgin wax, to waste myself and spend my life that I might give light and comfort to those that live under me."[57] Here, Elizabeth evokes the figure of the candle, rather than that of the wax heart. Yet once again, wax becomes a material associated with chastity; she is not simply wax, but a "taper of true virgin wax." As we saw in the introduction, such wax was most highly prized, in part because it gave off the purest light. Still, the value of the taper is called into question by the discourse of waste. Like the young man in Shakespeare's sonnet 1, Elizabeth "waste[s] [her]self." Yet where Shakespeare worries that the fair youth

"Feed'st [his] light's flame with self-substantial fuel, / Making a famine where abundance lies," Elizabeth claims this same self-consumption as a public good.[58] Her life brings "llight and comfort to those that live under [her]." For Elizabeth, chastity is a matter of wax, but that association has little to do with wax's malleability. Instead, the self-consuming taper becomes a kind of alternative to the malleable wax of impression.

Spenser, of course, wrote the *Faerie Queene* before Elizabeth gave that speech. Thus, when he imagines a shrine to chastity inside the queen's heart, he most likely is not imagining a virgin taper. However, since he finds that interiority of the heart precludes its study, we cannot know. We cannot look upon the "Soueraines brest" to study chastity (or its form). Instead, Spenser suggests that Ladies should "behould the portraict of her hart, / If pourtrayd it might be by any liuing art." Art, Spenser suggests, may provide a means for representing moral truths and teaching them. A "portraict" of Elizabeth's heart, at least according to this conceit, would be a representation that might provide access to some form of truth. Yet in the very next verse, Spenser discards such a possibility. He proclaims, "But liuing art may not least part expresse/ Nor life-resembling pencill it can paynt."[59] These lines reopen the question of the relationship between art and life (what exactly is the distinction being drawn between "liuing art" and "life-resembling pencill"?) and close down the possibility of representation. Spenser suggests that not only would a "portraict of her hart" be an imperfect representation, but also it "may not the least part expresse." Indeed, even if the artist were a god, "his daedale hand would faile, and greatly faynt, / And her perfections with his error taynt."[60] Here, "Daedale" means "skillful, cunning to invent or fashion," but it also invokes Daedalus.[61] The "error" introduced by the artist's skillful and cunning hand is also Daedalus's error, and an error of wax.

In these opening verses, we can see Spenser raising questions about art that eventually more explicitly mapped onto questions of materiality with the creation of the false Florimell. That these questions are initially raised around Elizabeth, a beautiful, powerful woman whose appearance and comportment are artfully orchestrated for political effect, is not incidental. Like Lucrece, or the Duchess of Malfi, Elizabeth's performance of femininity is a particular kind of gendered performance. These questions of gender, art, and representation are to some degree already wax in their early formulations. Yet they become more so when Spenser releases the false Florimell onto the landscape of Faerie Land. Comprised of wax and enabled by the wax arts of impression and imitation, the false Florimell differs from the true primarily through her wax materials—and yet that difference, as we shall see, threatens always to collapse.

Since the false Florimell is a copy of the true Florimell, we can only understand her by comparison. Within the poem, the two Florimells only meet once, a meeting that results in the spontaneous melting of the false Florimell. Yet before that meeting, each Florimell follows her own path, circulating through the poem's pages and interacting with a wide range of other figures. Looking at how each Florimell enters the poem reveals much about how Spenser uses them to create meaning. As readers, our first glimpse of the true Florimell coincides with the first sighting of that lady by the heroes of the poem: namely Britomart, Guyon, and Arthur. Spenser relays:

> Vpon a milkwhite Palfrey all alone,
> A goodly Lady did foreby them rush,
> Whose face did seeme as cleare as Christall stone,
> And eke through feare as white as whales bone:
> Her garments all were wrought of beaten gold,
> And all her steed with tinsell trappings shone,
> Which fledd so fast, that nothing mote him hold,
> And scarse them leasure gaue, her passing to behold.[62]

As A.C. Hamilton has noted, Spenser's description of Florimell at this moment shares many similarities with Ovid's description of the fleeing Diana.[63] Both authors associate the fleeing female body with chastity, despite the fact that female movement is generally associated, in the sixteenth century, with the absence of chastity rather than its presence.[64] The true Florimell is also, in Petrarchan fashion, portrayed through the objects and colors that Spenser associates with her here. Her purity is signaled by the whiteness of her Palfrey and her face, and her beauty by the value of gold and whales bone. By using blazons and constructing Florimell's character in part through material metaphors, Spenser also gestures at a kinship between Florimell and objects and by extension between women and things, as we shall see further in the discussion that follows.

When the witch crafts "another *Florimell*" to placate her son's amorous desire for the original, the false Florimell resembles the original, "in shape and looke / So liuely and so like, that many it mistook."[65]

Spenser emphasizes the materiality of the new Florimell, as the materials of her creation both aid in creating a likeness and make a perfect similitude impossible:

> The substance, whereof she the body made,
> Was purest snow in massy mould congeald,
> Which she had gathered in a shady glade
> Of the *Riphoean* hils, to her reuealed
> By errant Sprights, but from all men conceald:
> The same she tempred with fine Mercury,
> And virgin wex, that neuer yet was seald,
> And mingled them with perfect vermily,
> That like a liuely sanguine it seemd to the eye.[66]

Like the true Florimell, the false Florimell bears a white complexion. Yet while the true Florimell appears "through feare as white as whales bone," the false Florimell is pure white because she is made of "purest snow" gathered from an area beyond the knowledge of men and "virgin wex, that neuer yet was seald." False Florimell's whiteness and thus her symbolic purity can, on the basis of her materials, exceed the true Florimell's. When the pure wax and snow are "mingled... with perfect vermily" or vermillion—a pigment often mixed with wax to produce sealing wax and presumably used here to give color to the false Florimell's lips and cheeks—she further conforms to Petrarchan conventions of beauty.[67] Yet where a Petrarchan beauty might be rosy-cheeked or may turn red with a modest blush, the false Florimell seems frozen in that state, raising questions about what her redness might signify.[68]

Similarly, the yellow of the true Florimell's hair finds an echo in the false Florimell's "golden wyre."[69] Yet as Spenser insists there is an irreconcilable difference between gold and yellow.[70] Spenser suggests "golden wyre was not so yellow thryse / As *Florimells* fayre heare."[71] Over the course of these two stanzas, questions of materiality get mixed up with questions of superiority. Is it more beautiful to be pure white snow? Or flesh? Is it more beautiful to have hair? Or golden wire? The narrative voice cannot quite decide what constitutes beauty, suggesting first "that euen Nature selfe enuide" the false Florimell "And grudg'd to see the counterfet should shame / the thing it selfe" and then reminding us that gold can never be yellow.[72] Spenser's insistence on the difference between the two Florimells should remind us of his discussion of art at the opening of book 3. Just as it is impossible for any artist to figure Queen Elizabeth's heart perfectly, it is also impossible for the counterfeit Florimell to be a perfect copy of the original. The difference in materiality alone is sufficient to ensure meaningful difference.

If Florimell's character is portrayed through blazons, the false Florimell is literally made up of them. Thomas Roche has argued that the false Florimell is essentially a "'pin-up'; she is composed of sonneteers' epithets and represents the same type of wish-fulfillment and debasement of the female form as her modern counterpart."[73] She is, as Linda Gregerson suggests, "a likeness made of likeness, a composite beauty whose features derive from the interwoven similes of the Petrarchan sonneteers."[74] Mihoko Suzuki concurs, calling her "an amalgamation of literalized Petrarchan conceits."[75] Building on Nancy Vickers's seminal work on the blazon in Petrarch, Suzuki argues that "[t]hrough this creation of a counterfeit doll by joining various artificial body parts, Spenser exposes the violent appropriation of woman implicit in the *blason*."[76] Together, the two Florimells suggest that idealized femininity is always a construction that depends on a certain dehumanization. As Vickers says of Laura, these Florimells represent "a code of beauty, a code that causes us to seek, or to seek to be 'ideal types, beautiful monsters composed of every individual perfection.'"[77] Still, the materials that comprise the false Florimell matter not merely because Spenser seems to be mocking a particular poetic tradition or exposing its violence, but also for the ways that these particular materials work together to construct a particular woman. We may be able to trace Florimell's snowy complexion, her wax materiality, and her hair of golden wires back to specific sonnets, but we can also locate within Petrarchan sonnets countless other possibilities. Spenser's choice of snow, wax, and gold gains meaning within, beyond, and prior to their association with Petrarchan sonnets and these histories helped imbue them with symbolic resonances.[78]

Wax, in particular, becomes a material of the false Florimell because it is susceptible to being remodeled and melted, and its virgin status seems only temporarily ensured. As Rufus Wood argues, "there is a suggestion that it is only virgin because never before sealed, but will shortly be unsealed. Even the word 'wex' punningly draws out the sense in which wax is essentially malleable and unconstant."[79] According to Linda Gregerson, the wax materiality of Florimell's body gains meaning by comparison with Sidney's *New Arcadia*, in which "Philoclea's navel is blazoned as 'a daintie seale of virgin-waxe, / Where nothing but impression lackes.'"[80] Gregerson explains, "the virgin wax *invites* impression: 'lacking' is the work it does...'impression' is the stamp of [masculine] ownership. And pleasure (the contemplation of virgin wax, for example) requires that ownership be thwarted or precarious or not-yet-achieved."[81] The use of virgin wax suggests pliancy, femininity, iterability, artfulness, and possibilities of inscription that can be associated with fertility.

Some of these associations are Petrarchan. However, they also gain inflection through the association of wax with philosophy and wax's various deployments in the world as a material of writing and art. Wax only can figure virginity compellingly because it can be used to model reproduction. If, as Gregerson suggests, "the virgin wax might be a summary for the entire Petrarchan construct of desire," it might also be a summary of the entire project of constructing an artificial or artful female form.[82] Thus, while wax is only one of the many materials that comprise the false Florimell, it is a materiality that helps us understand her nature as an image of femininity. Moreover, wax can also help us understand the false Florimell as not simply an image, but a fully mobile automaton who resembles Florimell not only in appearance but also in behavior.

The false Florimell is both composed of wax and also shaped by wax arts. The witch models her creation after the impression she receives of the true Florimell, an impression not simply of appearance, but also of behavior. Indeed, since Florimell arrives at the witch's cottage weary from her travels and in a state of disarray, she wins entrance primarily through her display of distress. After explaining that she merely wants shelter from the storm, she wordlessly continues:

> With that adowne out of her christall eyne
> Few trickling teares she softly forth let fall,
> That like two orient perls, did purely shyne
> Vpon her snowy cheeke; and therewithall
> She sighed soft, that none so bestiall,
> Nor saluage hart, but ruth of her sad plight
> Would make to melt, or pitteously appall[83];

The witch witnesses first hand not only Florimell's beauty, but also her ability to wield that beauty to win over those that she encounters. For the false Florimell to substitute for the true one, she must be able to move and act in the world, just as the true Florimell does. As Karen

Raber suggests, "the most lifelike, the most lively, the most natural painted body is one in motion."[84] While other narratives might secure such motion by mechanization, here the witch summons "a wicked Spright yfraught with fawning guyle" who knows how "[h]im selfe to fashion likest *Florimell*."[85] The spright, like wax, epitomizes malleability and testifies to a certain vision of woman as inconstant, flirtatious, and wanton. Despite his masculine gender, he can form his actions and fashion himself to be "likest *Florimell*." He imitates Florimell so perfectly that the false Florimell rejects the witch's son, for whom she was created, "the more to seeme such as she hight" and ends up circulating from knight to knight, just as the true Florimell does, because the false Florimell plays the part of a damsel, becoming a woman to be rescued and won.[86]

Yet if the false Florimell wins her ability to pass as woman by being like wax, the true Florimell must reject any connection she might have with wax in order to escape Proteus. After rescuing Florimell, Proteus attempts to win her love by changing himself, "For euery shape on him he could endew."[87] When these attempts fail, he tries fear and finally eternal thralldom. But:

> Eternal thraldome was to her more liefe,
> Then losse of chastitie, or chaunge of loue:
> Dye had she rather in tormenting griefe,
> Then any should of falseness her reproue,
> Or loosenesse, that she lightly did remoue.[88]

The temptation Proteus offers is the temptation of wax. He can change shapes and take on any form that she might desire. All that is required of Florimell is that she "chaunge her love" and allow herself to be "false[ ]," like the false Florimell. When I discussed the proem's treatment of Queen Elizabeth's heart, I raised the possibility that for Spenser chastity might require not an absence of wax materiality, but rather a determination to prevent that wax location from being shaped or changed as the result of masculine pressures. Proteus's attempts to change Florimell along with her determination not to be changed suggest that chastity for Spenser might be exactly that: a capacity for change or malleability that can be refused through flight or some quality of will that Florimell seems to possess. Proteus's failure to "chaunge" Florimell suggests that her heart, already impressed by her love for Marinell, will not trade its print for Proteus, even after he places her in chains and despite the multitudes of forms he takes, including the form of "a Faerie knight."[89] She eschews the possibility of change signified by wax materiality, which is embodied at this moment by Proteus.

Still, if the two Florimells differ in their relationship to wax, and with it to art, truth, and virtue, those differences are not readily visible to the other inhabitants of Faerie Land. The false Florimell most clearly presents an interpretive problem for the figures within *The Faerie Queene* in book 4 when she tries to win the girdle of chastity and in book 5 when she is placed next to the real Florimell. In both of these moments, she is put under the critical scrutiny of the other allegorical figures, and when they first see her, they believe that they see Florimell. In book 4, Spenser relays, "all were glad there *Florimell* to see; / Yet thought that *Florimell* was not so faire as she."[90] Similarly in book 5, the spectators exclaim,

> ...that surely *Florimell* it was,
> Or if it were not *Florimell* so tride,
> That *Florimell* her selfe she then did pas.[91]

Both these scenes present moments of misrecognition coupled with a registering of difference that is not quite sufficient to upset the perceived recognition.

Other than the story of her creation, the most crucial moment for the false Florimell is her destruction in canto 3 of book 5. For the first time, the two Florimells occupy the same space, and simultaneously, both of them lay claim to the same name and the title of fairest. When the spectators see the Florimells, they cannot, as mentioned above, determine which is the true Florimell. Even Marinell, who has just married Florimell, begins to think that the false Florimell must actually be the true Florimell. The moment of revelation occurs when Artegall stands the two Florimells next to each other in book 5:

> Like the true saint beside the image set,
> Of both their beauties to make paragone,
> And triall, whether should the honor get.
> Streigh tway so soone as both together met,
> Th' enchaunted Damzell vanisht into nought:
> Her snowy substance melted as with heat,
> Ne of that goodly hew remayned ought,
> But th' emptie girdle, which about her wast was wrought.[92]

Although Artegall sets out to make "triall" of "their beauties," he is never given the chance. When the two Florimells encounter each other, it is not left to any outsider to judge which of the two is the true Florimell, or even which of the two is more beautiful. Instead, the snowy Florimell simply melts.[93] Spenser suggests that Artegall's act of setting the two women next to each other is like setting "the true saint beside the image." While this comparison suggests that the question comes down to one of truth and falsehood, original and counterfeit, it also invokes the fraught debate between Protestants and Catholics over the role of images, and, for that matter, saints in religion. The false Florimell, as an image of the true, still would have had significance in a Roman Catholic schema, while neither saint nor image would have mattered much to a Protestant. Still, the encounter between the two Florimells and the melting of the false Florimell suggests that there is something more authentic about the true Florimell than the false. Perhaps the difference between them is the difference of art, although such claims are complicated by the fact that both Florimells are allegorical figures, and that the true Florimell, while she does not melt, effectively disappears from the epic at this point.

Next to the false Florimell, we can place Spenser's man of iron, Talus, who also invites the question of the relationship between things and people, although his status within the poem and his material constitution are quite different from the false Florimell's. Where she represents something of the waxy falseness of art or femininity, he represents the iron hand of justice and materially embodies that figure. "[M]ade of yron mould"[94] and characterized as, "[i]mmoueable, resistlesse, without end,"[95] he is impenetrable and unrelenting, as devoid of wax as she is full of it. His iron nature informs his action in the play. As Jessica Wolfe suggests, Talus's metal materiality extends to "both… body and spirit," and leads to his "Terminator-like approach" to justice.[96] Yet it is not simply Talus's iron composition, but also his double claims to "yron mould" and "man" that impact his behavior in the poem, as many critics have noted. Lynsey McCulloch argues that Talus should be understood as a "killing machine" that is also simultaneously an "animated statue," occupying a status at once "sub- and superhuman."[97] Tiffany Jo Werth insists that his composite nature affords him multiple identities, suggesting he is simultaneously, "an iron man, a walking mineral, a stony human, human and mineral… irreducible neither to 'iron' or 'man.'"[98] For Jonathan Sawday, he is both "a perpetual motion machine" and "a figure of horror."[99] Building on these critics, I would suggest that like the false Florimell, Talus's constructed and mechanical nature is used to trouble the boundaries of the human, ultimately revealing our own inhumanity.

Talus moves through the poem without mercy and with an absolutist mentality. For example, when Artegall and Talus find that a Sarazin guards a bridge and demands passage money of travelers, Talus not only destroys the lord, but also kills his daughter, and razes his Castle, "euen from the sole of his foundation."[100] The punishment that Talus executes is extreme and cruel, "[t]hat there mote be no hope of reparation, / Nor memory thereof to any nation."[101] The death of the lady is particularly excessive. Despite her pleas for mercy, Talus cuts off her hands and feet, before drowning her in the mud. With a performance of justice as rigid as his body, Talus pursues his ends, "Yet for no pitty would he change the course / Of Iustice, which in *Talus* hand did lye."[102] Similarly, once Britomart has slain Radigund, Talus breaks into her fortress and:

> There then a piteous slaughter did begin:
> For all that euer came within his reach,
> He with his yron flaile did thresh so thin.[103]

Britomart has to order him to stop, "For else he sure had left not one aliue, / But all in his reuenge of spirite would depriue."[104] Left to his own devices, Talus slaughters in the name of justice because, like a machine, he is capable only of applying rules to situations and cannot bend them. Above we saw that the exacting hardness of justice is incompatible with the wax falseness of false Florimell. Here, we see that it is also incompatible with pity, a trait that in Shakespeare's *Rape of Lucrece* was also a trait of wax. Since sympathy depends on likeness and on the possibility of becoming like, to deny pity is to deny the power of wax. Justice without pity or wax seems to be the model condoned by both Talus and Artegall, who is the primary figure for justice within book 5.

Yet perhaps the biggest problem Talus presents lies in how little difference there actually is between him and the other knights. After Britomart has freed Artegall, he immediately returns to his quest, taking only Talus with him as "[t]he true guide of his way and vertuous gouernment."[105] What follows, almost immediately, is an encounter with a damsel in distress. Artegall sees "[a] Damzell, flying on a palfrey fast /

Before two Knights, that after her did speed"[106] and "Soone after these he saw another Knight, / That after those two former rode apace."[107] This latter knight, who we later learn is Arthur, manages to close the gap between himself and the two pursuing knights and engage one of them in combat. Artegall chases the other knight and also fights him. Both Artegall and Arthur win their battles. At which point, Arthur, confusing Artegall for one of the original villains, chases him down and they too begin battling. They are only stopped from killing each other by the intervention of the damsel, who they initially sought to protect. What difference is there between human knights and iron man at this moment? Both Arthur and Artegall act before gaining any understanding of the situation, and once in action, prove relentless. Their performance of knighthood seems as mechanical as Talus's performance of justice. Enshrined in armor, there would also be scarcely any visible difference between these knights and the iron man.

Indeed, as several scholars have argued, in armor, on horseback, the knights themselves may be something other than human. Jeffrey Jerome Cohen argues that "the horse, its rider, the bridle and saddle and armor together form the Deleuzian circuit or assemblage, a network of meaning that decomposes human bodies and intercuts them with the inanimate, the inhuman."[108] For Timothy Francisco, "the horsed soldier is cyborg-like: part man, part animal, and part metal."[109] While Raber, reading *1 Henry IV*, suggests that for the emissary, Lucy, "soldiers and armour are interchangeable, sharing more than metaphoric connection, since both are generated out of the requirements of battle, and the identities of both are subsumed by the apparatus that is war."[110] While each of these formulations differs in their inflections, they all read the knight and soldier as a being whose claim to humanity is complicated by its commitments to armor, horse, and war, and whose identity as an individual is called to question. Interestingly, while the false Florimell confuses the other characters within *The Faerie Queene*, Talus does not. Perhaps the moments of confusion and misrecognition do not occur precisely because his primary relationship to almost all the figures he encounters occurs on the battlefield, where only the trappings of armor, heraldic signs, and differing displays of skill differentiate one knight from another, and automaton and knight perform in precisely the same ways.

Talus's mechanicalness is different from the false Florimell's, and yet, they both represent gendered stereotypes and expose those stereotypes as mechanical forms. Talus's relentless application of justice and rigid performance of knighthood problematize masculine virtue in much the same way that the false Florimell's success at deploying feminine wiles and in winning contests of beauty calls into question the virtues of femininity. Spenser's treatment of gender in books 3–5 of *The Faerie Queene*, and his connection of gender to specific materialities, brings us back full circle to where we started this project with Shakespeare's wax women and the possibility that the ideal woman would be perfectly malleable and soft and consequently supremely vulnerable to masculine impression. More, just as Shakespeare portrays Tarquin as hard, Spenser's men (and sometimes his women), encased in armor, also threaten to be too impervious.[111] Britomart's turn to knighthood and her adoption of arms suggest the power offered by encasing flesh in armor, even when that flesh is female. At the same time, Talus's unfeeling responses to the situations he finds himself in show the dangers of that type of hardness, especially since Talus's behavior is at most a somewhat more extreme version of the other knights' actions.

In pursuing Spenser's treatment of automata through his depiction of Talus and the false Florimell, I have tried to show how materiality figures into the possibility and threat represented by artificial beings brought to life. That Spenser, writing in the 1580s and 1590s, takes up these questions reminds us that the story we have been telling is not a narrative of progress. Instead, wax materiality (or the lack thereof) connects moments from different times and illuminates conversations that persist across time. Spenser's concern about the false Florimell and her ability to pass is not all that different from Descartes' worry that the people he sees in the street might be automata. Of course since the false Florimell is animated by a spright, that is, by an intelligent being, she would pass Descartes' tests for a person. She has a command of language and the capacity to build knowledge that Descartes does not believe possible of an automaton. Yet she is still mere imitation. Her body is an imitation of the true Florimell's body, an imitation that might be understood best through the wax that gives her form: She is flexible, feminine, and human-like, yet her wax materiality also reminds us that she is fundamentally a figure of art like Pygmalion's wife, and as such, at least for Spenser different from a person. For Spenser, both "yellow" and "gold," nature and art, may exceed the other in some qualities, but they are never strictly equivalent, or at least their equivalence cannot be conveyed through simple representation and imitation, but instead requires an allegorical mode.

As we have seen, early modern writers thought about the nature of humanity in comparison with artificial constructions and use wax to explore possibilities of invention, imitation, and flexibility. Wax for Descartes seems to model what it means to be human, and for Spenser to represent pure mimicry and the artfulness of art. It thus exists as a threshold material, able to represent both human and nonhuman, organic life and artificial. It is a material of potential, representing the project of prosthetics and the artfulness of invention in Ovid, Paré, and Spenser. At the same time, its weakness, its susceptibility to pressure and heat, reveals early modern anxieties about the boundaries of art in those same texts. Through all these possibilities, wax provides a surprising thread, figuring both the expansive possibilities and threatening implications of hybrids and artificial humans, and suggesting that prosthetics, cyborgs, animated statues, and automata relate to the theorizations of art, gender, and epistemology that we have been tracing throughout the project.

Notes

1. Jane Bennett, *Vibrant Matter: A Political Ecology of Things* (Durham: Duke University Press, 2010), xvii.
2. Ian Bogost, *Alien Phenomenology, or What It's Like to Be a Thing* (Minneapolis: University of Minnesota Press, 2012), 8.
3. Eugene Thacker, *After Life* (Chicago: University of Chicago Press, 2010), xv.
4. N. Katherine Hayles, *How We Became Posthuman: Virtual Bodies in Cybernetics, Literature, and Informatics* (Chicago: University of Chicago Press, 1999).
5. Rosa Braidotti, *The Posthuman* (Cambridge, UK: Polity Press, 2013), 26.
6. Ovid, *Metamorphoses*, trans. A. D. Melville and E. J. Kenney (Oxford: Oxford University Press, 1986). Citations are to book and line. 8.188–189. In Latin: "et ignotas animum dimittit in artes naturamque novat," Ovid, *Ovid III: Metamorphoses, Books I–VIII*, ed. G. P. Goold, trans. Frank Justus Miller, 3rd edition, Loeb Classical Library (Cambridge, MA: Harvard University Press, 1984). All Latin transcriptions of book 8 follow this edition.
7. Ovid, *Metamorphoses*, 8.191–198. In Latin:

   ... nam ponit in ordine pennas

a minima coeptas, longam breviore sequenti,
ut clivo crevisse putes: sic rustica quondam
fistula disparibus paulatim surgit avenis;
tum lino medias et ceris alligat imas
atque ita conpositas parvo curvamine flectit,
ut veras imitetur aves.

8. Ovid, *Metamorphoses*, 8.217–220. In the original Latin:

hos aliquis tremula dum captat harundine pisces,
aut pastor baculo stivave innixus arator
vidit et obstipuit, quique aethera carpere possent,
credidit esse deos.

9. These figures also provide perspective in *Landscape with the Fall of Icarus* (1560s), long attributed to Bruegel and now believed to be an early copy of his original composition. In that painting, Icarus is portrayed as only a small pair of legs in the bottom right corner. His humanity is emphasized by both minimizing his form and emphasizing instead the shepherd and ploughman. Pieter Bruegel, attrib., *Landscape with the Fall of Icarus*, circa 1558, oil on canvas, 73.5 × 112 cm, Royal Museum of Fine Arts of Belgium. The authenticity of the painting was called into question following technical examinations in 1996. For a further discussion, see Lyckle de Vries, "Bruegel's 'Fall of Icarus': Ovid or Solomon," *Simiolus: Netherlands Quarterly for the History of Art* 30, no. 1 (2006): 4–18.

10. Ovid, *Metamorphoses*, 8.224–230. In the Latin:

cum puer audaci coepit gaudere volatu
deseruitque ducem caelique cupidine tractus
altius egit iter. rapidi vicinia solis
mollit odoratas, pennarum vincula, ceras;
tabuerant cerae: nudos quatit ille lacertos,
remigioque carens non ullas percipit auras,

11. Ovid, *Metamorphoses*, 8.195–200. In the Latin:

… puer Icarus una
stabat et, ignarus sua se tractare pericla,
ore renidenti modo, quas vaga moverat aura,
captabat plumas, flavam modo pollice ceram

12. Ovid, *Metamorphoses*, 8.204.199–200. In Latin: "mirabile patris...opus."
13. For more on such concerns, see Lorraine Daston and Katherine Park, *Wonders and the Order of Nature 1150–1750* (Cambridge, MA: Zone Press, 2001).
14. Ovid, *The. Xv. Bookes of P. Ouidius Naso, Entytuled Metamorphosis, Translated Oute of Latin into English Meeter, by Arthur Golding Gentleman, a Worke Very Pleasaunt and Delectable* (London: Willyam Seres, 1567). Sig. a3r.
15. Ibid.
16. Ibid.
17. Ibid.
18. *Oxford English Dictionary, s.v.* 'Mean.'
19. For a discussion of the Icarus myth in emblem books, see Carlo Ginzburg, "High and Low: The Theme of Forbidden Knowledge in the Sixteenth and Seventeenth Centuries," *Past and Present* 73 (1976): 28–41.
20. Rom. 2:20. Qtd. and trans. in Ginzburg, "High and Low," 28, 30.
21. Ibid., 28–31.
22. Andrea Alciati, *Emblematum libellus* (Paris, 1534), 57.
23. Trans. in Ginzburg, "High and Low," 34. In the Latin:

Icare, per superos qui raptus et aëra, donec
In mare praecipitem cera liquata daret.
Nunc te cera eadem, fervensque resuscitat ignis,
Exemplo ut doceas dogmata certa tuo.
Astrologus caveat quicquam praedicere: praeceps
Nam cadet impostor dum super astra vehit.

24. Julianus, "Emblem 107," in *The Greek Anthology*, trans. W. R. Paton, 5 vols (London, 1916), vol. 5, 219. The *Greek Anthology* is a collection of poems from the classical and Byzantine periods of Greek literature that was transmitted to Europe by Maximus Planudes. In the Greek: εἰς Ἴκαρον χαλκοῦν ἐν λουτρῷ ἱστάμενον.
25. Ibid. To create a finished bronze statue using lost wax casting, an artist first makes a preliminary model in wax and then creates channels for the wax to escape. Next, the artist encases the model with a ceramic coating. Once that has dried, the artist can melt away the wax and fill the mold with molten bronze. In the Greek: "ἤγαγεν εἰς μορφὴν αὖθις ὁ χαλκοτύπος."
26. Julianus, "Emblem 108," in *The Greek Anthology*, trans. W. R. Paton, 5 vols (London, 1916), vol. 5, 221. In the original Greek:

Ἴκαρε, χαλκὸς ἐὼν μιμνήσκεο: μηδέ σε τέχνη,
μηδ' ἀπάφῃ πτερύγων ζεῦγος ἐπωμάδιον.
εἰ γὰρ ζωὸς ἐὼν πέσες ἐν πελάγεσσι θαλάσσης,
πῶς ἐθέλεις πτῆναι χάλκεον εἶδος ἔχων.

27. Hayles, *How We Became Posthuman*, 3.
28. Ambroise Paré, *The Workes of That Famous Chirurgion Ambrose Parey Translated out of Latine and Compared with the French*, trans. T. Johnson (London, 1634). The English and Latin translations seem to have added much of the discourse around art and nature that I am interested in here.
29. Ibid., 4. In the Latin: "Sed quae, ceu primis ab incunabulis, ceu postea ex eventu desunt quantum ars et natura patiuntur ille reparat." *Opera Chirurgica* (Frankfurt: Ioannem Feyrabend, 1593), 2. The same section in the French *Ouevres* does not contain this sentence.
30. Ibid., 869. In the Latin: "alium factitium aureum, argenteúmve opere tectorio expositum, sic encausto pictum substitueris, ut nativi oculi perluciditatem et gemmeum decorem habere videatur" *Opera Chirurgica*, 648. In the French: "Partant où tel accident aduiendroit apres la curation de l'vlcere, on pourra adapter dans l'or bite vn œil faict par artifice comme ceuxcy figurez, qui font feulement pour l'orne ment du malade." And from the caption of a figure: "reux artificiels, defquels t'eft demonftré le deffus & le deffous qui feront d'or efmaillé, & de couleur femblable aux naturels."
31. Ovid, *Metamorphoses*, 10.284–287. In the original Latin:

ebur positoque rigore
subsidit digitis ceditque, ut Hymettia sole
cera remollescit tractataque pollice multas
flectitur in facies ipsoque fit utilis usu.

Ovid, *Ovid IV: Metamorphoses, Books IX–XV*, ed. G. P. Goold, trans. Frank Justus Miller, Subsequent edition, Loeb Classical Library (Cambridge, MA: Harvard University Press, 1916). All Latin transcriptions of book 10 follow this edition.
32. Ibid., 10.295–297. In the original Latin:

iamque coactis
cornibus in plenum noviens lunaribus orbem
illa Paphon genuit, de qua tenet insula nomen.

33. She is also used by Wendy Beth Hyman to represent automata and all non-human early modern animates and to explore the anxieties that such creations produce. See Hyman, ed., *The Automaton in English Renaissance Literature* (London and New York: Routledge, 2016), 1–3.
34. Donna Haraway, *Simians, Cyborgs and Women: The Reinvention of Nature* (New York: Routledge, 1991), 150.
35. Jonathan Sawday reads Shakespeare's Coriolanus as akin to Haraway's cyborgs in "'Forms Such as Never Were in Nature': The Renaissance Cyborg," in *At the Borders of the Human, Beasts, Bodies, and Natural Philosophy in the Early Modern Period* (Houndmills, Basingstoke, Hampshire: Palgrave, 1999), 171–195.
36. See Haraway, *Simians, Cyborgs and Women*, 149.
37. Joseph Campana, "Epilogue: H is for Humanism," in *The Renaissance Posthuman*, eds. Joseph Campana and Scott Maisano (New York: Fordham University, 2016), 294.
38. The version of this claim in *The Meditations* is "the proposition, *I am, I exist* is necessarily true whenever it is put forward by me or conceived in my mind," *Meditations on the First Philosophy*, ed. John Cottingham (Cambridge, England: Cambridge University Press, 1997), 51. In the Latin: "hac pronuntiatum, *Ego Sum, ego existo,* quotie a me profertur, vel mente concipitur, necessario esse verum" *Meditationes de Prima Philosophia*, vol. 7 of *Oeuvres de Descartes*, eds. Charles Adam and Paul Tannery (Paris: L. Cerf, 1897), 25. The claim "I think therefore I am" is actually articulated in his *Principles of Philosophy* "cogito ergo sum," *Oeuvres De Descartes*, eds. Charles Adam and Paul Tannery, vol. 8 (Paris: L. Cerf, 1910), 7 or in his *Discourse on the Method*, "Je pense, donc je juis" *Oeuvres De Descartes*, eds. Charles Adam and Paul Tannery, vol. 5 (Paris: L. Cerf, 1910), 32.
39. Descartes, *Mediations*, 54. In the Latin: "eadum [cera]" *Meditationes de Prima Philosophia*, 31. In the French: "la mesme cire," *Les Meditations Metaphysiques*, vol. 9 in *Oeuvres de Descartes*, eds. Charles Adam and Paul Tannery (Paris: L. Cerf, 1897), 25.
40. Descartes, *Meditations*, 55. In the Latin: "quandoquidem nullae rationes vel ad cerae, vel ad cuiuspiam alterius corporis perceptionem possint juvare, quin eadem omnes mentis meae naturam melius probent" *Meditationes de Prima Philosophia*, 33. In the French: "Puisque toutes les raisons qui feruent à connoistre, & conceuoir la nature de la cire, ou de quelque autre corps, prouuent beaucoup plus facilement & plus euidemment la nature de mon esprit" *Les Meditations Metaphysiques*, 26.
41. Ibid. In the Latin: "Dicimus enim nos videre ceram ipsammet, si adsit, non ex colore vel figura eam adesse judicare. Unde concluderem statim: ceram ergo visione oculi, non solius mentis inspectione, cognosci;

nisi jam forte respexissem ex fenestrâ homines in plateâ transeuntes, quos etiam ipsos non minus usitate quàm ceram dico me videre. Quid autem video praeter pileos & vestes, sub quibus latere possent automata? Sed judico homines esse. Io Atque ita id quod putabam me videre oculis, solâ judicandi facultate, quae in mente meâ eft, comprehendo" *Meditationes de Prima Philosophia*, 32. In the French: "car nous disons que nous voyons la mesme cire, si on nous la presente, & non pas que nous iugeons que c'est la mesme, de ce qu'elle a mesme couleur & mesme figure: d'où i.e. voudrois presque conclure, que l'on connoist la cire par la vision des yeux, & non par la feule inspection de l'esprit, si par hazard i.e. ne regardois d'une fenestre des hommes qui passent dans la rue, à la veuë desquels i.e. ne manque pas de dire que i.e. voy des hommes, tout de mesme que i.e. dis que i.e. voy de la cire; Et cependant que voy-je de cette fenestre, sinon des chapeaux & des manteaux, qui peuuent couurir des spectres ou des hommes feints qui ne se remuent que par ressors? Mais i.e. iuge que ce font de vrais hommes, & ainsi i.e. comprens, par la seule puissance de iuger qui reside en mon esprit, ce que i.e. croyois voir de mes yeux" *Les Meditations Metaphysiques*, 25.

42. Ibid.
43. Lisa Nocks, *The Robot: The Life Story of a Technology* (Westport, CT, 2007), 17.
44. Ibid.
45. See Sawday, "Forms Such as Never Were in Nature," 186–187 for further discussion of early modern automata.
46. For a discussion of attitudes toward automata during the Middle Ages and the Renaissance, see Alexander Marr, "*Gentillé curiosite:* Wonder-Working and the Culture of Automata in the Late Renaissance," in *Curiosity and Wonder from the Renaissance to the Enlightenment*, eds. R. J. W. Evans and Alexander Marr (Aldershot, England, 2006), 149–170. See also, Lorraine Daston and Katherine Park, *Wonders and the Order of Nature 1150–1750* (New York, 1998).
47. René Descartes, "To More, 5 February 1649," *The Philosophical Writings of Descartes*, ed. and trans. John Cottingham, Robert Stoothoff, Dugald Murdoch, and Anthony Kenny, 3 vols (Cambridge, England, 1991), vol. 3, 366. In Latin: "Deinde, quia rationi consentaneum videtur, cùm ars sit naturae imitatrix, possintque homines varia fabricare automata, in quibus fine ullâ cogitatione est motus, ut natura etiam sua automata, sed arte-factis longè praestantiora, nempe bruta omnia, producat" in *Oeuvres de Descartes*, eds. Charles Adam and Paul Tannery (Paris: L. Cerf, 1897), vol. 5, 277.

48. In *Shakespeare and Posthumanist Theory*, Karen Raber describes the early modern period as existing in "a world in which humanism, and the human at the supposed centre of humanist thought, is under constant pressure from technologies of all kinds, a 'human' and humanism that threatens to become fully mechanical," Karen Raber, *Shakespeare and Posthumanist Theory*, Shakespeare and Theory (London and New York: The Arden Shakespeare, 2018), 169. Certainly, Descartes' writings reveal that kind of pressure and a deep concern about how to differentiate the human from the mechanical.

49. Descartes, "To More," 366. In Latin: "certum est in corporibus animalium, ut etiam in nostris, esse ossa, nervos, musculos, sanguinem, spiritus animales, & reliqua organa ita disposita, ut se solis, absque ulla cogitatione, omnes motus, quos in brutis observamus, cire possint" *Correspondance: mai 1647-février 1650*, vol. 5 of *Oeuvres de Descartes*, eds. Charles Adam and Paul Tannery (Paris: L. Cerf, 1897), 277.

50. René Descartes, "Discourse on the Method," in *The Philosophical Writings of Descartes*, ed. and trans. John Cottingham, Robert Stoothoff, and Dugald Murdoch, 2 vols (Cambridge, England, 1985), vol. 1, 139. In the French, "considereront ce cors comme une machine qui, ayant esté faite des mains de Dieu, est incomparablement mieux ordonnée, & a en soi des mouvemens plus admirables qu'aucune de celles qui peuvent estre inventées par les hommes" *Discours de la Méthode et Essais*, vol. 6 of *Oeuvres de Descartes*, eds. Charles Adam and Paul Tannery (Paris: L. Cerf, 1897), 56.

51. Descartes, "Discourse on the Method," 139. In French, "s'il y en avoit qui eussent la ressemblance de nos cors, & imitassent autant nos actions que moralement il seroit possible" *Discours de la Méthode et Essais*, vol. 6 of *Oeuvres de Descartes*, eds. Charles Adam and Paul Tannery (Paris: L. Cerf, 1897), 56.

52. Ibid., 140. In French, "Car on peut bien concevoir qu'une machine soit tellement faite qu'elle profere des paroles, & mesme qu'elle en profere quelques unes a propos des actions corporelles qui causeront quelque changement en ses organes: comme, si on la touche en quelque endroit, qu'elle demande ce qu'on luy veut dire; si en un autre, qu'elle crie qu'on luy fait mal, & choses semblables; mais non pas qu'elle les arrenge diversement, pour respondre au sens de tout ce qui se dira en sa presence, ainsi que les hommes les plus hebetez peuvent faire. Et le second est que, bien qu'elles fissent plusieurs choses aussy bien, ou peutestre mieux qu'aucun de nous, elles manqueroient infailliblement en quelques autres, par lesquelles on découvriroit qu'elles n'agiroient pas par connaissance, mais seulement par la disposition de leurs organes" *Discours de la méthode*, 56–57.

53. Edmund Spenser, *The Faerie Queene*, ed. A. C. Hamilton (Abingdon, Oxon: Oxford University Press, 2013), 714.

54. Jonathan Goldberg, *The Seeds of Things: Theorizing Sexuality and Materiality in Renaissance Representations* (New York, 2009), 65. See also Thomas Roche, *The Kindly Flame: A Study of the Third and Fourth Books of Spenser's Faerie Queene* (Princeton, 1964), 14n.

55. Spenser, *The Faerie Queene*, 3.proem.1.1–2. Citations are to book, canto, stanza, and verse, unless otherwise noted.

56. Ibid., 3.proem.1.5–9.

57. Elizabeth I, "Queen Elizabeth's Final Speech before Parliament, December 19, 1601, Version 1," in *Elizabeth I: Collected Works*, ed. Leah S. Marcus, Janel Mueller, and Mary Beth Rose (Chicago: University of Chicago Press, 2002), 347.

58. William Shakespeare, "The Sonnets and 'A Lover's Complaint'," in *The Norton Shakespeare*, ed. Stephen Greenblatt et al. (New York: W. W. Norton, 1997), Sonnet 1, lines 6–7.

59. Spenser, *The Faerie Queene*, 3.proem.2.1–2.

60. Ibid., 3.proem.2.4–5.

61. *Oxford English Dictionary*, s.v. "deaedal, adj."

62. Spenser, *The Faerie Queene*, 3.1.15.2–9.

63. A.C. Hamilton, *The Spenser Encyclopaedia* (London, 1996), 209.

64. For a further discussion of Florimell and Diana, see Amy Margaret Braden, *As She Fled: Women and Movement in Early Modern English Poetry and Drama*. Diss. University of Southern California, 2010.

65. Spenser, *The Faerie Queene*, 3.8.5.8–9.

66. Ibid., 3.8.6.1–9.

67. Rufus Wood, *Metaphor and Belief in "The Faerie Queene"* (London, 1997), 117.

68. Wood suggests that the "snow is being mixed to produce a sanguine complexion," which can be humorally associated with "boldness, success and amourousness" (117). Regardless, the question of the false Florimell's complexion is quite interesting, as red is a color that is only explicitly associated with the true Florimell when she is brought to stand next to her counterpart in book 5. At that point "her bashfull shamefastness ywrought / A great increase in her faire blushing face; / As roses did with lilies interlace" (Spenser 5.3.23.3–5). While Florimell's blush increases her beauty, it also marks her shame. If the false Florimell's cheeks are always already red, then she is either always blushing or incapable of a blush, both of which could suggest immodesty.

69. Spenser, *The Faerie Queene*, 3.8.7.6.

70. The distinction between gold and yellow pigments applied in painting as well. The two colors were not generally interchangeable. As Paul Hills

explains gold was often used to provide background depth to mosaics: "browner than yellow, gold is an impure colour… the gold field is darker than the grey and white marbles used to highlight the figures, and for this reason nowhere does gold suggest an analogue for the even luminosity and infinite recession of the sky." Paul Hills, *Venetian Colour: Marble, Mosaic, Painting and Glass, 1250–1550* (New Haven: 1999), 47. In Venetian art, gold and blue were popular pairs, eventually replaced by blue and white. Yellow, on the other hand, was less affected by changes in light "tend[s] to stand out as a local colour disrupting any reading of pictorial light" (142–143). Hills posits that Bellini avoided yellow for this reason. Thus, gold is a color of painting and art more properly than yellow, and the two function very differently in paintings.

71. Spenser, *The Faerie Queene*, 3.8.7.7–8.
72. Ibid., 3.8.5.4–6, 3.8.7.7.
73. Thomas P. Roche, *The Kindly Flame*, 162.
74. Linda Gregerson, *The Reformation of the Subject: Spenser, Milton, and the English Protestant Epic* (Cambridge, England, 1995), 136.
75. Mihoko Suzuki, *Metamorphoses of Helen: Authority, Difference, and Epic* (Ithaca, NY, 1989), 176.
76. Ibid., 177.
77. Nancy Vickers, "Diana Described: Scattered Woman and Scattered Rhyme," *Critical Inquiry* 8, no. 2 (1981): 277. The quote within the quote is from Elizabeth Cropper's "On Beautiful Women, Parmigiano, *Petrarchismo*, and the Vernacular Style," *Art Bulletin* 58 (1976): 376.
78. The golden wires that comprise false Florimell's hair not only repeat the poetic fascination with blonde hair found in Petrarchan poetry, but also perhaps suggest the alchemical possibilities of gold, along with richness and largesse. Her snowy composition renders her not only fair, and lends her connotations of purity, but also connects her to a pristine natural landscape that is somewhat ephemeral in nature. While the snows of Riphoean hills may never melt in their natural clime, transposed into faerie land they are more precarious, as becomes evident when the false Florimell melts away in book 5.
79. Wood, *Metaphor and Belief*, 118.
80. Gregerson, *The Reformation of the Subject*, 137.
81. Ibid.
82. Ibid., 138.
83. Spenser, *The Faerie Queene*, 3.7.9.1–7.
84. Raber, *Shakespeare and Posthumanist Theory*, 178.
85. Spenser, *The Faerie Queene*, 3.8.8.1, 6.
86. Ibid., 3.8.10.4.
87. Ibid., 3.8.40.2.

88. Ibid., 3.8.42.1–5.
89. Ibid., 3.8.40.1.
90. Ibid., 4.5.14.8–9.
91. Ibid., 5.3.17.6–8.
92. Ibid., 5.3.24.2–9.
93. Throughout book 5, Spenser insists on the false Florimell's snowiness (and makes no mention of her waxiness). While wax and snow share many qualities, snow can more completely melt away, which perhaps explains why Spenser emphasizes it here.
94. Spenser, *The Faerie Queene*, 5.1.12.6.
95. Ibid., 5.1.12.7.
96. Jessica Wolfe, *Humanism, Machinery, and Renaissance Literature* (Cambridge, 2004), 203, 213.
97. Lynsey McCulloch, "Antique Myth, Early Modern Mechanism," in *The Automaton in English Renaissance Literature*, ed. Wendy Beth Hyman (Abingdon, 2011), 62, 64.
98. Tiffany Jo Werth, "'Degendered': Spenser's 'Yron Man' in a 'Stonie' Age," *Spenser Studies: A Renaissance Poetry Annual* 30 (2015): 393–413.
99. Jonathan Sawday, "Forms Such as Never Were in Nature," 190.
100. Spenser, *The Faerie Queene*, 5.2.28.2.
101. Ibid., 5.2.28.4–5.
102. Ibid., 5.2.26.1–2.
103. Ibid., 5.7.35.5–7.
104. Ibid., 5.7.36.8–9.
105. Ibid., 5.8.3.9.
106. Ibid., 5.8.4.2–3.
107. Ibid., 5.8.5.1–2.
108. Jeffrey Jerome Cohen, *Medieval Identity Machines*, Medieval Cultures, Vol. 35 (Minneapolis: University of Minnesota Press, 2003), 76.
109. Timothy Francisco, "Marlowe's War Horses: Cyborgs, Soldiers, and Queer Companions," in *Violent Masculinities: Male Aggression in Early Modern Texts and* Culture, eds. Jennifer Feather and Catherine E. Thomas (New York and Basingstoke: Palgrave Macmillan, 2013), 49.
110. Raber, *Shakespeare and Posthumanist Theory*, 187–188. See also Benjamin Bertram, *Bestial Oblivion: War, Humanism, and Ecology in Early Modern England* (NY: Routledge, 2018) for a further discussion on the soldier as assemblage.
111. For a further discussion of Britomart and what armor offers her, see Kathryn Schwarz, *Tough Love: Amazon Encounters in the English Renaissance* (Durham, NC, 2000), 137–174.

REFERENCES

Alciati, Andrea. *Andreae Alciati Emblematum Libellus*. Paris: Wechelius, 1534.

Bennett, Jane. *Vibrant Matter: A Political Ecology of Things*. Durham: Duke University Press Books, 2010.

Bertram, Benjamin. *Bestial Oblivion: War, Humanism, and Ecology in Early Modern England*. New York: Routledge, 2018.

Bogost, Ian. *Alien Phenomenology, or What It's Like to Be a Thing*. Minneapolis: University of Minnesota Press, 2012.

Braden, Amy Margaret. *As She Fled: Women and Movement in Early Modern English Poetry and Drama*. Los Angeles: University of Southern California.

Braidotti, Rosi. *The Posthuman*. Cambridge, UK; Malden, MA, USA: Polity, 2013.

Bruegel, Pieter. *Landscape with the Fall of Icarus*. circa 1558. Oil on canvas, 73.5 cm × 112 cm.

Campana, Joseph. "Epilogue: H Is for Humanism." In *Renaissance Posthumanism*, edited by Joseph Campana and Scott Maisano, 1st edition, 283–316. New York, NY: Fordham University Press, 2016.

Cohen, Jeffrey J. *Medieval Identity Machines*. Minneapolis: University of Minnesota Press, 2003.

Daston, Lorraine, and Katharine Park. *Wonders and the Order of Nature, 1150–1750*. New York; Cambridge, MA: Zone Books; Distributed by the MIT Press, 1998.

Descartes, Rene. "Discourse on the Method." In *The Philosophical Writings of Descartes*, edited by John Cottingham, Dugald Murdoch, and Robert Stoothoff, 1:111–51. Cambridge, England: Cambridge University Press, 1985.

———. "Meditationes de prima philosophia." In *Oeuvres de Descartes*, edited by Charles Adam and Paul Tannery, Vol. 7. Paris: L. Cerf, 1897.

———. *Meditations on First Philosophy: With Selections from the Objections and Replies*. Edited and translated by John Cottingham. Rev. edition. Cambridge, UK: Cambridge University Press, 1997.

———. "Meditations Touchant la Premiere Philosophie." In *Oeuvres de Descartes*, edited by Charles Adam and Paul Tannery, Vol. 9. Paris: L. Cerf, 1897.

———. *Oeuvres De Descartes*. Edited by Charles Adam and Paul Tannery, translated by Louis-Charles D'Albert Luynes, Vols. 5–9. Paris: L. Cerf, 1910.

———. "Principles of Philosophy." In *The Philosophical Writings of Descartes*, edited by John Cottingham, Dugald Murdoch, and Robert Stoothoff, 1:177–292. Cambridge, England: Cambridge University Press, 1985.

———. "To More, 5 February 1649." In *The Philosophical Writings of Descartes*, edited by John Cottingham, Dugald Murdoch, and Robert Stoothoff, 3:360–67. Cambridge, England: Cambridge University Press, 1991.

Elizabeth, I. "Queen Elizabeth's Final Speech Before Parliament, December 19, 1601, Version 1." In *Elizabeth I: Collected Works*, edited by Leah S. Marcus, Janel Mueller, and Mary Beth Rose, 346–50. Chicago: University of Chicago Press, 2002.

Francisco, Timothy. "Marlowe's War Horses: Cyborgs, Soldiers, and Queer Companions." In *Violent Masculinities: Male Aggression in Early Modern Texts and Culture*, edited by J. Feather and C. Thomas, 47–66. New York, NY: Palgrave Macmillan, 2013.

Ginzburg, Carlo. "High and Low: The Theme of Forbidden Knowledge in the Sixteenth and Seventeenth Centuries." *Past & Present* 73, no.1 (November 1, 1976): 28–41.

Goldberg, Jonathan. *The Seeds of Things: Theorizing Sexuality and Materiality in Renaissance Representations*. 1st edition. New York: Fordham University Press, 2009.

Gregerson, Linda. *The Reformation of the Subject: Spenser, Milton, and the English Protestant Epic*. Cambridge and New York: Cambridge University Press, 1995.

Hamilton, A. C. *The Spenser Encyclopaedia*. London: Routledge, 1990.

Haraway, Donna J. *Simians, Cyborgs and Women: The Reinvention of Nature*. London: Free Assn Books, 1996.

Hayles, N. Katherine. *How We Became Posthuman: Virtual Bodies in Cybernetics, Literature, and Informatics*. 1st edition. Chicago, IL: University of Chicago Press, 1999.

Hills, Paul. *Venetian Colour: Marble, Mosaic, Painting and Glass, 1250–1550*. New Haven, CT: Yale University Press, 1999.

Hyman, Wendy Beth, ed. *The Automaton in English Renaissance Literature*. London and New York: Routledge, 2016.

Marr, Alexander. "Gentille Curiosité: Wonder-Working, and the Culture of Automata in the Late Renaissance." In *Curiosity and Wonder from the Renaissance to the Enlightenment*, edited by R. J. W. Evans and Alexander Marr, 149–70. Aldershot, England: Ashgate, 2006.

McCulloch, Lynsey. "Antique Myth, Early Modern Mechanism: The Secret History of Spenser's Iron Man." In *The Automaton in English Renaissance Literature*, edited by Wendy Beth Hyman, 61–76. Literary and Scientific Cultures of Early Modernity. Surrey, England: Ashgate, 2011.

Nocks, Lisa. *The Robot: The Life Story of a Technology*. Westport, CT: Greenwood Press, 2007.

Ovid. *Metamorphoses*. Edited by E. J. Kenney, translated by A. D. Melville. Oxford: Oxford University Press, 1998.

————. *Ovid III: Metamorphoses, Books I–VIII*. Edited by G. P. Goold, translated by Frank Justus Miller, 3rd edition, Loeb Classical Library. Cambridge, MA: Harvard University Press, 1984.

————. *Ovid IV: Metamorphoses, Books IX–XV*. Edited by G. P. Goold, translated by Frank Justus Miller, Subsequent edition, Loeb Classical Library. Cambridge, MA: Harvard University Press, 1916.

————. *The. Xv. Bookes of P. Ouidius Naso, Entytuled Metamorphosis, Translated Oute of Latin into English Meeter, by Arthur Golding Gentleman, a Worke Very Pleasaunt and Delectable*. London: Willyam Seres, 1567.

Paré, Ambroise. *Les oeuvres d'Ambroise Paré ...* Jean Gregoire, 1664.

————. *Opera Chirurgica*, 1594.

————. *The Workes of That Famous Chirurgion Ambrose Parey Translated Out of Latine and Compared with the French by Th: Johnson*. Edited by Thomas Cecil. London: Printed by Th: Cotes and R. Young, 1634.

Paton, W. R, ed. and trans. *The Greek Anthology, Vol. 5*. Loeb Classical Library. London: Harvard University Press, 1918.

Raber, Karen. *Shakespeare and Posthumanist Theory*. Shakespeare and Theory. London and New York: The Arden Shakespeare, 2018.

Roche, Thomas P. *The Kindly Flame; a Study of the Third and Fourth Books of Spenser's Faerie Queene*. Princeton, NJ: Princeton University Press, 1964.

Sawday, Jonathan. "'Forms Such as Never Were in Nature': The Renaissance Cyborg." In *At the Borders of the Human: Beasts, Bodies and Natural Philosophy in the Early Modern Period*, edited by Erica Fudge, Ruth Gilbert, and Susan Wiseman, 171–95. New York, NY: Palgrave, 2002.

Schwarz, Kathryn. *Tough Love: Amazon Encounters in the English Renaissance*. Durham, NC: Duke University Press Books, 2000.

Shakespeare, William. "The Sonnets and 'A Lover's Complaint.'" In *The Norton Shakespeare*, edited by Stephen Greenblatt, Walter Cohen, Jean E. Howard, and Katherine Eisaman Maus, 1915–90. New York: W. W. Norton, 1997.

Spenser, Edmund. *The Faerie Queene*. Edited by A. C Hamilton. London and New York: Longman, 1980.

Suzuki, Mihoko. *Metamorphoses of Helen: Authority, Difference, and the Epic*. Ithaca: Cornell University Press, 1992.

Thacker, Eugene. *After Life*. Chicago: University of Chicago Press, 2010.

Vickers, Nancy J. "Diana Described: Scattered Woman and Scattered Rhyme." *Critical Inquiry* 8, no. 2 (Winter 1981): 265–79.

Vries, Lyckle de. "Bruegel's 'Fall of Icarus': Ovid or Solomon 30/1/2 (2006): 4–18." *Simiolus: Netherlands Quarterly for the History of Art* 30, no. 1/2 (2006): 4–18.

Werth, Tiffany Jo. "'Degendered': Spenser's 'Yron Man' in a 'Stonie' Age." *Spenser Studies: A Renaissance Poetry Annual* 30 (2015): 393–413.

Wolfe, Jessica. *Humanism, Machinery, and Renaissance Literature.* 1st edition. Cambridge and New York: Cambridge University Press, 2004.

Wood, Rufus. *Metaphor and Belief in The Faerie Queene.* New York: St. Martin's Press, 1997.

CHAPTER 7

Epilogue: A Figure of Wax

Over the course of this book, we have moved from the golden age of Elizabethan literature to the edges of the seventeenth century and back again. We have wandered to Italy and France, and returned to England, following wax impressions and figures into the various cultural spaces and literary texts that they inhabit. Like Descartes' purportedly errant consideration of wax, our study of wax has not simply been a wandering but has brought us some version of truth, proving the lie of the false etymology of "sincere" that would connect truth to a lack of wax through the Latin "sin cera."[1] Certainly, pursuing wax has revealed a nexus of questions about gendered bodies, the nature of the mind, the relationship between the mind and other objects, the nature of writing, and of art, and imitation rendered more broadly. It also has led us to considerations of what makes us human and how that question is complicated by technology and the promise (or threat) of prosthetics and automata. While wax may not have fully revealed the answers to those questions, it has allowed us to see more clearly how sixteenth- and seventeenth-century thinkers grappled with them. Moreover, by tracing the complex ways in which these thinkers engage wax, we have seen that these questions overlap and threaten at times to merge to become the same question, like pieces of wax pushed together, melted and solidified into new shapes. The malleability of wax allows it to speak to the messiness of the very questions that it authorizes and also allows it to tell a nonlinear

© The Author(s) 2019
L. M. Maxwell, *Wax Impressions, Figures, and Forms in Early Modern Literature*, Early Modern Cultural Studies 1500–1700,
https://doi.org/10.1007/978-3-030-16932-9_7

version of history. Thus, wax offers us different stories and different truths than more traditional narratives.

As I suggested in the introduction, this project itself can be conceptualized as a wax sculpture, a sculpture that takes its shape from the way different moments, texts, art forms, and thoughts connect across time. In traveling along its surfaces, following wax into various discursive spaces, we have, perhaps, been standing too close to it to see its contours fully. Or perhaps, more aptly, we have not actually been looking at the wax figure at all, but rather tracing our fingers blindly along its contours. Now that we have traversed the surface of the wax, what can we say about the shape or shapes that have emerged? What can we say about the figure of wax in the period? We certainly have not discovered its full extent. We have touched only its surface, and while our fingers have moved purposefully and searchingly along its contours, there are still other paths we could have followed. Nor, perhaps, can we name the figure that has emerged; it is the shape of malleability, and also a malleable shape. It is the shape of memory, writing, and art. It is almost human and yet not, a gendered shape that also speaks about the artificiality of gender and exposes the limits of those constructs.

Still, even as the paths offered by wax may fail to resolve into a nameable figure, we can say something about our experience tracing them. We have been studying a figure of some complexity, with curves of varying intensity. Sometimes in tracing one shape or curve, we have found ourselves back traversing familiar surfaces, re-encountering questions that we thought left behind. We have discovered that our figure is one of folds, connections, and overlaps. With our journey at an end, we can say something more of the greater contours and of the paths that traverse our figure as a whole.

One of the major paths offered by this project has been the figuration of gender and particularly women through wax. In Chapter 2, when we took up the figure of the wax seal, we asked what happens to female agency when women are associated with wax and found that often wax is deployed as one half of a binary opposition, pitted against marble or a signet ring in order to suggest female vulnerability and weakness to masculine impression. Yet as we pressed on Shakespeare's wax and his women, we found that neither were so soft or yielding as such an opposition might suggest. We discovered that his trope bent to accommodate same-sex relations, and that agential women such as Viola could come to occupy the "masculine" half of the trope. We also found that

Shakespeare was critical of men who failed to soften or show pity—who set their print "by force, by fraud, or skill," and that being soft or impressible in Shakespeare might signal one's humanity. In Chapter 3, questions of gender lay on the edge of our inquiry, as we took up wax minds in relation to memory, education, virtue, and subjectivity. Gender became more central again in Chapter 4, where we examined Donne's *Sappho to Philaenis*. There Donne uses wax to figure Sappho's heart and also her project of re-seducing Philaenis. The association of wax with women and the impossibility of wax impressing wax become a problem for Sappho, who seeks new possibilities of drawing Philaenis or restoring the image of Philaenis on her own heart without a signet. Margaret Cavendish's natural philosophy, and particularly her theory of patterning, provide exactly those possibilities, as we saw in Chapter 5. Patterning posits agency in all positions and suggests that wax is never impressed but instead shapes itself after the signet. By rewriting the physics of the encounter between signet and wax, Cavendish also rewrites what it means to be a wax self and that rewriting also has implications for gender. Finally, in Chapter 6, we returned to the problem of female wax through Spenser's false Florimell, a figure whose performance of femininity seems contingent on perfect malleability accomplished through wax.

Another path that we traced throughout this project concerns the purpose and limits of art. At first, that path was subtle, a gentle ridge running along our consideration of gender, emerging first as a meditation on the art of writing. Both *The Rape of Lucrece* and "Sappho to Philaenis" consider the power of the writing. For Lucrece, writing offers the possibility of narrating her own story, but also the possibility of being misread. Her suicide becomes a form of writing that makes legible the violence of Tarquin's rape, but also forever silences Lucrece's voice. In Donne's "Sappho to Philaenis," on the other hand, verse is imagined to have a "holy fire" capable of enflaming the beloved's passions and the ability to inscribe and attract the beloved's heart.[2] Whether Sappho's address to Philaenis will succeed in recapturing Philaenis's heart is not resolved within the poem, but Sappho certainly believes that art can be transformative. At the same time, the power of the authorial voice is called into question by the association of Lucrece and Sappho with wax. Shakespeare raises the possibility that Lucrece's voice is no longer her own after her mind has been impressed by the force of Tarquin's rape. Likewise, when Sappho looks inward at her melting heart to find inspiration for her poem, she instead discovers that she is "robbed of picture, heart and sense."[3] In other places, the path we traced offered by art became more pronounced. In Chapter 5, we asked how Ferdinand's wax sculptures work on the Duchess's psyche and how art objects relate to the subjects they depict. In Chapter 6, we explored some of the concerns that artistic achievement raises as the possibility of imitating human form threatens to become the possibility of modifying or creating human bodies. By looking at Ovid's myths, Ambroise Paré's *Workes,* and Spenser's *Faerie Queene,* we were able to consider early modern fears about the limits of knowledge and human invention and their relationship to questions of art. Moreover, when we took up Descartes' consideration of automata and Spenser's treatment of Talus and the false Florimell, we were able to consider how questions of materiality and invention intersect with questions about the nature of humanity.

In the course of this study, we have returned repeatedly to wax as philosophical model and wax as literary topos. These two paths ran intertwined through the discussion of gender and came together again around our consideration of subjectivity in Shakespeare, Tourneur, Donne, Cavendish, and Descartes. The path of wax as philosophical model was well defined at times, outlined explicitly in the introduction, in Chapter 3, and in Chapter 4. We saw that wax functioned as a philosophical model in ancient Greece and Rome and continued to function as such through our period. We also saw that seventeenth-century thinkers (both philosophic and literary) found in wax a material that could be re-molded and used to offer new narratives about gender relations, the nature of the mind, and the physical underpinnings of the universe. In our final chapters, the path of wax as philosophical object was more muted, yet in our consideration of the limits of humanity in Chapter 6, we touched on the path of wax as philosophical model again as we juxtaposed the wax Florimell and the mechanical Talus. Throughout this work, wax was also always a literary topos, and in each of these literary deployments, the meaning of wax shifted. It stood for softness, malleability, the threat of loss and death, the promise of mimesis, and continuity in change. Perhaps then wax in literature is less a topos and more a shifting landscape of meaning and possibility.

Running our fingers along the wax, we have returned most persistently to wax's capacity to interrogate the nature of humanity. Thus, as I mentioned earlier, our wax figure seems at times to be almost human in shape. In Chapter 6, we looked at how wax is explicitly used to consider the limits of humanity when it is applied to a discussion of prosthetics and automata. But the connection of wax to the question of what it means to be human has been a path that we have been exploring since the beginning of the project. Our consideration of wax and gender and the ramifications of wax hearts and wax minds in Shakespeare, Donne, Cavendish, and Descartes began that work. When we moved on to consider wax's role in art both as a material of creation and a material that facilitates artistic conception and mediates between nature and ideals, we continued to ask about the limits of humanity. What we found throughout was that wax proves a material suited to representing what it means to be human and also to testing those limits. Wax's ability to mimic skin, represent the body and womb, and figure the mind and heart, make it a material of humanity. Still, its lack of life and its status as copy set it apart from human experience.

While these paths might be more suggestive than concrete, raising questions more than providing answers, wax with all its malleability could never promise anything else. As we have traced the contours of wax in the period through this project, the heat of our fingers on the surface of wax has threatened already to change its shape. There are more paths offered by wax than this project shows and more shapes this project could have taken. We could, for example, have more thoroughly traced religion through wax. While the topic of religion and wax emerges in both the introduction and Chapter 3, I could have written an entire chapter around wax and impression in the Bible, and in Catholic and Protestant teachings. We could also have looked at how the Reformation might be understood through wax. Prior to the Reformation, the largest consumer of wax in England was the Catholic church, which consumed great quantities of wax during Masses and encouraged devotees to light candles to aid a lost soul's movement out of purgatory. Yet with the Reformation, the use of candles in churches was severely restricted. For example, Thomas Cromwell's *Injunctions to the Clergy* declared that the clergy "shall suffer from henceforth no candles, tapers, or images of wax to be set afore any image or picture, but only the light that commonly goeth across the church by the rode-loft, the light before the sacrament of the altar, and the light about the sepulchre, which for the adorning of the church and the divine service, ye shall suffer to remain still."[4] The Reformation can be understood, in part, as a movement away from wax. Not only because of the restriction of candles, but also in the elimination of images. In Italy, wax ex-votos "anatomized and configured the human body as a palpable presence and they celebrated votary identity in proximity to holy objects in consecrated spaces."[5] Yet these ex-votos are exactly the type of images critiqued by both Protestant and Catholic reformers as idolatrous. Even tracing the path of religion in this rudimentary way along the surface of wax raises tantalizing possibilities that could no doubt be explored further.

Another path not traced in this project is the path that would have carried us beyond the seventeenth century into later manifestations of wax. Throughout our discussion has been limited to the sixteenth and seventeenth centuries, and to a lesser extent to their appropriation of the waxworks, wax technology, and philosophies of the classical and medieval periods. Yet wax does not disappear at the end of the seventeenth century. Instead, its possibilities mutate and expand. If we pursued wax figures further into the future, we encounter the eighteenth-century wax anatomical figures and the way they construct and intervene in the medicalized human body, and particularly again in the construction of the feminized body.[6] We also encounter the wax figures of Madame Tussaud, figures of spectacle built on the bloodshed of the French Revolution. In the modern wax museum, we can locate an aggressive collision of pop culture and the ancient traditions of the death mask. To wander a wax museum is to confront uncanny replicas of dead and living celebrities frozen in time.

A 2018 exhibit at the Met Breuer, *Like Life: Sculpture, Color, and the Body (1300–Now)* brought together sculptures from the past 700 years. The exhibit, like this book, chose not to move chronologically, but rather to link sculptures across time that speak to each other and ask similar questions about what it means to be human. Perhaps it is not surprising that in such an exhibit wax sculptures figured prominently. I want to highlight two of them here, to show how wax continues to trouble the meaning of art, life, and the limits of the human. *Sleeping Beauty*, a reproduction of a 1765 wax sculpture by Madame Tussaud's uncle, Philippe Curtius, is a wax sculpture of Madame du Barry, who was a mistress of Louis XV. The wax woman is exquisitely beautiful. Her hair drapes in golden ringlets and her delicate features are caught in a form of repose. She lies on a velvet chaise, her head nestled into the crook of her elbow, wearing an intricate golden dress that is hardly suitable attire for sleep. The sculpture's beauty arrests the eye, yet not as much as the subtle rise and fall of its diaphragm. Curtius's wax woman breathes. The exhibit's online catalog connects *Sleeping Beauty* to a larger cultural practice of displaying sleeping women and sculptures at fairgrounds in the eighteenth century.[7] These fairground shows invited audiences, and particularly male audiences to survey the female form and try to differentiate between life and art.[8] As Karen Hoffman explains, "A tableau vivant show was always about plays of counterfeits, of body and art, static image and breathing flesh... Whatever was in the case was a fairground front act that caught the play between reality and its simulacrum that was central to fairground display, and used that play, configured in the shape of a pretty girl, to draw customers into the show."[9] Curtius's *Sleeping Beauty*, with her aristocratic clothes, beautiful features, and lifelike posture, invites audiences to gaze with pleasure, to enjoy the counterfeit, and almost believe that she is real. The fact that Madame du Barry, the model for the sculpture, was killed by the guillotine, adds an element of macabre that might further titillate. Even more than most wax sculptures, this wax woman raises questions about what it means to be simulacra or to gaze with pleasure upon one. Her subtle breathing troubles our understanding of how sculptures work and blurs the lines between sleep, death, and art.

Another unsettling work in the exhibit is the *"Auto-Icon" of Jeremy Bentham*. This sculpture is the preserved skeleton of Jeremy Bentham, dressed in his own clothes which have been stuffed to make him appear living. The sculpture is completed with a wax head that was added after efforts to preserve his actual head failed. Seated in the philosopher's own chair, with his staff draped across his lap, the figure is ready to meet with his "personal friends and other disciples" if they should gather "on some day or days of the year for the purpose of commemorating the founder of the greatest happiness system of morals and legislation."[10] If *Sleeping Beauty* raises questions about the lines between a sleeping woman, a corpse, and a sculpture, the *"Auto-Icon" of Jeremy Bentham* is undeniably both corpse and sculpture. Made according to his will and intended for display, the Auto-Icon participates in Bentham's larger project of utilitarianism by alleviating some of the financial burdens of death, and also as Amy L. Gates argues, "keep[ing] the dead visibly present and actively participatory among the living by commanding attention, raising questions, and inciting imaginative responses and reconsiderations."[11] Bentham imagined that other corpses would also be transformed into auto-icons and serve various societal functions—the remains of criminals could serve as warnings, while other remains could amuse and inspire. Wax here, while seemingly incidental, does the important work of making the corpse look alive by substituting for the poorly preserved head. Appearance is more important than truth here—the *"Auto-Icon"* needs to look like a living Bentham, more than it needs to be his corpse. Again, the sculpture troubles the boundaries of art and raises questions about how the dead might interact with the living.

Next to these wax sculptures, we could place many more. While scholars in other periods have studied these works, more needs to be done to reach across time periods and consider what broader narratives could be offered about wax and its relation to culture and the production of knowledge. A panel entitled "Theorizing Wax" at the 2011 annual conference of the Association for Art History called for more attention to be paid to the unique challenges of studying wax. According to the organizers, the panel's "twofold aim is to broaden the study of the function and meaning of wax, as well as seek ways of finding alternative art historical approaches by taking rare and marginalized wax artifacts as point of departure, for which current methodologies developed for portraiture or sculpture do not suffice."[12] This call to arms suggests that much work still needs to be done in theorizing and studying wax objects and in recovering the history of those objects, since "the history of wax has been a history of disappearance, partly due to the perishable quality of the wax."[13] If wax is a medium that has not sufficiently been explored in art history, the connections between wax objects, philosophical models, and literary metaphors have been even less explored. This project offers to fill that gap for the sixteenth and seventeenth centuries, but more work must be done to address the absence of similar projects in later periods.

Stepping back further, if this project can be understood as a wax sculpture, there are other objects that could be displayed alongside it, other studies that would resonate with our study of wax, and which are to a degree invited by it. Much of this project dealt with wax as an impressible medium, a medium that shares important similarities with other impressible mediums, such as clay and snow. These alternatives have both made appearances in this project, but neither has been fully explored. As we saw in the introduction, clay connects to wax as a medium for artistic models. Moreover, clay might also connect to wax through the mentioned but unexplored connections between wax and religion as, according to *Genesis*, God formed Adam out of clay and also in his image. Thus, as materials of model making, wax and clay carry different religious inflections.

Snow has made more of an appearance in this project than clay. As I mentioned in Chapters 4 and 5, the trope of footprints in the snow is employed frequently in close proximity to the trope of the signet–seal and often seems in conversation with that trope. We found the two together in Margaret Cavendish's *Philosophical Letters* and John Donne's "Sappho to Philaenis," and. Moreover, in Chapter 6, we saw that in Edmund Spenser's *Faerie Queene*, wax and snow combine with gold wire to make up the substance of the false Florimell's body. Throughout I have tried to be attentive to the significance of this coupling of snow and wax; yet because my project is centered on wax, I have not fully explored the potential depth offered by snow or by the trope of the footprint. A project that took on snow-related tropes could prove enlightening and could further complicate the relationship that I have narrated between tropes of wax and snow.

While snow and clay immediately suggest themselves for further study, other materials also share qualities with wax and could be discussed alongside it. For example, plaster casts are a mimetic art form founded on impression and a study of plaster could have much to say to our study of wax. Moreover, substances with less connection to wax might also be pursued along similar lines of inquiry. Perhaps studying the movement of gold, iron, or marble through similarly diverse cultural registers would reveal compelling intersections and narratives. As I suggested in the introduction, one of the goals of this work has been to provide a new methodology for interdisciplinary research. Other studies that explore the way materials are used in philosophy, literature, and the real world could greatly enhance our understanding of the way objects circulate and the importance of materiality in philosophy and literature, as could studies that looked at wax alongside other technologies of image repro-duction such as photography. Any of these projects would share some contours with our wax figure, despite the differences of materials, and invite conversations about the ways in which materiality matters.

Let us look one last time at our piece of art, the figure of wax we have been exploring, the figure that has helped us think through and concep-tualize the work that wax does in the period. It is, of course, itself, a rhetorical construction that figures other rhetorical, literary, philosophi-cal, and cultural constructions. In doing so, it has taught us many truths about how wax manifests itself in those spaces. Perhaps, though, it has one final lesson to teach, the lesson offered by its own wax materiality. If this project is a wax sculpture, its materiality can remind us of the infinitude of possibilities inherent in the study of the history of literature, philosophy, and art. While this project, embodied as wax, has a specific shape that we have traced and re-traced, as I suggested in my reading of Shakespeare's tropes of impression, the mutability of wax insists that any shape it takes is provisional. Wax always can be re-molded, twisted into new shapes, used to tell new stories. Still, whatever form it takes, it is still "the same wax," just as the objects we study continue to exist no matter what stories we tell about them.[14]

NOTES

1. *Oxford English Dictionary*, 'sincere.'
2. John Donne, "Sappho to Philaenis," in *The Major Works*, ed. John Carey (Oxford, UK, 1990), 1. All citations to 'Sappho to Philaenis' are to line number.
3. Ibid., 12.
4. Thomas Cromwell, "Number XI. Injunctions to the Clergy Made by Cromwell," in *A Collection of Records Letters and Original Papers with Other Instruments*, ed. Gilbert Burnet, vol. 4 (Oxford, UK: Clarendon, 1865), 343.
5. Megan Holmes, "Ex-Votos: Materiality, Memory, and Cult," in *The Idol in the Age of Art: Objects, Devotions, and the Early Modern World*, eds. Michael W. Cole and Rebecca Zorach (Farnham: Ashgate, 2009), 160.
6. Wax anatomical figures predate the eighteenth century, but the collection of wax anatomical figures in Bologna and Florence began in the 1740s.
7. "Philippe Curtius | Sleeping Beauty | French | The Met," The Metropolitan Museum of Art, i.e. The Met Museum, accessed January 28, 2019, https://www.metmuseum.org/art/collection/search/736081.
8. For more on fairground sleeping beauties see Kathryn A. Hoffman,"Sleeping Beauties in the Fairground: The Spitzner, Pedley and Chemisé Exhibits." *Early Popular Visual Culture* 4, no. 2 (2006): 139–159.
9. Ibid., 140.
10. Jeremy Bentham, Will of Jeremy Bentham of Westminster Middlesex, 21 June 1832, MS, The National Archives, Kew, Richmond, Surrey, UK, PROB 11/1801.
11. Amy L. Gates, "Fixing Memory: The Effigial Forms of Felicia Hemans and Jeremy Bentham," *Women's Writing* 21, no. 1 (2014), 66.
12. Allison Goudie and Hanneke Grootenboer, "Theorizing Wax: On the Function and Meaning of a Disappearing Medium," in *AAH 2011*,

Association of Art Historians 37th Annual Conference Call for Papers (The University of Warwick, 2011), 96. See also the special issue "Theorizing Wax: On the Meaning of a Disappearing Medium," eds. Allison Goudie and Hanneke Grootenboer, Oxford Art Journal, 36, no. 1 (2013).

13. Goudie and Grootenboer, "Theorizing Wax," in AAH 2011, 96.

14. Descartes, Meditations on First Philosophy: With Selections from the Objections and Replies, trans. and ed. John Cottingham, Cambridge Texts in the History of Philosophy, revised edition (Cambridge, UK: Cambridge University Press, 1997), 20. In the Latin, "remanet cera". Meditationes de Prima Philosophia, vol. 7 of Oeuvres de Descartes, eds. Charles Adam and Paul Tannery (L. Cerf: Paris, 1897), 30. In the French: "la mesme cire demeure" Meditations Touchant la Premiere Philosophie, vol. 9 in Oeuvres de Descartes, eds. Charles Adam and Paul Tannery (L. Cerf: Paris, 1897), 24.

REFERENCES

Cromwell, Thomas. "Number XI. Injunctions to the Clergy Made by Cromwell." In A Collection of Records Letters and Original Papers with Other Instruments, edited by Gilbert Burnet, 4:341–46. Oxford, UK: Clarendon, 1865.

Descartes, René. "Meditationes de prima philosophia." In Oeuvres de Descartes, edited by Charles Adam and Paul Tannery, Vol. 7. Paris: L. Cerf, 1897. http://archive.org/details/oeuvresdedescar08desc.

Descartes, René. Meditations on First Philosophy: With Selections from the Objections and Replies. Edited and translated by John Cottingham. Revised edition. Cambridge, UK: Cambridge University Press, 1997.

Descartes, René. "Meditations Touchant la Premiere Philosophie." In Oeuvres de Descartes, edited by Charles Adam and Paul Tannery, 9:13–123. Paris: L. Cerf, 1897. http://archive.org/details/oeuvresdedescar08desc.

Donne, John. "Sappho to Philaenis." In The Major Works, edited by John Cary, 65–67. Oxford and New York: Oxford World Classics, 1990.

Gates, Amy L. "Fixing Memory: The Effigial Forms of Felicia Hemans and Jeremy Bentham." Women's Writing 21, no. 1 (February 2, 2014): 58–73.

Goudie, Allison, and Hanneke Grootenboer. "Theorizing Wax: On the Function and Meaning of a Disappearing Medium." In AAH 2011, Association of Art Historians 37th Annual Conference Call for Papers, 96. University of Warwick, 2011.

———, eds. "Theorizing Wax: On the Meaning of a Disappearing Medium." Oxford Art Journal 35, no. 1 (2013).

Hoffmann, Kathryn A. "Sleeping Beauties in the Fairground: The Spitzner, Pedley and Chemisé Exhibits." *Early Popular Visual Culture* 4, no. 2 (2006): 139–159.

Holmes, Megan. "Ex-Votos: Materiality, Memory, and Cult." In *The Idol in the Age of Art: Objects, Devotions and the Early Modern World*, edited by Michael W. Cole and Rebecca Zorach, 1st edition. Burlington, VT: Routledge, 2009.

"Philippe Curtius | Sleeping Beauty | French | The Met." The Metropolitan Museum of Art, i.e. The Met Museum. Accessed January 28, 2019. https://www.metmuseum.org/art/collection/search/736081.

"Will of Jeremy Bentham of Westminster Middlesex," June 21, 1832. PROB 11/1801/468. The National Archives, Kew.

Index

Printed by Printforce, the Netherlands